The Comic Offense from Vaudeville to Contemporary Comedy

The Comic Offense from Vaudeville to Contemporary Comedy

Larry David, Tina Fey, Stephen Colbert, and Dave Chappelle

RICK DESROCHERS

BLOOMSBURY

NEW YORK · LONDON · NEW DELHI · SYDNEY

Bloomsbury Academic

An imprint of Bloomsbury Publishing Inc

1385 Broadway	50 Bedford Square
New York	London
NY 10018	WC1B 3DP
USA	UK

www.bloomsbury.com

Bloomsbury is a registered trade mark of Bloomsbury Publishing Plc

First published 2014

© Rick DesRochers 2014

Library of Congress Cataloging-in-Publication Data
DesRochers, Rick.
The comic offense from vaudeville to contemporary comedy : Larry David, Tina Fey, Stephen Colbert, and Dave Chappelle / Rick DesRochers.
pages cm
Includes bibliographical references and index.
ISBN 978-1-4411-3232-1 (hardback) — ISBN 978-1-4411-6087-4 (paperback)
1. Comedians — United States — History–20th century. 2. Vaudeville — United States— History — 20th century. 3. Vaudeville — Social aspects—United States. I. Title.
PN2285.D455 2014
792.7'60973—dc23
2014003010

ISBN: HB: 978-1-4411-3232-1
PB: 978-1-4411-6087-4
ePub: 978-1-4411-6193-2
ePDF: 978-1-4411-6718-7

Typeset by RefineCatch Limited, Bungay, Suffolk
Printed and bound in the United States of America

The secret of success is to offend the greatest number of people.
—George Bernard Shaw

Jesters do oft prove prophets.
—King Lear

Contents

Illustrations

Acknowledgments

First and foremost to my editor at Bloomsbury, Katie Gallof, who championed this book from its inception and a fateful meeting in San Antonio, Texas, at the PCA/ACA conference, where this all began. Many thanks to Drs. James Wilson, Henry Jenkins, and Alison Forsyth for their support and insightful comments on this project in its initial stages. During my time at the CUNY Graduate Center several professors were also influential in guiding my research interests and process including Morris Dickstein, Jean Graham-Jones, Judy Milhous, and Jim Wilson—*encore*. A special tribute is in order for the late Daniel Gerould whose support of my scholarship in popular comic entertainments over my six years at the Graduate Center enabled me to pursue my interest in this field.

And to my colleagues at Long Island University Post—professors Jon Fraser, Cara Gargano, Maria Porter, Noel Zahler, and the many students over the years that have sustained my passion for the practice and scholarship of theater. I need to thank Paul Meshejian for the endless hours we have spent talking theater and collaborating on amazing new plays for the past ten years for the PlayPenn New Play Development Conference.

I need to acknowledge the generous support of the Long Island University Post research grant committee who provided much-needed funding for this book, especially professors Nancy Frye and Heather Parrott, as well as the American Travel Research Fund (the CUNY-sponsored Tackel Grant), and the multiple CUNY Graduate Center Salk Travel Grants, and several Long Island University Post Travel Grants that made it possible to do the archival research necessary for this book. And for the research assistance of Thomas Lisanti at the New York Public Library.

And finally I want to extend my deepest gratitude and love to my family— my daughter, Lucy Frances, who keeps me smiling and laughing in the darkest moments when I think I can't go on—I go on—and the love of my life and partner in crime—Ashley Semrick DesRochers.

Preface

All the human race demands of its members is that they be born. That is all vaudeville demanded. You just had to be born. You could be ignorant and be a star. You could be a moron and be wealthy. The elements that went to make up vaudeville were combed from the jungles, the four corners of the world, the intelligentsia and the subnormal. An endless, incongruous swarm crawled over the countryside dragging performing lions, bears, tigers, leopards, boxing kangaroos, horses, ponies, mules, dogs, cats, rats, seals, and monkeys in their wake. . . . Vaudeville asked only that you [. . .] have a minimum of talent or a maximum of nerve.[1]

Writing in 1956, Fred Allen, a former vaudevillian turned radio comedy star of the 1940s, was looking back on what made vaudeville an all-embracing and encompassing American popular art form. Another former vaudevillian, and a contemporary of Allen's, Groucho Marx, would famously say, "I would never want to belong to a club that would have me as a member."[2] Vaudeville was the club that Groucho would not only belong to but also become one of its most distinguished members, whether he liked it or not. The comedians discussed in *The Comic Offense from Vaudeville to Contemporary Comedy* worked with a vaudeville aesthetic that connected this widely diverse membership of one of the most inclusive and entertaining clubs that the United States has ever produced.

Comedy at the turn of the twentieth century was constructed from sociocultural stereotypes inherited from nineteenth-century performance forms including minstrelsy (blackface performance based on racial stereotypes), medicine shows (traveling shows that sold bogus cure-alls), burlesque (sensual female dancers interspersed with comics), the variety theater (a male-oriented mélange of ribald singing and dancing acts), and its cleaned-up cousin—vaudeville—created to attract a middle-class family audience. This new development in humor was centered around a vaudeville aesthetic that, according to stage and media theorist Henry Jenkins, was characterized by "a different performer–spectator relationship, a fragmented structure, a heterogeneous array of materials, and a reliance upon crude shock to produce emotionally intense responses."[3]

The evaluation of how the vaudeville aesthetic evolved and has influenced comedy in America from the late nineteenth century to the early twenty-first century will be the focus of *The Comic Offense*. This book examines present-day writer-performers, and how they are influenced by comic vaudevillians. It also discusses how they continue to expand and explore the history and legacy of vaudeville-era performance. Beginning with the iconic comedians Groucho Marx, Mae West, Will Rogers, and Bert Williams—moving from their stage acts of the 1910s and 1920s to the next generation of radio and television during the following three decades, represented here by Fred Allen, Lucille Ball, Sid Caesar, Phil Silvers, and the creators of *The Amos 'n' Andy Show*, Freeman Gosden and Charles Correll—this study examines how the vaudeville aesthetic emerged at the turn of the twentieth century and was carried forward to contemporary comedy. The present-day comedians considered here are Larry David—from failed stand-up comic to television writer, producer, and director of two wildly popular shows in *Seinfeld* and *Curb Your Enthusiasm*; Tina Fey—from touring the improv stages of the Midwest to head writer of *Saturday Night Live*, and creator and star of the critically acclaimed *30 Rock*; Stephen Colbert—from second stringer at Chicago's Second City to the internationally successful *The Colbert Report*; and Dave Chappelle—from the small-time comedy clubs of Washington, DC, to a $50 million television contract after only two seasons of *Chappelle's Show*. These comedians continue to create variations of the vaudeville aesthetic inherited from their early twentieth-century forebears.

How these stage and screen "new" vaudevillians reinforced, confronted, and deconstructed stereotypes of ethnicity, race, gender, and class, will be at the core of this project.[4] The heritage of comic vaudeville is evaluated here by delineating the tradition of the confrontational comedy of offense. Examining the parallels and differences in American comic writing and performance from the vaudeville stage to the present, this book traces the influence of comic acts derived from the *tummler* (the tumult or noise-maker) of the Yiddish stage tradition, comic female performers in burlesque, medicine show con-men and their stump speeches (monologues that mocked political speeches or religious sermons), and the blackface performers of minstrel shows. Each of these popular entertainment forms influenced vaudeville, beginning with the stage to the media inventions of radio and television of the mid-twentieth century to the new media platforms of today.

Vaudeville comedy painted quick and easily identifiable character types and scenarios that produced a varied series of acts. These performances were rendered through hyperbolic accents, heightened makeup and costuming in exaggerated contours, that were meant to reflect cultural stereotypes intended primarily to make audiences laugh. Vaudeville also required a shared performer–spectator relationship that appealed to the senses through an intense amalgam of physical and verbal humor. The variety and innovation of these acts was tantamount to success on the vaudeville stage.

Starting with the transition of stage to radio and television, the vaudeville aesthetic will be observed from the 1880s to the mid-twentieth century in America. It is evidenced by the freedom of experimentation and improvisation of comic vaudevillians, as this new brand of humor was translated through stage comedians who became writers, directors, and producers in addition to being celebrated performers in these new media formats. Connected by the vaudeville aesthetic, the humorists discussed offered an alternative view of American society and culture, predicated on where and from what circumstances they originated. As one generation moved to the next, whether on stage, radio, or television, they carried this aesthetic with them. The evolution of this comic aesthetic through multiple eras serves to connect the chapters throughout this book.

The vaudeville-inspired comedians who participated in the new media of the 1940s and 1950s will serve as a bridge between the stage work of Groucho Marx, Mae West, Will Rogers, and Bert Williams, beginning with the radio comedians Freeman Gosden and Charles Correll, Fanny Brice, and Fred Allen, and then television with Sid Caesar, Phil Silvers, and Lucille Ball. During the late 1950s and 1960s, stage comedians Mort Sahl and Lenny Bruce challenged authoritarianism in American life with the vaudeville aesthetic. It continued on television with *The Smothers Brothers* and *Rowan & Martin's Laugh-In* during the late 1960s with comedians who represented a post-Vietnam War America. A new generation of comedians in Richard Pryor and Gilda Radner moved this aesthetic from small clubs to comedy recordings to television and film in the 1970s and 1980s depicting the disaffection of ethnic-, racial-, and gender-minorities. The book concludes as the 1990s gave way to the next wave of the vaudeville aesthetic with Larry David, Tina Fey, Stephen Colbert, and Dave Chappelle who would dominate the comedic form into the new millennium.

The contemporary vaudeville comedians examined here dissented by questioning and deconstructing institutional authority and reverent social rituals by being intentionally disrespectful and disruptive. They exposed the hidden agendas that were meant to keep socio-political-cultural fantasies alive. By unsettling these agendas, these comedians demystify what Stephen Colbert calls "truthiness": a false sense of knowledge and understanding that relies on intuition that derives from "the gut."[5] How the vaudeville aesthetic evolved and challenged the status quo of the "truthiness" of American mores and societal standards is a unifying theme throughout this book. By examining how the vaudeville aesthetic was developed and found its way into the work of comic writer-performers like David, Fey, Colbert, and Chappelle, this project examines how this legacy of comedy has changed in the new millennium due to cultural and media shifts in comic performance, including Internet streaming, especially from popular venues like *YouTube* and *Facebook*, as a new kind of vaudeville entertainment for the digital age.

The Comic Offense discusses how new media evolutions influence each other, and ultimately merge to create a subversive outsider critique through the unique comic sensibility inspired by the vaudeville aesthetic. There is a natural progression from vaudeville to radio and television and the Internet that is accessible to comic performers and utilizes their skills born of the early twentieth-century stage. The performers and their techniques discussed here expand upon each other and support the notion that the dissemination of controversial and satirical acts has a vital and complex history in American popular entertainment. The "new" becomes the challenge to the entrenched establishment who clings onto a "classical" narrative past that supports heterogeneous notions of culture and society. As each novel medium and comedian is introduced, original ways of confronting these institutionalized notions of ethnic identity and stereotyping (Groucho Marx/Larry David), gender roles and behaviors (Mae West/Tina Fey), social and political messaging (Will Rogers/Stephen Colbert), and racism and interracial conflicts (Bert Williams/Dave Chappelle) are sought after.

This book is not a simple compare and contrast of comedians from different time periods to see how similar or different the humorists in question are to and from each other, but aims to show their connection throughout one hundred and twenty-five years of comedy history. Comedians that share in the vaudeville aesthetic face similar issues and challenges in their work in spite of the context of the times discussed. It is not enough to say that these issues still exist (although in some cases they are strikingly similar) but to show how these comedians deal with social paradigm shifts through vaudeville-inspired humor over a century in the making.

Chapter 1, "The vaudeville aesthetic and the migration to radio and television," describes how vaudeville was absorbed by radio during the late 1920s and into the 1930s, and its transition from stage to radio and television in the mid-twentieth century. Formative figures such as Freeman Gosden and Charles Correll (*The Amos 'n' Andy Show*), Groucho Marx (*You Bet Your Life*), and Sid Caesar (*Your Show of Shows*) are evaluated, along with how television and radio engaged with former vaudevillians in these new media forms. This chapter works from the idea of the vaudeville aesthetic as it is defined by performance historian and theorist Henry Jenkins. I extend this notion of the vaudeville aesthetic as it influenced comedy in radio and television into the new media of the twenty-first century.[6]

Contemporary case studies of how Larry David, Tina Fey, Stephen Colbert, and Dave Chappelle use the vaudeville aesthetic in television and live performances are the focus of Chapters 2 through 5. Each chapter will recognize various "bridge" performers like Phil Silvers, Fanny Brice, Lucille Ball, Fred Allen, and Richard Pryor to negotiate the transition from one medium to the next. Using the memoir of former vaudevillian Joe Laurie Jr. and his definitions of vaudeville acts, these chapters examine how these acts were, and continue to be, appropriated and modified by comedians in the digital age.

Chapter 2, "'What's real got to do with what we do?'—Groucho Marx to Larry David" focuses on these performers and their use of the "two-man act," and the influence of the *tummler* in their respective work. Chapter 3, "'The Girlie Show' as the new burlesque—Mae West to Tina Fey," traces the legacy of female comic writer-performers from Mae West to Lucille Ball to Tina Fey, and how women entered the male-dominated world of comedy through burlesque humor. Chapter 4, "Truth and truthiness go to Washington—Will Rogers to Stephen Colbert," looks at satire as political commentary and action through the "truthiness" of "fake" news shows like *The Colbert Report* and their antecedents beginning with the "all I know is what I read in the papers" philosophy of trick-roper-turned-cowboy-philosopher, Will Rogers. Chapter 5, "The mask of minstrelsy—Bert Williams to Dave Chappelle," looks at the legacy of the black comedian from vaudevillian Bert Williams and his stardom on the white-dominated *Ziegfeld Follies* stage. Richard Pryor provides the link to the television and live acts of Dave Chappelle through the heritage and struggle with minstrelsy and blackface performance. These case studies examine how the vaudeville aesthetic has developed and found its way into early twenty-first-century comic performances through stage and multimedia formats by its transformational figures.

Working from popular vaudeville acts beginning at the turn of the twentieth century, this book traces the vaudevillian as sociocultural commentator through improvisation, mimicry, and archetypal characterizations that defined comedy during this era. Also surveyed will be how popular comic entertainers negotiated censorship, bigotry, and sexism, even as they strove to engage audiences, and create successful professional careers. The overarching subject of *The Comic Offense* concerns the diversity of performers and performance techniques derived from vaudeville acts and, ultimately, how the vaudeville aesthetic lives on in these myriad performers and media platforms in contemporary comic popular entertainment.

Notes

1 Fred Allen, "The Life and Death of Vaudeville," in *The American Stage: Writings on Theater from Washington Irving to Tony Kushner*, ed. Laurence

Senelick (New York: The Library of America, 2010), 85. An examination of Fred Allen's radio comedy will be featured in Chapter 4.

2 The quote is attributed to Groucho Marx in *Annie Hall*, directed by Woody Allen (1977; Santa Monica, CA: MGM Home Entertainment, 2000), DVD.

3 Henry Jenkins, *What Made Pistachio Nuts?: Early Sound Comedy and the Vaudeville Aesthetic* (New York: Columbia University Press, 1992), 22–25.

4 My use of the term "new" vaudevillians is not in reference to the new vaudeville movement of the 1990s in the United States featured in the stage performances of Bill Irwin and Geoff Hoyle, but denotes a continuum of the vaudeville aesthetic into the new millennium.

5 Stephen Colbert, "Truthiness," *The Colbert Report*, episode 1 (New York: Comedy Central, October 17, 2005), DVD.

6 Jenkins, *What Made Pistachio Nuts?*, 63.

1

The vaudeville aesthetic and the migration to radio and television

During the filming of the 1928 Marx Brothers' movie *The Cocoanuts*, Groucho Marx defended his use of the stage aside saying,

> I frequently stepped out of character and spoke directly to the audience. After the first day's shooting on *Cocoanuts*, the producer . . . said, 'Groucho, you can't step out of character and talk to the audience.' Like all the people who are glued to tradition, he was wrong. I spoke to them in every picture I appeared in.[1]

Direct address and commentary on the proceedings would enter Groucho's comedy vocabulary in his radio and television performances as well. Ungluing his audience from their ingrained traditions would become his trademark. Groucho's training in comedy came from his nearly three decades on the vaudeville stage. Two stage shows that he starred in with the Marx Brothers, *The Cocoanuts* and *Animal Crackers*, would be directly transferred from the stage to film, and Groucho brought his vaudeville aesthetic with him.

Although the Marx Brothers' films are ubiquitous, and Groucho's iconic image is still represented with his "Groucho glasses"—with black bushy mustache and eyebrows—in children's toys and adult costumes throughout the world, what is less well recognized is that Groucho was able to transfer his vaudevillian skills to radio and television. The transition of the vaudeville aesthetic to sound film comedy is well documented particularly in performance scholar Henry Jenkins' *What Made Pistachio Nuts?* and Robert C. Knopf's *The Theater and Cinema of Buster Keaton*. This chapter will focus on the transfer of the vaudeville aesthetic from stage to radio and television. I argue that the vaudeville aesthetic as it moved to these mid-twentieth-century new media forms was even more successful as witnessed in three landmark programs: Freeman Gosden and Charles Correll's *The Amos 'n' Andy Show*, Groucho Marx's *You Bet Your Life*, and Sid Caesar's *Your Show of Shows*. Seemingly counterintuitive, the vaudeville aesthetic was quite conducive to the new media platforms of radio and television. These technological innovations recreated the interplay between audience and performer through its "liveness"[2] and informal series of short sketches, interviews, and reporting of cultural events.

The vaudeville aesthetic was initially predicated on the notion that there ought to be "something for everybody" in stage entertainment as propounded by stage impresario Edward F. Albee. In 1923, Albee was quoted in *Variety* saying, "Thus, in the arrangement of the ideal modern vaudeville program, there is one or more sources of complete satisfaction for everybody present, no matter how 'mixed' the audience may be." Albee's contention became overstated as he went on to say that vaudeville provided entertainment for all, "just as in every state and city, in every county and town in our democratic country, there is opportunity for everybody, a chance for all."[3] Vaudeville comedians performed for diverse audiences of men, women, and children through a variety of comic acts.

* * *

The Marx Brothers stage act exemplified vaudeville performances that reached the wide-ranging audience that Albee hoped for, consisting of a unique interplay between their diverse comedic skills. They were originally billed as the Four Marx Brothers—Groucho, Chico, and Harpo, and included Gummo, who was later replaced by Zeppo. In an interview for the *Utah Democrat*, the Marx Brothers revealed their performance strategy to an entertainment reporter:

> Since some people like one style of comedy and don't care for another, it behooved the Marx boys, if they wanted to stick to their agreement, to offer every style of comedy known to the stage; if one of the brothers did not please, one of the other three would be sure to; and thus the four brothers, individually and collectively, would be credited with being a "hit." Accordingly, they divided up the field of comedy among themselves thus: Julius [Groucho] took up eccentric comedy; . . . Arthur [Harpo], nut comedy; and Leonard [Chico], boob comedy.[4]

Harpo portrayed a silent form of comedy that seemed to have no logic in its completely chaotic physicality—what *avant-garde* Italian performance theorist F. T. Marinetti attributed to the variety theater of the nineteenth century as *fisicofolia* or body-madness. Chico Marx presented himself as a "boob" to Harpo's "nut." He pretended to be a simple Italian peasant who could not understand basic concepts while actually being willfully ignorant in order to get out of doing something he did not want to do—usually work. But Groucho's "eccentric" comedy was a combination of the physical body-madness, represented in his signature bizarre dances and crouching "Groucho walk," and the easily duped "boobs" like the authority figures of Captain Spaulding and President Rufus T. Firefly. He added to this with his unique barrage of non-sequitur dialogue (most often improvised) that overwhelmed his listener reducing him or her to a flummoxed, gibbering fool. Zeppo played the comic foil and straightman to his brothers. These outwardly varied forms of comedy came to create a distinctive style when melded together. It truly was vaudeville comedy with "something for everyone." If one type of comedy did not please, another was soon to be on the way. Groucho Marx, along with other performers like Mae West, Will Rogers, and Bert Williams—who are discussed in subsequent chapters—beginning in the late nineteenth century to the mid-1920s, crafted their vaudeville aesthetic after almost thirty years on the stages of the United States.

Vaudeville acts consisted of a series of five-to-twenty-minute acts in no particular order except to represent a wide range of performances so that audience members could drop in at any point in the proceedings and be able to follow the action onstage. Acts included performers trained in commercial theater, holdovers from nineteenth-century minstrel and variety shows, and young people direct from the streets who developed acts on their own. Included were cabaret singers, male and female impersonators, tap dancers—known as "hoofers," acrobats, animal trainers, prizefighters, and strong men. There were "dumb" (silent) acts, singers of popular songs, opera, jazz, and musical revue tunes, dances ranging from ballet to eccentric self-styled choreography, juggling, fire-breathing, bogus "mystics," mind readers, escape acts, Shakespearean soliloquies, solo comics, and comedy teams of multiple performers. As long as the bill was arranged so as not to repeat the same type of act back to back, there was no regard for narrative throughline, only the inevitable build-up of excitement for the headliners who ended the shows.

In order to evaluate the vaudeville aesthetic, I first look to the work of comedy legend, Buster Keaton. The early stage career of Keaton serves as the apotheosis of vaudeville's humor both on stage and screen. Keaton is one of the acknowledged masters of silent-film comedy, however he began his comedy apprenticeship on the vaudeville stage with his parents in an act called the Three Keatons.[5] Buster Keaton serves as a superlative illustration of how vaudeville comedy was performed during the first two decades of the twentieth century.

Keaton's vaudeville stage acts are recorded in his short silent film *The Playhouse* (1921). This film shows him as a trained stage vaudevillian playing multiple roles both on- and backstage. Keaton's vaudeville gags and scenarios can be evaluated by reading this early silent-movie text to see how popular comic stage entertainments came to dominate his work. All the elements of the comic vaudeville stage and its roots can be witnessed in this film. Written, produced, directed (nominally with Eddie Kline), and starring Keaton, *The Playhouse* is a microcosm of the vaudevillian's world and encapsulates the vaudeville aesthetic.[6]

The film features the dreamlike series of scenes of a working-class man who toils unrecognized backstage while fantasizing about being successful onstage, winning the girl, becoming the hero-savior of his fellow vaudevillians, and entertaining a paying audience of various classes. *The Playhouse* can be viewed as the American dream embodied by a comic vaudevillian whose fantasy becomes reality on the vaudeville stage. However, Keaton's vision takes place in a much more ambivalent landscape of the underclass at the beginning of the twentieth century, documenting American illusion as delusion.

The Playhouse begins as a monodrama of a stagehand who keeps daydreaming of himself as the actors, musicians, and even audience he is performing for. The protean personae of the hallucinatory reality in which Keaton discovers himself metamorphose from one state to another, whether onstage, backstage, in the audience, or at the box office. Even Keaton's presumed safe haven of his bedroom becomes yet another set, and the prop room—filled with objects that presumably ground him in reality that serves as his refuge from the dream world—cannot be trusted as stable. Keaton's anxiety about being lost and disoriented in a theatrical world that has no foundation is reflected in this dreamscape where he must perform the roles of an entire minstrel show—including the interlocutor, end men (Tambo and Bones), complete with blackface and tap dancing, and even portrays a trained monkey—to keep up with the constant changes that present themselves to Keaton.

True to the vaudeville aesthetic, everything that can go wrong does go wrong with the various acts, as these theatrical worlds collide in a seemingly chaotic juxtaposition. The disruption of gags in and of themselves, sidetracked and derailed by other even more bizarre gags, is a comic innovation for the vaudeville stage and later slapstick silent films. One such scene from *The Playhouse* depicts the working-class aggression of Keaton's character as a put-upon stagehand. In a sequence that features his resentment at being a wage slave, he punches a time clock by actually hitting it with his fist. Another moment comes when Keaton, again as stagehand, sets the beard of the stage manager on fire. The stage manager happens to be Keaton's boss. To help his immediate superior, Keaton punches another object this time around—the glass case that houses a fire axe—and uses the axe to knock out the stage manager, proceeding to "shave" his burning beard and potentially decapitate the literal and figurative head of this backstage world. The aggression of Keaton's subservient character is exposed by his actions as he resists his working-class position and the bullying of those in authority over him in the theater's hierarchy.

Another gag sequence shows Keaton using the backdrop of a painted ocean and piercing this fantasy landscape by jumping through it as if swimming in an actual ocean. Then we go behind the curtain to see him beat on the stage manager through the same opening in the backdrop. The fantasy ocean becomes a reality after Keaton smashes open a water tank during an escape act reminiscent of Houdini's medicine-show routines with Keaton's real-life father, Joe. After the escape artist becomes trapped inside the "mermaid" tank, Keaton breaks the glass with a giant mallet, and the water from the tank gushes into the orchestra pit and onto the audience. As the spectators flee from the flood, Keaton escapes from the bully-stage manager using a bass drum as a boat in the now-flooded pit. The stage has now become a literal ocean, and the audience, as well as the onstage and backstage realities, come together in a final act that collides and confuses the theatrical fantasy with reality. The film ends with the stagehand, after surviving multiple disasters, eluding the bully and marrying his dream girl, but not before marking her neck with an *X* to avoid confusing her with her twin sister—another routine straight out of vaudeville.

The vaudeville stage that Keaton grew up on is reflected in this montage of staged realities. In Keaton, this produces a comic juxtaposition of acts that showcase his physical skills as he portrays a hapless stagehand who loses his bearings and identity in this parody of the world as a vaudeville theater that is barely under control. Walls that are actually stage flats drop away, and certainties shift from one state to another as in an anxiety dream.

As Keaton attempts to keep up with these unstable existences, the physical comedy comes from his desperation and apprehension of performing the various duties of actor, spectator, stagehand, trained monkey, and bewildered lover. The perpetual motion of these vaudeville acts keeps Keaton in a state of constant problem-solving, and the speed with which his reality keeps changing produces a desperation that creates comic physical distress; one of the signatures of the popular stage—body-madness.[7]

Keaton's *The Playhouse* combines the onstage disruption of narrative through a series of comic vaudeville gags that serve as an overarching structure without logical continuity. His control over the narrative dissolves into a series of disrupted and unforeseen events. The entire performance is a comic burlesque of a professional vaudeville show gone wrong. What constitutes "the show" is the deliberate disorder of the performance that culminates in a theater full of water and an audience running for the exit to escape this stage world from literally and metaphorically engulfing them. Keaton's vision of the vaudeville act as gag-driven entertainment is a film record of what his work was like on the comic vaudeville stage. It also serves as an archive of the vaudeville aesthetic.

After several successful short silent films like *One Week* (1920) and *Sherlock Jr.* (1924), culminating in his feature-length silent masterpiece, *The General* (1926), Buster Keaton had to face the reality of sound comedy films. In 1928, Keaton signed a contract with MGM, after having his own production company, Buster Keaton Comedies, since 1920. The vaudeville comedians, like Keaton, who were contracted to Hollywood studios soon found out that their brand of humor was on the wane. In an interview toward the end of his life, Keaton discussed why vaudevillians found the transition to the sound screen difficult: "Sound came in. New York stage directors, New York writers, dialogue writers, all moved to Hollywood. So the minute they started laying out a script, they're looking for those funny lines, puns, little jokes, anything else."[8] The focus on being "witty" with a set script by playwrights made it virtually impossible to maintain the physical and improvisational comedy that Keaton, and other vaudevillians discussed here like Bert Williams, were able to put over onstage.[9] The vaudeville construction of films like *The Playhouse*, with their gags and short comic acts with little to no connection to logic or storytelling progression, would be replaced by highly scripted and set narratives as sound comedies progressed into the 1930s and 1940s.

The demise of vaudeville, beginning in the mid-to-late-1920s, was concurrent with the birth of early sound film comedy effectively ending this "golden era" of comedy as it had existed on the American stage since the 1880s. As the Great Depression took hold, film comedy began to eclipse the voices of rebellion as it was being transformed into a new kind of humor. Although some of the vaudeville comedy acts were successful in sound film, they were best when they eschewed narratives and character development for the vaudeville aesthetic of unrelated comic sequences. For the more dialogue-driven comedians like Groucho Marx, Mae West, and Will Rogers, this transition was not as difficult, and in fact initially enhanced their careers. However after some film successes early on in their sound careers, even these verbal acts lost their allure, as their comedy after the mid-1930s became far less effective when studio executives forced them into formulaic story-oriented vehicles. Ultimately even these three iconic comedians lost control over the content of their pictures rendering them simply and even embarrassingly not funny.

The 1930s saw the advent of the screwball comedy that featured beautiful movie stars speaking witty dialogue and engaging in a traditional storyline that could be followed in a linear fashion. According to Depression-era cultural historian Morris Dickstein: "Culturally, 1934 was a key year for Hollywood" as the Production Code (a Hollywood censorship organization run by Will Hays) "replaced direct eroticism with explosive verbal and cultural energy and made the war between the sexes an unexpected metaphor for social conflict and concord" with the advent of screwball comedy.[10] This new form of film comedy, with its emphasis on sexual tensions portrayed through dialogue-driven sparring between highly attractive white actors, "replaced" and lessened the overt confrontation and commentary of ethnicity, class, gender, and the hegemony of Anglo-American sociocultural values, that the comic vaudevillians explored in this project, created for the vaudeville stage.

The feature-length format and stories that accompanied sound film were not the ideal presentation platform for former vaudevillians trained in the immediate, attention-getting short acts that characterized their stage work. As the 1930s progressed, radio and television would become the principal medium for these acts, particularly in comedy. Many comic vaudevillians were easily translated to radio, like Groucho Marx (*You Bet Your Life*, 1947), W. C. Fields (with Edgar Bergen and Charlie McCarthy on *The Chase and Sanborn Hour*, 1936), and Will Rogers (*The Gulf Headliners*, 1930). As the 1920s came to a close and the vaudeville stage began losing its performers to the burgeoning sound film industry, comedians became of particular interest to radio and later, to television producers. The vaudevillians had established stage careers and a fan base already built into their work; however, the one thing they also brought with them from the vaudeville stage was the autonomy of developing an act that they could sell with little change in format and content.

Vaudeville stage comedy and slapstick silent film relied on the disruption of the gag that intentionally derails the narrative structure of storytelling that came to characterize film. Radio and television would become the new home for the vaudeville-trained stage comedians and their gags. With these media came a shorter framework and a variety entertainment format, in order to place commercials and allow audiences who dropped in on these shows a way to access them without the context of an extended storyline. They could enter the sketch or monologue anywhere during the short program and be able to follow it. Segments would last from five to fifteen minutes with characters that could be easily identified by their simplistic outlines and recognizable types. Comic Hollywood films and Broadway plays had to sustain interest over a ninety-minute to two-hour performance requiring character development and a carefully plotted structure. Radio and television moved in the opposite direction with expansive characterizations and nonlinear, unconnected sequences. Vaudevillians who had been trained in the short sketch, the comic monologue, or the two-person act were right at home in radio and television.

In 1956, popular-entertainment critic Gilbert Seldes noted that the arrival of radio and television into what he called the "public arts" was a powerful sociocultural tool that had the potential to inform and entertain, or conversely become a banal, anesthetizing panacea. Taking the former, more optimistic position, Seldes cited two major figures in the public arts, Edward R. Murrow and Jimmy Durante, and their importance to radio and television as seemingly polar yet mutually supportive popular art forms.

> Our dependence, for our pleasures and for our ideas on the popular arts, on the movies and radio and television particularly, gives another significance to the word "public." [Murrow and Durante] represent institutions as powerful in shaping our lives as our schools, our politics, our system of government—and anything that affects the entire public is by nature compelled to serve the public.[11]

Although seemingly from the two different worlds of journalism and comedy, Murrow and Durante each shared a mutual responsibility, according to Seldes. "For the comedian creates an audience and hands it over to the news analyst," he argued, "and when that audience has met statesmen and philosophers and demagogues and poets it returns to the comedian, living more fully, using more of its faculties."[12] As radio and television comedy increased in importance beginning in the 1930s and throughout the 1940s and 1950s, it began with former vaudevillians who used these novel media—as Seldes had advocated— as a platform for "living more fully, using more of [the audience's] faculties," and, more significantly, confronting Americans with social critiques of pre- and postwar anxieties.

Radio dominated in the US from 1922 until the arrival of television in the early 1950s. In successive years, NBC Radio (1927) and CBS Radio (1928) began regular nationwide broadcasting, and with this new programming the number of radio sets increased at an extraordinary rate. At the beginning of the decade, circa 1922, three million American households had radio receivers, and sales of radio sets amounted to $60 million. However, by 1929, with a radio in one out of three homes in the United States, sales increased to $842,548,000— nearly 1,400 percent.[13] By the end of the decade, the radio became just another appliance, like refrigerators and vacuum cleaners, for middle-class living.

Vaudevillians were able to make the change to this new medium in large part because it relied on live broadcasts of short sketches, monologues, and interviews. The ability to work in a live format through improvisation and creating novel characterizations and easily recognizable types through simple voice inflection, accents, and vocabulary, was familiar to former vaudevillians.[14] The serialized comedy, like *The Amos 'n' Andy Show*, relied not on character development or nuance but on situations identifiable with the audience (being tricked out of money, problems with a job or a boss, and the daily maintenance of relationships and survival) that "created a new kind of relationship between audience and medium."[15] Comedy in the variety and quiz show format like *Your Show of Shows* and *You Bet Your Life* was perfect for the short programs, allowing for a similar structure to that of its predecessor in vaudeville.

One of the first branches of vaudeville to find its way to radio was minstrelsy. Both Gilbert Seldes and radio historian Michele Hilmes cite minstrel shows and their formats as being especially easy to transfer from stage to radio.[16] The significant difference from the visually oriented stage performance of race through the blackface mask, and the radio performance of blackness was that blackface visual comedy was superseded by the black-"voice" auditory identification of the "Negro" characters.

Performing in blackface in the first decades of the twentieth century was carried over from nineteenth-century-American minstrelsy that emerged in the 1830s. The minstrel show was structured as a semicircle of four or five (sometimes more) white male performers marked with the racial "blacking-up" of greasepaint or burnt cork and adorned in absurdly oversize or ragged "Negro" costumes.[17] The minstrel performers played a variety of instruments, including banjo, fiddle, bone castanets, and tambourine. The show was divided into three parts, the first of which was a random selection of songs interconnected with stereotyped Negro jokes and foolishness; the second part (called the "olio") featured performers who specialized in comedic dialogues, malapropism-laden stump speeches, and cross-dressed wench routines. The third part was a scenario, usually set in the South, comprised of music, dance, and burlesque.[18] It was the minstrel shows' structure and stereotyped characterizations that vaudeville would inherit and refine into the early twentieth century.[19] *The Amos 'n' Andy Show* would become the most successful transfer of minstrelsy first with radio and then later in television.

As comedy moved from the stage to radio, its influence and far-reaching audience appeal was witnessed with the phenomenal achievement of the 1928 debut of *The Amos 'n' Andy Show*. Popular-culture historian Arthur Wertheim confirms the unprecedented fame of this broadcast right from its inception: "The telephone company claimed that calls declined during the show's fifteen minutes on the air. . . . Motion picture theaters installed loud speakers in lobbies so that fans could hear the program over a radio placed on the stage."[20] The resurgence of the vaudeville aesthetic through radio had begun in earnest with the advent of *Amos 'n' Andy* and continued until the next media phenomenon of television in the early 1950s. The playwright and critic George Bernard Shaw summed up his impressions of the United States by writing, "There are things I shall never forget about America—the Rocky Mountains, Niagara Falls, and *Amos 'n' Andy*."[21]

The Amos 'n' Andy Show began as a radio comedy series debuting on January 12, 1926 under its original title of *Sam 'n' Henry*. It became an instant sensation in the Midwest and grew to be so popular that in 1927, Gosden and Correll asked Chicago radio station WGN to distribute it to other stations on phonograph records in an early version of syndication. After this proposal was rejected by WGN, Gosden and Correll left the show in July 1928. The characters that they created contractually belonged to WGN, so when WMAQ, the *Chicago Daily News* station, hired Gosden and Correll to create a radio serial in the same vein as *Sam 'n' Henry*—offering them significant salary increases and the right to the "chainless chain" notion of syndication—they gladly renamed the characters Amos and Andy, later noting that they chose these names after overhearing two elderly blacks greet each other by these names in a Chicago elevator.[22]

Amos 'n' Andy began its unprecedented run on radio on March 19, 1928, on WMAQ, written and voiced by Gosden and Correll. The radio program ran as a nightly series from 1928 to 1943, then as a weekly series from 1943 to 1955, and finally as a nightly disc jockey program from 1954 to 1960. The television adaptation of the series began on CBS-TV, airing from 1951 to 1953 and continuing in syndication from 1954 to 1966 with black actors Alvin Childress and Spencer Williams in the titular roles. It was produced at the Hal Roach Studios for CBS-TV. On radio, Gosden and Correll had voiced all the male roles (170 characters in all) for the show's first decade; however, when it was adapted for television, the newly hired black actors were instructed to keep their speech patterns and vocal qualities as close to Gosden and Correll's as they possibly could.

Amos 'n' Andy broadcasts, particularly during the Depression era, reaffirmed to American listeners that faith in the country's institutions was not misplaced. The Depression was seen by some middle-class Americans as an instructional tool teaching and reminding Americans to look to the ideals associated with the American way of life.[23] *Amos 'n' Andy* depicted two contrasting characters—one, a get-rich-quick schemer in Andy, and the other, an honest, hardworking, and trustworthy friend and colleague. As introduced by the announcer, Andy was described as "not especially fond of hard work," while Amos was a "hard working little fellow who tries to do everything he can to help others and to make himself progress." The self-important Andy appointed himself president of the Fresh Air Taxi Company, while the conscientious Amos was the "chief mechanics mate, fixer of automobiles, head driver . . . and chief bizness gitter."[24] Gosden and Correll used the character of Amos to confirm American values of liberality, conscientiousness, and sincerity that many Americans wished to restore during the trying times of the Great Depression.[25]

Much like its forerunner, *Sam 'n' Henry*, the characters of *Amos 'n' Andy* have moved from rural Georgia to the urban North (first Chicago, then Harlem) to look for work. Reflecting a time when employment was difficult to find, especially for two black Southerners, Andy conceives of becoming an entrepreneur to "make a lot o' money":

ANDY: Wait a minute—I got an idea.

AMOS: Whut is it, whut is it—'splain it to me.

ANDY: We kin start sumpin' new—be diff'ent dan anything else in de country—we kin clean up a fortune—make barrels of money—be millionaires—have de biggest comp'ny in de world.

AMOS: Wait a minute—wait a minute—'splain dat to me—how we goin' do it?

ANDY: You say de car aint got no top on it.

AMOS: Dat's de trouble wid it—it ain't got no top on it—but we kin git de car on time.

ANDY: We'll buy dat automobile an' start up a comp'ny called de Fresh Air Taxi Comp'ny.

AMOS: Boy, dat's a idea—Um—Um—de Fresh Air Company—Um—Um.[26]

However, being their own bosses came with constant harassment by creditors and lawsuits, as they failed to pay their income taxes because they did not understand the forms. Andy in particular was vulnerable to huckster salesmen, especially the character of Kingfish—a Zip Coon prototype from minstrelsy, played by Tim Moore—who took advantage of their naïveté and invested their money on schemes that were mostly failed business ventures.

Broadcast historians including Melvin Patrick Ely, Michele Hilmes, Arthur Frank Wertheim, and Elizabeth McLeod have weighed in on the virtues and detriments of the show's black characterizations, particularly when performed by the white actor-writers on radio.[27] The racism of these central character types carried over from minstrel shows cannot be denied, however many secondary characters in the black social club, known as the fraternal order of the Mystic Knights of the Sea, were cast as physicians, lawyers, accountants, and business owners creating a more sympathetic and complex depiction of blacks in popular entertainment. The typage of minstrelsy was slowly giving way to a more diverse portrait of black life in urban centers like Chicago and New York. If we see popular entertainments and audience's reactions to them as reflections rather than creations of social realities, then *Amos 'n' Andy* reflected a time when Americans were grappling with the integration of blacks and whites and the perceptions of race that were about to explode onto the streets of Middle America in the 1960s.

The sensation of radio comedy was absorbed into television during the late 1940s. In 1945, fewer than ten thousand television sets were part of American homes; however, fifteen years later that number would reach sixty million. At present there are more than a quarter-billion televisions in the United States, with about 97 percent of all households owning at least one—not including personal computers, tablets, myriad "i-devices," and cell phones, which are replacing the television as sources of popular entertainment and the "public arts."[28] The unprecedented increase in new media technology during the 1920s through the 1950s would increase the profile of humor in the United States. Gilbert Seldes commented that during the mid-twentieth century, comedy had become "the axis on which broadcasting revolves."[29] Radio and then television comedy drew from the vaudeville aesthetic by using social satire of middle-class Americans, ethnic and race acts that featured stereotyped behavior as social commentary, the burlesque of gender roles, and the growing divide between female and male sociocultural constructs.

Stage comedians were most suited to television since this new medium retained the structure and "liveness" of vaudeville. Performance historian and theorist Philip Auslander makes a compelling case that "[t]elevision was imagined *as theatre*."[30] The broadcasting of programs directly into the home allowed viewers to experience the feeling of theater as if they were actually there. Film allowed audiences to voyeuristically view a scene in the darkness separated from the larger-than-life fantasy action on the sixty-foot-tall silver screen, whereas television would give spectators the feeling of being part of the presentation as if the actors were speaking directly to them in the intimacy of their own home. Writing in 1940 during the formative years of television broadcasting, Hans Burger in *Theatre Arts* notes that actors performed to cameras as if they were playing to "the fourth wall . . . much as it is on stage."[31] The vaudeville aesthetic was most easily transferred to television as it became a new form of theater without actually leaving the personal domain of the home.

A 1958 book titled *A Primer for Playgoers* in which the case for theater as television is advocated notes:

The tremendous personal comfort of relaxing at home in an easy chair and seeing some of the top names in the theatre world perform in a variety of three or four programs in a single evening. This involves a greater degree of physical comfort than to come home weary from the day's work, wash, dress, hurry, drive through heavy traffic, find a place to park, walk to the theatre, pay an ever-increasing admission, sit on the same seat for two hours, then fight traffic and arrive home very late.[32]

Former vaudevillians like Groucho Marx embraced this idea of the "liveness" of television as a natural progression from stage comedy to the televisual medium. His second act success on *You Bet Your Life* would not only revive Groucho's career but solidify his iconic image created on the vaudeville stage even more readily than the Marx Brothers' films had. Accessing Groucho on television would be easier and more ubiquitous on the small screen, as he reached into middle-class American homes, both in its original broadcasts and through syndication for years to come.

Groucho Marx made the transition from stage and film to radio first. His radio show was designed as a quiz show called *You Bet Your Life*. It debuted on ABC Radio in October 1947, then moved to CBS Radio in September 1949 before making the transition to NBC-TV in October 1950. It was broadcast simultaneously on radio and television.

Isidore Lindenbaum, the president of Film Craft Productions, which produced *You Bet Your Life* for NBC-TV,[33] discussed the reasoning behind making the popular quiz show "the first TV program ever filmed before a live audience" in a one-hour take that could be edited before it was broadcast. According to Lindenbaum, Groucho, "the comedian, wished to play to his audience" and needed "their laughs, their applause, even the general feel of audience presence."[34] In other words, for his television debut, Groucho decided to return not to his film roots but to his vaudeville stage past to structure his comedy. Putting the program in sequence like a stage show allowed Groucho to play to a live audience through an improvisatory series of interviews with contestants.

The real focus of the program was not the quiz show portion, which was almost an afterthought, taking up only a quarter of the hour-long show, but Groucho's command before a live audience. Groucho's relationship with his contestants on *You Bet Your Life* was an adversarial one that often forced a truthful confession out of seemingly middle-class, ordinary citizens. Groucho's attack extended to institutional authority represented by individuals from the professional classes (lawyers, doctors), middle-class office employees (insurance salesmen were a particular favorite target), and religious leaders. According to biographer and comedy historian, Joe Adamson, "Once a clergyman came on his television show glowing and declared 'Groucho, I want to thank you for all the enjoyment you have given the world.' Groucho shot right back, 'And I want to thank you for all the enjoyment you've taken out of it.' "[35] Contestants for the game show were chosen and vetted by the producers and Groucho to maximize the use of his ability to respond in the moment as he had on the vaudeville stage.

Groucho put questions and comments into a spontaneous format that ebbed and flowed according to audience reactions and built his humor throughout the broadcast much like he had onstage with the Marx Brothers during the 1910s and 1920s. As Lindenbaum noted, it was not the network's decision to produce the show this way, but rather at the request of its star and co-producer, Groucho,[36] who insisted on this structure as a result of his twenty-plus-year stage experience in vaudeville. Groucho cited the lack of spontaneity and audience reaction that had begun to dull the Marx Brothers' film work, particularly at MGM in the mid-to-late-1930s and 1940s. "[Groucho Marx] also has required continuity of the program," acknowledged Lindenbaum. "He doesn't want it broken up for light changes, camera positions changes, film magazine changes, or for any other reason. He wants the entire program shot in sequence. . . . He wants no interruptions to cool the audience or his own enthusiasm."[37] This continuity with vaudeville and its audience interplay proved Groucho's prescience in this untested medium for his brand of humor: You Bet Your Life ran on NBC-TV and Radio from 1950 to 1961. According to Lindenbaum, Groucho "wants undivided attention"[38] and received it for over a decade in both radio and television.

Groucho became a primary influence on television's most successful star in the 1950s, Sid Caesar. Like Gosden and Correll, and Groucho Marx, Caesar made direct use of the vaudeville format with his program, Your Show of Shows. Sid Caesar took the vaudeville aesthetic to its logical conclusion with this hit television show. Caesar, as a pioneer of early television comedy, is another direct link to vaudeville, using its structure and tropes to create a new television format soon to be known as variety television. From 1950 to 1958, Caesar would dominate television comedy with Your Show of Shows (NBC, 1950–54), Caesar's Hour (NBC, 1954–57), and finally Sid Caesar Invites You (ABC, 1958). His influence was felt into the 1960s when cast member and co-writer Carl Reiner would create The Dick Van Dyke Show; co-writer Neil Simon would become a significant playwright of Broadway comedies until the 1990s; staff writer Woody Allen would begin his impressive fifty-year career, first onstage, then in filmmaking, which continues today; and Mel Brooks, as writer-producer of iconic comic films and stage shows that have become future Broadway musicals, like Young Frankenstein (2007–9) and The Producers (2001–present). Indirect but just as influential would be Caesar's influence on Rowan & Martin's Laugh-In in the 1960s, and Lorne Michaels's Saturday Night Live in the 1970s.

Caesar's vaudeville format included burlesques—in the nineteenth-century meaning of parody—featuring silent-film and film noir send-ups; Italian opera produced in Caesar's ad-libbed, faux-Italian double-talk; and "double acts" about middle-class tribulations of married life, featuring collaborator Imogene Coca—whose role was later taken over by Nanette Fabray. Caesar's variety programming, including Borscht Belt *tummler*, burlesque, and vaudeville playlets and sketches, featured the ethnic humor of the early twentieth century.

Caesar was born in 1922 to Jewish immigrant parents living in Yonkers, New York. His father, Max, had emigrated from Poland; his mother, Ida (née Raphael), from the former Russian Empire. Caesar's parents ran an all-night luncheonette where a young Sid waited on tables and learned to mimic the ethnic accents and patois of its diverse customers. It was there that he developed the comic technique of "double-talk," which was popular with vaudeville comedians like Chico Marx and the duo of Joe Weber and Lew Fields. Caesar was "fluent" in ad-libbed Polish, Russian, Hungarian, French, Spanish, Lithuanian, and Bulgarian, which he used on his show throughout the 1950s.[39]

Caesar's acknowledged debt to former vaudevillians of the 1910s and 1920s is evidenced in his autobiography, *Caesar's Hours*:

> The key to the success of the show was very simple, if not amazingly challenging to execute week after week—we had the ability to extract humor out of everyday life. The humor sprang from everyday events and was a mixture of the sad and funny. The guy in trouble is a very funny guy. Chaplin [and Keaton] knew that in 1910 and we knew that in 1950.[40]

The aphorism "comedy is a man in trouble" shows Caesar's everyman who encounters the daily life of the middle-class husband and employee in his sketch comedy. The Hickenloopers would become a recurring sketch for Caesar and Coca (and later, Fabray) in which the beleaguered male was in a constant struggle to maintain his middle-class status and the respect of his wife and colleagues. In one scenario, Caesar and Fabray live in a typical overly small, overly expensive Manhattan apartment, refusing to move to the suburbs in an effort to be cosmopolitan. The couple hosts a dinner party for three other couples in their tiny one-room studio. Caesar, in an effort to ignore the obvious and act with normalcy, attempts to carve a turkey on a card table with all the guests crushed around it. With the food in their laps and the threat of decapitation from the carving knife in such close proximity, Caesar tries to appear triumphant when all the plates are filled with food, but no one can eat because they all have their hands full holding their heaped plates.

This sketch was reminiscent of the "stateroom" scene in the Marx Brothers' *A Night at the Opera* (1935), in which a small berth aboard an ocean liner is overrun with the ship's staff, passengers, and the stowaways themselves—the Marx Brothers. As food is delivered to the overfull room of strangers, Harpo is placed on platters while sleeping and moved hand over hand like a roasted suckling pig. Caesar translated vaudevillian scenarios like this Marx Brothers' classic to the ordinary experiences of the middle-class Jewish married couple and their "bedroom" communities. The Sisyphean tasks of the quotidian overwhelm the Hickenloopers depicting an existential angst that contradicted the American dream of the suburban 1950s.

As the decade came to a close, Caesar's career would come to a grinding halt. Although he would do guest appearances on other television shows and featured roles in films, Caesar's vaudevillian humor would quickly disappear from the American landscape. As Caesar himself notes in *Caesar's Hours*,

> There was no one reason but a number of them, each true to varying degrees, why the show was losing its steam and slipping in the ratings. For one thing, as the television audience was expanding outside of the big cities, audience tastes were changing and attention spans were shrinking. They didn't understand the foreign movies we were parodying. We were writing high-class comedy and were not willing to dumb it down.[41]

As America moved toward more homogenous cultural trends, comedy moved in this direction as well, and Caesar's more challenging and complex commentary on the plight of the average man came to an end.

Television comedy, in the early 1950s, would incorporate stage and radio performers. The vaudeville aesthetic would thrive with its variety of short acts comprised of comic sketches, songs, and stand-up monologues, that fit the framework of the half-hour show with commercial breaks.[42] Initially television's target audience was the educated and upper-middle classes who could afford a television set. But as the price of television sets dropped and as middle-class affluence rose, television reached a less "sophisticated" audience of lower, middle, and working classes in the United States.

By the late 1950s, the new middle class had moved to the suburbs and the dream of middle-class family success was transferred to television families as the Cold War era took hold and a homogenized Anglo-American middle-class was represented on television by *Father Knows Best* and *Leave it to Beaver*. The vaudeville format of *You Bet Your Life* and *Your Show of Shows* was replaced by what became known as the situation comedy (sitcom) of families, friends, and colleagues, and their everyday existences.

During the formative years of radio and television, comic vaudevillians were in demand for the comedy skills that made them vaudeville stage successes. Comic vaudevillians whose techniques created the breakthroughs that led to the popularity of radio and television comedians like Freeman Gosden and Charles Correll, Groucho Marx, and Sid Caesar, were able to bridge the live comic stage to the new media. These comedians were joined by Fred Allen, Fanny Brice, Lucille Ball, and Phil Silvers who dominated comic popular entertainment during the 1940s and 1950s. The 1960s through the 1980s would see the return to the vaudeville aesthetic in comic performers like Mort Sahl, Lenny Bruce, Gilda Radner, and Richard Pryor. These comic innovators will be discussed in subsequent chapters as they provided the bridge from the vaudevillians Groucho Marx, Mae West, Will Rogers, and Bert Williams, to the world of comedy in the twenty-first century.

Gilbert Seldes noted that the public arts of the 1950s of radio and television "discovered the manipulation of symbols and the use of entertainment itself to create the atmosphere in which our ideas are formed."[43] As comedy evolved from the mid-twentieth century it would not remain simply a popular entertainment in the public consciousness but also a source for sociocultural critique in the United States. The vaudeville aesthetic and its "atmosphere in which our ideas are formed" was revived by producer Lorne Michaels with *Saturday Night Live* (*SNL*) and the Canadian comedy-variety show, *Second City Television* (*SCTV*)—both televised offshoots of Toronto and Chicago's Second City improvisation-comedy companies—and Keenan Ivory and Damon Wayan's *In Living Color*.[44] Alumni from these shows included Dan Aykroyd, John Belushi, John Candy, Jim Carrey, Stephen Colbert, Tina Fey, Joe Flaherty, Jaime Foxx, David Alan Grier, Eugene Levy, Jennifer Lopez, Andrea Martin, Rick Moranis, Tracy Morgan, Bill Murray, Catherine O'Hara, Gilda Radner, Chris Rock, Martin Short, and the family act of the Wayans Brothers—Keenan Ivory, Damon, Marlon, and Shawn—all of whom have either appeared as guest hosts on *SNL*, *SCTV*, and *In Living Color*, or worked as part of these show's ensembles.

The comedic tradition of the vaudeville aesthetic has created a theatricality and communication between past and present that characterized vaudeville comedy from the advent of the modernist era to the present. How radio and television used the vaudeville aesthetic will form the basis of examining the changes and crossovers of vaudevillians and their acts to the new media performers of the twenty-first century as they are evaluated in the following chapters through the work of Larry David, Tina Fey, Stephen Colbert, and Dave Chappelle.

Notes

1 Groucho Marx, *Groucho and Me* (New York, Bernard Geis Associates, 1959), 225.

2 See Philip Auslander's *Liveness* (London and New York: Routledge), 1999.

3 Edward F. Albee, "Twenty Years of Vaudeville," *Variety* 72, no. 3 (September 6, 1923): 18.

4 Unidentified reviewer, "Review of *Home Again*," *Utah Democrat*, March 9, 1917.

5 Robert Knopf provides one of the most complete examinations of Keaton's vaudeville years, although his primary focus is Keaton's later film work. Robert Knopf, *The Theater and Cinema of Buster Keaton* (Princeton, NJ: Princeton University Press, 1999), 36–37.

6 All references to Keaton's film come from *The Playhouse*, directed by Buster Keaton, in the *Buster Keaton Collection* (1921; Montreal, Canada: St. Clair Vision, 2007), DVD.

7 F. T. Marinetti, "The Variety Stage," in *Critical Writings*, ed. Gunter Berghaus (New York: Farrar, Straus, Giroux, 2006), 185–92.

8 Buster Keaton, "The Knockabouts," *Make 'Em Laugh: The Funny Business of America*, episode 3 (New York: Rhino Entertainment, 2008), DVD.

9 Bert Williams and his stage career are discussed in detail in Chapter 5.

10 Morris Dickstein, *Dancing in the Dark: A Cultural History of the Great Depression* (New York: W. W. Norton, 2009), 441–42.

11 Gilbert Seldes, *The Public Arts* (New York: Appleton-Century-Crofts, 1958), vi.

12 Seldes, *The Public Arts*, vii.

13 George Soule, *Prosperity Decade: From War to Depression: 1917–1929* (New York: Reinhart, 1947), 147–51; Frederick Lewis Allen, *Only Yesterday: An Informal History of the 1920s* (New York: Harper and Brothers, 1931), 137–38; Arthur Frank Wertheim, *Radio Comedy* (New York: Oxford University Press, 1979), 16–17.

14 Radio programs often went unrecorded and thus the ephemeral nature of the stage and radio were linked as well.

15 Michelle Hilmes, *Radio Voices: American Broadcasting, 1922–1952* (Minneapolis, MN: University of Minnesota Press, 1997), xix.

16 Minstrelsy is discussed in Chapter 5.

17 Very rarely were there female performers in the antebellum minstrel show.

18 Eric Lott, *Love and Theft: Blackface Minstrelsy and the American Working Class* (New York: Oxford University Press, 1995), 5–6.

19 Minstrel shows will be discussed in detail in Chapter 5.

20 Wertheim, *Radio Comedy*, 48–49.

21 Wertheim, *Radio Comedy*, 48–49.

22 Hilmes, *Radio Voices*, 384; quoted from John Dunning, ed., *On the Air: The Encyclopedia of Old-Time Radio* (New York: Oxford University Press, 1998), 840.

23 Wertheim, *Radio Comedy*, 40; Hadley Cantril and Gordon W. Allport, *The Psychology of Radio* (New York: Harper and Brothers, 1935), 24.

24 Wertheim, *Radio Comedy*, 42–43; *Andy 'n' Andy* script no. 1 (March 19, 1928), 1, script no. 29 (April 27, 1928), 2, Freeman Gosden and Charles Correll Collection, Department of Special Collections, Doheny Library, University of Southern California, Los Angeles.

25 Wertheim, *Radio Comedy*, 44; *Andy 'n' Andy* script no. 836 (November 27, 1930), 3–4, Gosden and Correll Collection.

26 *Amos 'n' Andy*, script no. 23 (April 19, 1928), 4–5, Gosden and Correll Collection.

27 Ely, Hilmes, and Wertheim are cited above. Elizabeth McLeod, *The Original Amos 'n' Andy: Freeman Gosden, Charles Correll and the 1928–1943 Radio Serial* (Jefferson, NC: McFarland, 2005).

28 Stephen Apkon, *The Age of the Image: Redefining Literacy in a World of Screens* (New York: Farrar, Straus and Giroux, 2013), 32–33.

29 Seldes, *The Public Arts*, 133.

30 Auslander, *Liveness*, 23.

31 Hans Burger, "Through the Television Camera," *Theatre Arts* (March 1, 1940): 209.

32 Edward A. Wright, *A Primer for Playgoers* (Englewood Cliffs, NJ: Prentice-Hall, 1958), 222–23; I gratefully acknowledge Philip Auslander's *Liveness* which was invaluable in bringing this discussion to my attention and the works cited here on television production during the 1950s, particularly Hans Burger and Edward A. Wright.

33 *You Bet Your Life* had a long life on radio, being simultaneously programmed first on ABC, then on CBS Radio (1947–50), and finally on NBC Radio (1950–60) until 1960.

34 Isidore Lindenbaum, "Film on the Marx," *Television Magazine*, August 1952: 31.

35 Joe Adamson, *Groucho, Harpo, Chico, and Sometimes Zeppo* (New York: Simon and Schuster, 1983), 36–37.

36 Groucho owned 50 percent of the production rights to *You Bet Your Life*.

37 Lindenbaum, "Film on the Marx," 31.

38 Lindenbaum, "Film on the Marx," 31–32.

39 Sid Caesar, with Eddy Friedfeld, *Caesar's Hours: My Life in Comedy with Love and Laughter* (New York: Public Affairs Books, 2005), 16–17.

40 Sid Caesar, with Eddy Friedfeld, *Caesar's Hours*, 91.

41 Sid Caesar, with Eddy Friedfeld, *Caesar's Hours*, 115.

42 Many of the references to television history cited in the conclusion come from: Gerald Nachman, *Seriously Funny: The Rebel Comedians of the 1950s*

and 1960s (New York: Pantheon Books, 2003), and David Marc, *Comic Visions: Television Comedy and American Culture*, 2nd ed. (Malden, MA: Blackwell Publishers, 1997), 44–45.

43 Seldes, *Public Arts*, 66.

44 *Saturday Night Live* (October 11, 1975–present), *Second City Television* (September 21, 1976–July 17, 1984), and *In Living Color* (April 15, 1990–May 19, 1994).

2

"What's real got to do with what we do?"

Groucho Marx to Larry David

I find television very educating. Every time somebody turns on the set, I go into the other room and read a book.

GROUCHO MARX

In an episode titled "The Bare Midriff" during season 7 of *Curb Your Enthusiasm*, Larry David requests that a character on the "Seinfeld Reunion" episode be cast with an unknown, "because you believe that it's real." Jerry Seinfeld responds, "What's *real* got to do with what *we* do?" According to David, the show's executive producer, star, and creator, *Curb* uses scenarios that come from David's life and are improvised by professional actors in front of cameras. Not only does this give the show its spontaneous feeling, it simulates a kind of reality that makes it seem as if the characters are not working from scripts. *Curb* traffics in iconographic American social patterns and behaviors in relationship to events like weddings, funerals, dating, marriage, and religious affiliations, and how people belie what is accepted as "real" by their unexpected and often seemingly unbelievable actions and reactions. *Curb* has the feeling and veneer of reality but is a crafted and intentional popular entertainment, as well as a social commentary that questions the rituals of contemporary Americans.

For Groucho Marx and Larry David, their social criticism is not so much political as it is personal. In David's case, unlike that of his topical contemporary peers Stephen Colbert, Bill Maher, and Jon Stewart, he can be seen as fellow comedian Jeff Garlin describes him on *Curb*, as "a social assassin."[1] Jerry

Seinfeld explains the humor of *Seinfeld*, which he and David co-wrote and produced, this way: "Larry was a guy open to discussing virtually any human dilemma, as long as it was something that not a lot of other people were interested in. I was exactly the same way. We weren't interested in what was on the front page of the newspaper."[2] Taking into consideration their early careers, beginning chronologically with Groucho Marx and then moving to Larry David, as comics in vaudeville and stand-up, we can see how they were influenced by the vaudeville aesthetic and how cultural awareness began to take shape in the work of these social assassins.

The comedian as social assassin can be traced from the history of subversive comedy beginning with the *tummlers* of villages with large Jewish populations known as *shtetls*. Eastern European and Russian Jews from the *shtetls* who immigrated brought with them the *tummler*, a popular entertainment type that would become part of comic diversions in the resorts of upstate New York known colloquially as the Borscht Belt. The *tummler* ridiculed and taunted guests at traditional Jewish weddings in the *shtetls* and eventually became prominent in New York with the mass immigration of Slovak and Russian Jews in the late nineteenth century. *Tummler* comes from a Yiddish word, *tumler*, meaning "one who makes a racket," and *tummeln*, "to go among the people, cavort."[3] The *tummler* traveled with immigrants and found a place in the Yiddish theater of New York's Lower East Side and American vaudeville with comic solo acts and monologists like Fanny Brice, Eddie Cantor, Danny Kaye, Groucho Marx, and Sophie Tucker, as well as double acts like Joe Weber and Lew Fields.

Tummlers became part of the early twentieth-century new humor of cynicism, aggression, and humiliation that was a significant part of popular stage comedy. By 1900 the comic actors of the Yiddish theater were becoming as popular as their more mainstream rivals in the American vaudeville form of comedy, and in 1905, scholars of the settlement-house movement commented that saloons and dance halls were being converted at an alarming rate, as "every important street on the Lower East Side has its glaring electric sign which announces 'Jewish Vaudeville House' or 'Music Hall.'"[4] Sixty percent of the vaudeville audience in 1910 was working class, according to a settlement-house survey, with only 36 percent composed of the "clerical class." Yiddish vaudeville was more often than not located in the commercial entertainment areas, either within or at least bordering working-class neighborhoods. Theaters in Manhattan alone were founded in large numbers in such impoverished locations as 14th Street, 125th Street, Eighth Avenue, Grand Street, and the Bowery.[5]

The Yiddish theater would come under scrutiny as early as 1905. Ethnic performances were thought to be coded through foreign languages and stage traditions that encouraged the immigrant-friendly audiences to question their assimilation to the American middle class. Responding to the Yiddish Music Hall comic performers, one settlement worker observed: "The songs are suggestive of everything but what is proper, the choruses are full of double meanings, and the jokes have broad and unmistakable hints of things indecent."[6] The presumed collusion between performer and spectator by reform-minded Americans revealed a prejudiced distrust of ethnic vaudevillians—particularly those who made reference to a cultural heritage that they could not understand and consequently feared. One of the many stage techniques that the Yiddish comic theater used that authorities perceived as suspect, yet would become a successful tool on the vaudeville stage, was performer–audience interaction. For the *tummler*-influenced comedians of Eastern European heritage, the development from Yiddish theater and the language of the *shtetl* and its Anglo-American confrontation became the comic's battleground. As sociologist John Murray Cuddihy writes with regard to Jewish versus Gentile representations in American society in the early immigrant days of the twentieth century: "The 'serious and restrained' words of your liberal-Reform Jews will 'pass,' but the mocking impudence of your *schlemiels . . .* will not pass."[7]

An example of *shtetl* humor can be observed in the vaudeville act of Groucho Marx captured in the Marx Brothers' 1932 film, *Horse Feathers*. In a scene when Groucho and Chico are pretending to give a young woman (Thelma Todd) a singing lesson, a jealous boyfriend asks Groucho why he is at the event. He replies, "I'm the plumber. I'm just hanging around in case something goes wrong with her pipes." Groucho pauses and then acknowledges his bad joke by turning to the audience/camera in an aside and says, "That's the first time I've used that joke in twenty years." As Chico continues to play the piano, Groucho stands up and walks directly to the camera, and in another aside to the theater's audience, says, "I've got to stay here. But there's no reason you folks shouldn't go out into the lobby until this thing blows over."[8] Groucho's self-deprecating commentary on his attempts at humor and the absurdity of the whole scene asks the audience not to take him seriously and, in fact, not to bother with sitting and watching the scene at all.

These comic vaudevillian insults and asides were derived from the tradition of taunting and teasing audiences as with the *tummlers*. The legacy of the *tummler* can be witnessed from Groucho Marx to Larry David through the alter-ego characters of "Groucho" and "Larry"—Groucho Marx and Larry David are referred to as "Groucho" and "Larry" when discussing the characters they play as opposed to them as writer-performers. Both "Groucho" and "Larry" are unexpurgated versions of the real-life Groucho Marx and Larry David; they are honest but selfish, sincere but coercive, yet are ultimately themselves as they really would like to be in the quotidian world. They are direct and unfiltered and speak what they truly think and feel through these characters.

For "Groucho" and "Larry," telling it like it is can be perceived as insensitive and even offensive, but fans enjoy their caustic humor through these characterizations. They re-enact how audiences would like to be able to behave socially. During a televised interview with fellow comedian and sitcom creator Ricky Gervais, Larry David notes that in real life, you cannot always say what is actually on your mind, and as a comedian, "if you're any good, you kinda have to have a compulsion to tell the truth." "And without guilt," Gervais concurs. "This is guilt-free truth."[9] Looking at the work of Groucho Marx and Larry David—both of whom are connected by their outsider status in an insider's world and by their respective personas on- and offstage—reveals how they use the vaudeville aesthetic as a form of biography, as well as of cultural critique.

Groucho Marx's transition from vaudeville to film reveals a significant factor in his stage work and the nature of his outsider-as-insider character. A story from his autobiography, *Groucho and Me*, begins to tease out the question of audience reception and participation with regard to live versus filmed vaudeville acts:

> When *Animal Crackers* closed [on Broadway] and we went west for Paramount, our first movie was to be [*The*] *Cocoanuts*. Soon after we arrived I was called into a conference and informed that I would have to discard the black, painted mustache. When I asked why, they explained, "Well, nobody's ever worn a black painted mustache on the screen. The audience isn't accustomed to anything as phony as that and just won't believe it." "The audience doesn't believe us anyhow," I answered. "All they do is laugh at us and, isn't that what we're getting paid for?"[10]

Groucho Marx's mustache establishes the fiction that is the essence of the ubiquitous character known as "Groucho." This anecdote referring to the "Groucho" greasepaint mustache as a mask that has to fool the audience with its reality, weakens the notion that the film-studio executive thinks he is tricking the gullible audience into believing in a fictional construct. However, that same "fooled" audience appeared well aware of the character's phoniness as portrayed by Groucho Marx. The audience's enjoyment lies in the make-believe of show business, and their complicity in the joke makes his mustache funny while it symbolizes a bogusness that gets passed off to those in authority as real. Ultimately, the "Groucho" mustache incident reveals the obtuseness of the entertainment industry's hierarchies. Recalling Seinfeld's admonition of "Larry," the significance of the greasepaint mustache engages the question, "What's *real* got to do with what *we* do?"

Groucho Marx and Larry David began their careers as small-time stage performers. Groucho was born and raised in New York City of Eastern European immigrants, Minnie and Sam "Frenchie" Marx. He was one of five brothers all of who were part of the Marx Brothers' stage act at some point in their history. Larry David was brought up in middle-class Sheepshead Bay, Brooklyn, to Rose and Morty David, and followed a typical path of an American youth attending high school and then graduating college. He then tried to break into show business by living in Manhattan while taking random jobs to support himself. Groucho and Larry's blunt, cynical, and improvisatory styles were developed after many years on stage. Groucho in vaudeville and Larry in stand-up comedy.

Beginning with the third-tier vaudeville career of Groucho, we can witness the trajectory of a successful show business legend that spans stage, film, radio, and television, and made "Groucho" an iconic character whose signature glasses, heavy black greasepaint eyebrows and mustache, and ever-present cigar, part of the landscape of popular culture from the early twentieth century to the present. Groucho Marx began his stage career as a teenager using his birth name of Julius. He was the first Marx brother to work in vaudeville beginning in 1905 at the age of fifteen, when he joined an act called the Leroy Trio.[11] According to Marx, he discovered an ad in the *New York Morning World* stating: "Boy singer wanted for star vaudeville act. Room and board and four dollars a week."[12] Robin Leroy, a middle-aged singer-dancer and self-proclaimed vaudeville star, hired the fifteen-year-old Marx as a singer, along with a teenage male dancer named Johnny Morris, to complete the trio. Marx observes his youthful exuberance for his newfound profession in his autobiography: "I was in show business, even if it was only two weeks. . . . I felt for the first time in my life I wasn't a nonentity. I was part of the Larong [*sic*] Trio. I was an actor. My dream had come true."[13] To give a sense of what this small-time act was like, Marx describes the end of his first vaudeville tour in Grand Rapids, Michigan.

Larong [*sic*] closed the act dressed as the Statue of Liberty and holding a torch in his hand. Morton and I were decked out as Continental soldiers, guarding Miss Liberty from her unseen enemies. The unseen enemies turned out to be the audience, and only the fact that the theatre was almost empty by this time saved us from being stoned.[14]

The reality of show business became clear to Groucho Marx when they played their final engagement in Cripple Creek, Colorado, and found that Leroy had skipped town with the act and Groucho's pay. "I don't know where dire straits is," reflects Groucho, "but I certainly was now in that neighborhood. No money, no job, a minimum of talent and far, far from home. It was no use writing my mother and father for money. They didn't have any, either."[15]

Soon after his ignominious return from the road, Julius Marx's development as a vaudevillian would become closely aligned through his early collaboration with his brothers and their act put together by his mother, Minnie, in 1907. Minnie Marx, seeing no prospects for her public-school-dropout sons, was buoyed by the success of Julius' vaudevillian uncle, Al Shean, who was himself a popular show-business figure, starring with his partner Edward Gallagher in a vaudeville double act called Gallagher and Shean.[16] Minnie decided that a show-business career was a way out of poverty for her family. She created an act out of a conventional group of singers and dancers first known as the Three Nightingales. This trio consisted of Julius, his brother Milton, and a young female singer named Mabel O'Donnell.[17] As the act progressed, it would become the Four Nightingales, adding Arthur as a fourth member. Eventually, Minnie's marketing plan for the act would include adding more performers, including Leonard, and renaming the act the Six Mascots—regardless of how many performers there were actually in the act at any given time. Faced with stages that often were really unstable benches at one end of an open hall, dressing rooms that were really backyards, and pay that they often never received, the Nightingales/Mascots ultimately became the Four Marx Brothers by adding Herbert in 1917 when Gummo left the act to enlist in the army during World War I. The Marx Brothers ultimately distanced themselves from their Jewish immigrant roots by renaming themselves: Julius became Groucho, Milton became Gummo, Leonard became Chico, Arthur became Harpo, and Herbert became Zeppo.

The pressure of pleasing audiences through improvisational and nonsensical comedy only improved the Marx Brothers' craft of disruptive humor. According to Groucho, for the Marx Brothers the intensity of a diverse vaudeville-touring schedule became the key to their success. It allowed them to hone their skills in front of rural and middle-class audiences who were often indifferent if not hostile to their act. Groucho developed his improvisational quick-thinking and one-liners that made each performance a unique experience from show to show. On the road, the Marx Brothers created their now iconic characterizations, along with their eccentric, absurd, and unexpected brand of humor. It also allowed Julius to cultivate his self-critical, sarcastic, ad-libbed commentary that would follow him to film, radio, and television comedy. Groucho recalled that, "We played three days in Burlington, Iowa, caught the train overnight and played the following four days in Waterloo. This was very hard work: four-[shows]-a-day for five days equals twenty shows; five-a-day for two days equals ten more shows, for a total of thirty shows per week."[18] It was this intense schedule that provided Groucho with his comic schooling.

A review from this period comments on the importance of their far-reaching and distinctive appeal: "the Marx Brothers introduce a variety of amusements, indeed it is hard to find a theatrical accomplishment they do not excel in that is not incorporated in their performance."[19] Groucho would become the central driving force of the Marx Brothers. His consistently futile attempts to control and manipulate his brothers were coupled with his stream of consciousness monologues that overwhelmed his rivals by deconstructing the socially acceptable ideas and morality of authority. Groucho developed his comic techniques in vaudeville where the live audience gave him the chance to improvise and interact with their daily responses. He became the de facto leader of this merry band of anarchists known as the Marx Brothers.

Initially the Marx Brothers' success appeared to defy explanation. The inability to qualify their act was crucial to its popularity. The Marx Brothers began to realize this while on vaudeville tours and, according to Groucho and Harpo's autobiographies, the audiences loved them for their inexplicable humor. The Marx Brothers complemented each other through creating their own off-beat logic and the enjoyment of their willful destruction of vaudeville's prescribed acts along with the literal destruction of the comic stage.

An apocryphal show business story, found in both autobiographies *Groucho and Me* as well as *Harpo Speaks!*, reinforces the notion that their comedy relied on an intensely energized forward motion and in-the-moment inspiration. Harpo once found a cockroach crawling across the stage, and Groucho instantly became a racetrack announcer encouraging all the brothers to get down on their knees and place bets on how long it would take the roach to cross it.[20] This disruption of any given vaudeville act was not for the audience's enjoyment so much as it was a way to amuse themselves. As Groucho told the *New York Times* in 1928, "We always played to ourselves, never the audience. Sometimes we got to laughing so hard at ourselves we couldn't finish."[21] A final unmotivated improvisation that would find its way into Groucho's stage as well as film and television performances was the arbitrary aside to the audience that stopped the stage action dead in its tracks. Groucho's asides, taking shots at the self-seriousness of other vaudeville acts and the legitimate theater, translated from stage to film, radio, and television, became one of the many skills he learned on the road.

The Marx Brothers finally found their footing in vaudeville, when they broke away from programming with acts of varying quality that offered little but standard fare.[22] They independently produced a show in Philadelphia that became *I'll Say She Is*. The show was developed on the road in small US towns as a compilation of their best scenarios and gags with musical comedy numbers added to the mix.[23] It also included a significant amount of reworked material from their vaudeville shows as well. The show opened at the Walnut Street Theatre in Philadelphia in the summer of 1923. It was an instant success and ran for almost a year both in Philadelphia and on a national tour before opening on Broadway on May 19, 1924.[24] *I'll Say She Is* was ultimately praised by the New York critics when it played the Shubert's Casino Theatre for almost two years.[25] *I'll Say She Is* was recognized by the New York critical establishment and Broadway audiences in what influential theater critic Alexander Woollcott described in his review:

> As one of the many who laughed immodestly throughout the greater part of the first performance given by a new musical show, entitled, if memory serves, "I'll Say She Is," it behooves your correspondent to report the most comical moments vouchsafed to the first nighters in a month of Mondays. It is a bright colored and vehement setting for the goings on of those talented cutups, the Four Marx Brothers.[26]

Becoming their first Broadway success, it showcased Groucho's writing, improvisational skills, and the eccentricity of his comic non-sequiturs.

I'll Say She Is was loosely draped over the structure of a narrative concerning "a thrill-seeking rich girl . . . presented with various adventures from a courting doctor, lawyer, merchant, chief, rich man, poor man, beggar man, and thief. Eventually she is allowed to imagine herself as Napoleon's wife Josephine."[27] A telling sequence entitled "Cinderella Backwards" adds to the rich-girl fantasy of having a working-class fairy godmother—here played by Groucho and reversing the image of the fairy godmother as a man with a greasepaint mustache and cigar firmly planted in mouth—that will deliver her to a poor but handsome lover. Groucho, as lead writer and improviser of the sketches in *I'll Say She Is*, utilized the burlesque satire of upending the conventions of the fairytale and sentimental stories with happy endings. The reversal of the Cinderella figure is complicated by the fact that Groucho spends most of the scene mocking and undercutting her fantasy. He comments on the entitlement of the rich encroaching and displacing all aspects of society even the most downtrodden. The scene begins with the "Beauty" (Lotta Miles) conjuring her "Fairy Godmother" (Groucho)[28]:

> BEAUTY: I have always been miserably rich. I long to be wretchedly poor like everybody else. I am striving for a goal.
> GROUCHO: Well, stop striving or I shall be forced to knock you for one.
> BEAUTY: Haven't you ever wanted something you couldn't get?
> GROUCHO: Yes, we have no bananas. But I can give you anything your heart desires. I will wield my magic wand. I will make you Ella Cinder. If you want to mingle with hoboes come with me to Hoboken.[29]

Ella Cinder says that she longs "to be wretchedly poor like everybody else." Groucho reverses the demands of the rich by saying that it is beneath him,

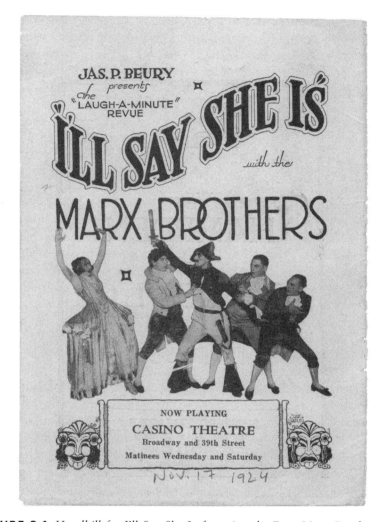

FIGURE 2.1 *Handbill for* I'll Say She Is *featuring the Four Marx Brothers; their first vaudeville show to open on Broadway at the Shubert's Casino Theatre (1924).*
Source: *Billy Rose Theatre Division, The New York Public Library for the Performing Arts, Astor, Lenox, and Tilden Foundations.*

"the head fairy," to meet her request. He delegates, to his "assistant fairies," in true authoritative fashion even this simple action, creating a satirical reversal of power typical of Groucho's later stage, film, and television characters.

Although Groucho (with Tom Johnstone) wrote the next sequence, Chico is charged with introducing it. "Napoleon Meets His Waterloo" begins with

Chico's signature intentional misunderstanding (via the immigrant's pidgin English) of language and logic. He begins the scene as a huckster "hypnotist," direct from the lowbrow world of the carnival, in a dialogue (with another actor simply called, "Richman") that would echo Chico's later interactions with Groucho. Richman enters and immediately calls Chico out as a fake, asking him to "thrill this woman [Ella Cinder]!" Chico claims that he will "make her think she is Josephine, wife of Napoleon Bonaparte, Empress of the World." Then Chico and Richman go into a sexually explicit discussion of how when Napoleon (Groucho) goes off to war, three lovers (Chico, Harpo, and Zeppo) replace his bedroom door with a revolving door like one found in a department store that does not stop until he returns from battle. As Richman says, "while Napoleon is at the front . . .," Chico chimes in with, "They come in the back." It finishes with a joke typical of Groucho's style that culminates in the payoff line, "He went away a Frenchman and came back a Russian. That's what you call hypnotism!"[30]

The frank discussion of promiscuous wives, the foolish behavior of revered historical figures, and ethnic humor, all under the guise of a vaudeville-hypnotist act, come together in a juxtaposition of time periods and locations, and theatrical genres, including, fairy tales, carnival charlatanism, and vaudeville one-liners. The bizarre interplay between these seemingly disparate comic structures is what made Groucho's writing and improvisations stand out from the offerings of other comedic acts of the time.

The sketch that follows is called, "Napoleon Meets His Waterloo." It reinforces Groucho's vaudeville aesthetic as it is without narrative, structure, or story and relies on sexual innuendo and double entendre. To reinforce the improvisational nature of these sketches, and how they changed throughout the run of the show, there are three official versions of the script; not to mention the many more unofficial ones that were never written down.[31] The sketch begins with Napoleon going off to war and bidding goodbye to his Josephine, as his courtiers look on anxiously:

[*All the brothers kiss the Empress Josephine—played by Lotta Miles. As Napoleon—played by Groucho—tries to wedge his way in to get to her.*]

NAPOLEON: There is a lot of heavy lipping going on around here, but somehow or other I got shoved out of it. Forgive me, my Queen. I don't doubt your love. When I look into your big blue eyes, I know that you are true to the Army. I only hope it remains a standing Army. Fortunately France has no Navy, but then every man has qualms. Even an Emperor.

JOSEPHINE: Ah! Ah! Napoleon.

NAPOLEON: But I must not tarry. I must be off. Josephine, if I leave you here with these three snakes—chiselers—I must be off. I must be off to make Russia safe for sinus trouble. To make Russia safe for the five-year plan.[32] That's how I bought this furniture.

JOSEPHINE: Napoleon, when you go, all France is with you.

NAPOLEON: Yes, and the last time I came home all France was with *you*. [*Beat.*] And a slice of Italy too.

[*Napoleon exits as the other courtiers/brothers surround Josephine again.*]

After a series of false exits and re-entrances by Napoleon while catching Josephine in compromising positions with each of his courtiers, Groucho makes a series of rapid and verbally athletic speeches in order to confront these progressively awkward situations. Below are three of these speeches in sequence of how they build to a comic crescendo:

NAPOLEON: [*Re-entering. To Harpo.*] Hey, wait until I'm through. Hereafter, gentlemen, the line forms on the right. Farewell, my Queen. Beyond the Alps lies more Alps, and the Lord 'Alps those that 'Alps themselves. Vive la France! [*Groucho exits.*]

Followed by:

[*Groucho re-enters even more quickly. Chico and Zeppo hide.*]

JOSEPHINE: Oh! It's you. I thought you were at the front.

NAPOLEON: I was, but nobody answered the bell, so I came around here.

JOSEPHINE: Well, what are you looking for?

NAPOLEON: My sword. I lost my sword.

JOSEPHINE: There it is, dear, just where you left it.

NAPOLEON: How stupid of you. Why didn't you tell me? Look at that point. I wish you wouldn't open sardines with my sword. I am beginning to smell like a delicatessen. My infantry is beginning to smell like the Cavalry. Farewell, my Queen, farewell. I'm going any minute now, farewell. It's ten cents a dance. I run on the hour and the half hour. Get a load of this footwork. Get me while I'm hot, Josie.

And finally ending with:

[*Napoleon exits only to re-enter immediately finding all three brothers once again making love to Josephine.*]

NAPOLEON: [*Realizing this is his Waterloo.*] Our just is cause. We cannot lose. I am fighting for France, Liberty, and those three snakes hiding behind the curtain. Farewell, vis-à-vis Fifi D'Orsay. If my laundry comes, send it

general delivery, care of Russia, and count it—I was a sock short last
week. [. . .] Farewell, my Queen. Vive la France!
[*Music cue and Groucho exits.*][33]

The success of *I'll Say She Is* on Broadway, and its national tour, shows
Groucho's humor was not confined to any one class or region of audience. The
Napoleon sequence was so successful it was recreated in their film *Horse
Feathers* (albeit in a contemporary setting of a college) as the famous "Iceman"
scene this time with Thelma Todd portraying the woman in question.

After two more successful Broadway shows in *The Cocoanuts* (1925) and
Animal Crackers (1928)—both of which would be subsequently produced by
Paramount Pictures in 1929 and 1930 respectively—and several internationally
recognized films including *Monkey Business* (1931), *Horse Feathers* (1932),
and *Duck Soup* (1933), and for MGM with *A Night at the Opera* (1935) and *A
Day at the Races* (1937), the Marx Brothers would wind down with some
middling films that signaled the dwindling interest of the Marx Brothers for
Hollywood filmmaking, and the disbanding of the remaining brothers Chico,
Harpo, and Groucho. Groucho, although not interested in films anymore after
many years of disappointments and executive interference with his material,
would find a new career in two groundbreaking comedy media simultaneously.
He would bring his vaudevillian sensibility to both radio and television with *You
Bet Your Life* as these media evolved in the mid-twentieth century to become
staples of popular entertainment.[34]

Groucho's show *You Bet Your Life* was the most popular and lucrative of
his ventures in popular entertainment. He would attribute this to the nature
of comedy and its role in truth telling. As he revealed in an interview with
the *Saturday Evening Post*, "The first thing which disappears when men are
turning a country into a totalitarian state is comedy and comics. Because
we are laughed at, I don't think people really understand how essential we
are to their sanity."[35] Groucho's rejection of the totalitarian state and the
"truthiness" of its leaders is summed up in their 1933 film, *Duck Soup*.
One of the famous lines from this film, when all three Marx Brothers are
pretending to be Groucho and a rich dowager (Margaret Dumont) does not
seem to recognize the true Groucho, is "Who are you going to believe? Me?
Or your own eyes?"[36] This vaudevillian one-liner is an insightful look into how
Groucho sees his middle-American contestants on *You Bet Your Life*. Not
understanding, and even willfully misunderstanding, words and meanings
that are communicated both verbally and physically, is the key to Groucho's
comic commentary. For Groucho Marx, it is also a way to test his audience to
see how gullible they are with respect to authority. Who can you believe?
Groucho, or your own eyes?

FIGURE 2.2 *Groucho Marx on the set of* You Bet Your Life *for NBC-TV (ca. 1950s).*
Source: Billy Rose Theatre Division, The New York Public Library for the Performing Arts,
Astor, Lenox, and Tilden Foundations.

Groucho Marx would in turn influence Phil Silvers who would also become
a key inspirational figure for Larry David. Silvers serves as an interesting bridge
figure between Groucho Marx and Larry David. He serves as an illustration of
how the *tummler*, the vaudevillian, and the burlesque comic came together to

make a perfect storm of television comedic performer. *The Phil Silvers Show* (1955–59) featured Silvers as a Jewish army staff sergeant along with an ethnically and racially diverse barracks full of soldiers. The character of Bilko as created by Phil Silvers and writer Nat Hiken would come to be a significant influence on the work of Larry David, particularly with his alter ego of "Larry" on *Curb Your Enthusiasm*.[37]

Phil Silvers' parents were Russian Jewish immigrants who fled the Cossacks for New York City and ended up in the Brownsville section of Brooklyn. Silvers was discovered early on by Gus Edwards, the producer of numerous vaudeville comedy sketches, including *Gus Edwards' Protégés of 1923*, featuring a callow Phil Silvers singing "School Days." A school-age Silvers played a naive pupil until his voice changed. However, because of his success in this show, Silvers was remembered by producers for later stage opportunities—also playing a callow boy in "short pants"—and thus began his comic stage career in vaudeville into his early twenties. Silvers was featured in a vaudeville show called *Any Apartment*. A typical scene from this show played as follows:

[*Scene: a kitchen.*]

SILVERS: [*running on*] Mama, Mama, Mama, Mama! I lost Papa!

MAMA: Where?

SILVERS: The last time I saw him, he was standing in front of the Palace [or whatever theater they were playing then] looking at a picture of a girl in the lobby, and he was saying, "Oh, Mama, why did I ever leave you?"

MAMA: Go do your homework. [*The boy goes off, and Papa enters with a big hello. Mama bawls him out. Silvers returns with a toy train and plays with it behind them.*]

SILVERS: Mama! The train won't go! The train won't go!

As Silvers relates in his autobiography, *This Laugh Is on Me*, "I cannot tell anybody why that was so funny," but it received a "tremendous laugh."[38] Silvers' next break came in the Catskills Mountains as a *tummler*. As he describes it, "The comedian had to work with the social director as the hotel buffoon, the *tummeler* [*sic*], the noisemaker who would do anything to keep the guests from checking out."[39] The *tummler* would become a later signature characteristic of Silvers' work as Sergeant Ernie Bilko on *The Phil Silvers Show*.

Beginning in 1934, Silvers would spend the rest of the decade in burlesque. After vaudeville gave way to film and radio, burlesque became the only stage forum for comics who had not yet made the transition to Hollywood or the legitimate New York theater. This offshoot of the comedian in the variety theater and early burlesque of the late nineteenth century had become by the Depression era what can only be described as a break between strippers. Originally, burlesque was, as the name indicated, a satirical form of comedy that burlesqued legitimate theater, musicals, and revues like the *Ziegfeld Follies*. The comedians included the singers and dancers—women like Lydia Thompson, Eva Tanguay, Sophie Tucker, and Mae West, who all honed their comedy craft in burlesque. But as vaudeville fell on hard times, so did burlesque, and it reverted to its roots in the saloons of variety theater to become a platform for buxom women to titillate a mostly male, working-class audience. The comedians became a distraction and transitional act between the "girls" who were the main attraction. However, it inadvertently proved to be a training ground for comedians like Fanny Brice and Eddie Cantor, as well as for Phil Silvers.

The comedy was fairly mundane and old fashioned. According to Silvers, "The management was not interested in how funny you were, just how often you were funny. You had to appear in at least three sketches. They were all traditional, in the public domain, handed down by generations of unnamed, underpaid comics."[40] But burlesque also gave comedians like Silvers a lot of room to "improvise anything I wished—a new bit here, a couple of lines there didn't matter to the others in the scene, as long as you got us all to the blackout." It gave Silvers a chance to create his own material, since it did not concern management what the routines were, as "the only critic was the audience."[41] The jokes were expected to be ribald and full of sexual double entendre that were aimed at a broad spectrum of male patrons who were only waiting for the next dancer to disrobe.

For Phil Silvers, one of the advantages of burlesque was that "it used the *promise* of nudity, suggestion, double-meanings. . . . In the 1930s the audience—and the police who enforced the standards of taste—really believed in surface propriety. We worked within their frame of conventional morality." But for comedians serious about their craft, the burlesque stage offered lessons in how to put over an act that true comedians were after. Silvers notes that this was a school for acting, as well as comedy, since "so much of humor is the contrast between real life and the artificial rules we live by. When you destroy those conventions, what can you play satire against?"[42] If anything, the burlesque of the 1930s gave future radio and television stars like Silvers a place to merge their skills as *tummlers* and comic actors, as well as to meet their working-class audiences who demanded to be entertained.

Like the humorists from the *shtetls* of Eastern Europe and the ghettos of the Irish- and Jewish-dominated immigrant neighborhoods of the Lower East Side and Brooklyn before them, this new generation of soon-to-be television sitcom and variety entertainers began to comment on 1950s Americanization driven by their experience as outsiders performing for insiders. Phil Silvers' anti-authoritarian Bilko character would become the hallmark of his career. He makes clear that his time in burlesque houses and growing up in the slums of New York at an early age created his attitude toward comedy. "The general approach I use," according to Silvers, "on [the Bilko] show in particular, is to knock down authority. That appeals to practically everybody."[43]

The original title of Silvers' new television vehicle was, ironically, *You'll Never Get Rich*, then retitled as *The Phil Silvers Show* as he became well known and well off. Though it never had huge ratings, the show was considered by critics as one of the top television comedies of the era, in a league with *I Love Lucy*. The show was nominated for Emmy Awards for both Comedy Writing and Best Series in each of its four seasons, winning both awards in 1956, 1957, and 1958. *The Phil Silvers Show* received nine other nominations during the 1950s, with Silvers winning one individual Emmy for his performance and Nat Hiken winning one for direction.

The appeal to audiences, according to comic television star Steve Allen, was that Phil Silvers' speech retained "an earthy New Yorkishness," and like his fellow comedians who "seem to be grown-up pool-room habitués, card sharps, race-track touts, 'regular guys,' for in reality they may be intelligent and/or well educated."[44] Larry David uses Silvers' character of the New York Jew transplanted to Los Angeles for inspiration in *Curb Your Enthusiasm*. David plays a "regular guy" version of himself—albeit a rich television show creator-producer, but as his friends say about David, he remains his insecure, neurotic, New York Jewish self. Larry David has said of his character on *Curb*, "I'm playing—yes—I am playing myself. I'm playing the part of myself that doesn't censor my thoughts."[45]

In addition to the *tummler*-inspired comedy of Phil Silvers, the stage and early television work of Groucho Marx has had a tremendous influence on comedians because of their ability to command multiple media platforms. The careers of Groucho Marx and Phil Silvers lead to a better understanding of how the vaudeville aesthetic has made Larry David an international success with his own comedy. Improvisation, unmotivated action, and unannounced asides and rants, coupled with the insults of the social assassin, would also become the hallmarks of Larry David.

Juxtaposing the outlier career of the stand-up comedian turned television star of Larry David with Groucho Marx, we witness how the American vaudeville aesthetic informed both comedians. Comparing David's work as a comic actor-writer-producer to early twentieth-century vaudevillian Groucho Marx is to trace the legacy of vaudeville into the early twenty-first century. How Groucho Marx and Larry David disrupt and demolish the social proprieties associated with middle- and upper-class Anglo-Americans reveals the influence of this legacy through the vaudeville aesthetic.

Larry David came to comedy via his middle-class upbringing in Brooklyn and on New York City stages with his stand-up routines. Friend and fellow comedian Richard Lewis, who came up through the comedy ranks with David in the New York comedy scene of the late 1970s and early 1980s, has described David as a "comic's comic." Lewis remembered one evening when David went up to do his routine, took one look at the audience, decided he did not like the look of the crowd, said "fuck it," and walked offstage.[46] As Jerry Seinfeld would confirm about his former partner, "Larry had the material, but he never had what you would call the temperament for stand-up."[47]

In 1988, Seinfeld was pursuing a successful stand-up career, and as a result, NBC offered him a chance to make a pilot for a television show based on his comedy. The only problem was that Seinfeld had no ideas for a sitcom, which requires storytelling and dialogue skills, neither of which were his strong suit. Seinfeld turned to fellow comedian Larry David, as someone who had written for television—first for a short-lived variety show called *Fridays* (1980–82) and then a year-long stint on *Saturday Night Live* (1984–85). He was only able to get one sketch on during that *SNL* season, which prompted him to quit after one year of writing there.

Seinfeld has explained in many interviews that he and David were in a Korean grocery in Manhattan and began making funny comments about the strange things that were on the shelves.[48] Seinfeld remembers a typical dialogue with David that would revolve around various exotic products: "There's always these things here like, here's some Korean ginseng royal jelly. Comes in a jelly now. [*Pauses.*] So you can spread it." Seinfeld says David created the idea for the sitcom in that moment, as David announced, "This is what the show should be. Just, you know, making fun of stuff." NBC was skeptical about this idea, as well as about David himself, whom they did not respond well to, since he was adamant about what the show should be and defied their notions of how a sitcom should be structured and what it should be about. David claims that he kept telling the executives that their ideas were not what he and Jerry wanted, saying over and over to them, "No, this is *not* the show." But because the NBC executives liked Jerry Seinfeld and his success as a comedian, they decided to trust his instincts regarding David, and one of the most successful sitcoms in television history was born, making both Jerry Seinfeld and Larry David billionaires in the process.

When Ricky Gervais interviews Larry David about his technique of comic provocation through his character of "Larry," David responds, "That's why I like *that* 'Larry' better than I like *this* Larry"—meaning himself in real life.[49] Ultimately, David wishes he could be as forthright and honest as the character he has created. David's confrontational character of "Larry" has his roots in the *tummler*. The *tummler*, informed by cynicism, aggression, and humiliation that was an integral part of popular stage entertainment as evidenced with Groucho Marx and Phil Silvers, was to guide Larry David's work as a writer and performer. Larry David continues the tradition of the *tummler* first with his stand-up comedy, then in his writing for *Seinfeld*, particularly with the character of George Costanza as portrayed by Jason Alexander and his parents played by vaudeville-inspired Borsht Belt comics Estelle Harris and Jerry Stiller. The legacy of the offensive insult comic became part of the mainstream of American culture on television in the 1990s with the introduction of *Seinfeld* as created, written, and produced by Larry David and Jerry Seinfeld, and into the first decade of the twenty-first century with *Curb Your Enthusiasm*, courtesy of David now solo.

Larry David cites as his influences the television situation comedy of the 1950s, specifically that of *The Phil Silvers Show*. With Silvers, the insult humor of the *tummler* is combined with the rejection of authority also found in Groucho Marx's characters. "I loved Sergeant Bilko," says David. "It was easily my favorite TV show. Bilko was this con man who did things you weren't supposed to and got away with it. . . . Probably the first time I watched somebody doing despicable things and loved him for it."[50] In *Curb Your Enthusiasm*, David presents a twenty-first-century combination of Phil Silvers and Groucho Marx.

Where David would make a huge leap forward with his work on *Curb* was by using improvisation and the jazz riff, lacing these into the "Groucho" and "Bilko" sensibility of the *tummler* as Jewish truth teller. The rhythm of Yiddish-influenced speech patterns coupled with the jazz improvisation that began to change the face of entertainment in the 1950s and 1960s, with the comedy of Mort Sahl and Lenny Bruce, would come to influence David in the 2000s and break open the highly controlled scripting of television comedy. Larry David's freedom in being able to embrace improvisational stand-up comedy has made him one of the first writer-performer-producers of contemporary comedy to make this legacy of the *tummler* a mainstream success, as his eight seasons of *Curb* and his multiple awards attest.

One of the staples of vaudeville humor was the two-man act. Using opposite types of characters who are in constant conflict with each other, has made the careers of comedy duos discussed in this study as diverse as Weber and Fields (the "Double-Dutch" act), Lucille Ball and Desi Arnaz (*I Love Lucy*), and Tina Fey and Alec Baldwin (*30 Rock*). Opposites conflict but they also attract, making for the tension necessary in comedy.

Groucho Marx and Larry David also make use of the two-man act of contrasting characters whose misunderstandings and frustrations create funny riffs of nonsense logic. They form a version of reality that is both comic and acts as social commentary. The comic vaudevillians of the turn-of-the-twentieth century openly challenged American customs onstage and off, as does David beginning with *Seinfeld* and more dramatically and openly with *Curb Your Enthusiasm*. Their weapons are the verbal and physical gags as depicted in the two-man act format in which social rituals are deconstructed and challenged by the "nonsense" humor of comedians in the tradition of the Marx Brothers. Larry David, following in this heritage, incorporates the vaudeville aesthetic, creating a new kind of vaudeville stage for television.

The two-man act was a foundation of the Marx Brothers' international film successes, reaching its full potential in 1935 with *A Night at the Opera*. The Marx Brothers, encouraged by MGM producer Irving Thalberg, went on the road in 1934 to test out scenes for this new picture in front of live audiences. *A Night at the Opera* features elements of their humor from previous films like *Animal Crackers, Monkey Business*, and *Horse Feathers*, including vaudeville scenes like "the state room" that had inspired Sid Caesar, and a sequence simply known as "the contract scene." In this scene, Groucho and Chico are two theatrical agents who create a contract for an opera singer. As Groucho reads the contract to Chico, the following dialogue between the brothers ensues:

> GROUCHO: The party of the first part shall be known in this contract as the party of the first part. Would you like to hear it again?
> CHICO: No. Just the first part.
> GROUCHO: What do you mean? The party of the first part?
> CHICO: No, just the first part of the party of the first part.

After moving on to the second clause of the contract, which features the party of the second part, Chico says, "I don't like the second party either," to which Groucho replies, "Well, you should have come to the first party. We didn't get home till four in the morning. [*Beat.*] I was blind for three days." Chico ends the contract negotiation with "Hey, look! Why can't the first part of the second party be the second part of the first party? Then you got something."[51] In this exchange the Marx Brothers deconstruct the contract that binds two parties and combine the notion of the party as social event and political membership. The contract scene is a final remnant of a vaudevillian career that began twenty-five years earlier.

The two-man act remains a standard for comic writer-performers and is integral to the humor of Larry David. A prime example of this act can be seen in season 6 of *Curb Your Enthusiasm* as "Larry" confronts his new houseguest, Leon, played by comedian J. B. Smoove. Leon is a thirty-something, single black man from Los Angeles whose family (the Blacks, refugees from a Hurricane Katrina-type disaster) are staying with the Davids. After his first night in Larry's house, he has to confront Leon about a stain that was found on his bed the next morning while his wife Cheryl was changing the sheets:

LEON: What kind of stain was it?
LARRY: Ejaculate.
LEON: Aaah—what?
LARRY: Ejaculate.
LEON: Ah-jack-ah-lit?
LARRY: Not *ah*-jack-ah-lit. *E*-jack-u-late.
LEON: E-jack-a-lit.
LARRY: [*Pause.*] Cum stain. Cum?
LEON: Cum stain. What kind of cum was it?
LARRY: What do you mean what kind of cum was it?! Cum's cum.
LEON: Cum is not cum, Larry.
LARRY: Cum's cum.
LEON: Well, it couldn't have been mine, Larry. You know why? Because I brings a ruckus to the ladies![52]

The vaudeville aesthetic also featured double-entendre dialogue that used sexual innuendo much like that of the "Larry" and "Leon" confrontation. A typical ribald vaudeville two-man act called "The Scrutinizing Scene" was played between a "Straightman" and a "Comic" with a misunderstanding of the word *scrutinize* used to make it sound erotic. In the following excerpt, the "Comic" helps the "Straightman" handle three hundred women who send him letters every week:

STRAIGHTMAN: When a woman comes in, I'll be sitting over there. [*Points to a settee.*] And you stand her over there so I can scrutinize her.
COMIC: So you can what?
STRAIGHTMAN: So I can scrutinize her.
COMIC: How the hell can you reach her from over there? It can't be done.
STRAIGHTMAN: Why I can scrutinize a woman from here clear across the street.
COMIC: It's different with me. I can't scrutinize them even when I get them right up against me.
STRAIGHTMAN: You ought to see my father! He can scrutinize them around the corner.
COMIC: Now that's what I call a man!
STRAIGHTMAN: But you ought to see my uncle.
COMIC: The hell with your uncle, your old man is good enough for me.[53]

The exaggeration of sexual prowess is also a feature of the two-man act. The fact that Leon can bring a "ruckus to the ladies" and the "Straightman" can "scrutinize" across a street and around a corner is an absurd contention. Groucho Marx performs a similar scenario in the Marx Brothers' film *Horse Feathers* during the "Iceman" sequence, as follows:

> [*Professor Wagstaff (Groucho) enters the boudoir of a young widow, Connie Bailey (Thelma Todd), as the Iceman (Harpo) exits after throwing a block of ice out the window.*]
>
> WAGSTAFF: Who was that?
>
> CONNIE: The Iceman.
>
> WAGSTAFF: Is that so? Well you can't pull the wool over my eyes.
>
> [*Connie, exasperated, sits and sighs.*]
>
> WAGSTAFF: [*sitting on Connie's lap.*] That Iceman stuff leaves me cold. [*After an interruption by Zeppo, who gets thrown out by Groucho, he returns to sit in Connie's lap.*]
>
> WAGSTAFF: Let's see, where were we? Oh yes, I was sitting on your lap. And doing pretty well as I recall it. [*A knock at the door startles Wagstaff.*]
>
> CONNIE: Quick, get out. Hurry. And remember stay undercover.
>
> WAGSTAFF: You have more students than the college. [*He exits through another door, as Ravelli (Chico) enters with another block of ice.*]
>
> RAVELLI: Here, lady, you dropped your ice.
>
> CONNIE: But I don't want any ice.
>
> RAVELLI: Neither do I. [*Goes to the window and drops the ice out. He runs back to sit on the couch with Connie and begins to wrap his arms around her and violently attempts to kiss her. Pauses.*] Now do you want any ice?
>
> CONNIE: No!
>
> RAVELLI: Ah, you are beautiful! [*Sweet-talks her in faux double-talk Italian. Pauses.*] Lady, I like you. You got something, but I don't know what it is.
>
> [*Wagstaff reenters, sits on the couch, and accidently cuddles with Ravelli thinking it's Connie.*]
>
> RAVELLI: Oh, professor, I don't see you. What are you doing here?
>
> WAGSTAFF: Nothing right now. But I was doing all right till you came in.
>
> [*Harpo as the "Iceman" re-enters with yet another block of ice and runs over the couch with the three lovers still on it, goes to the window, and drops the ice once again. He then goes out over the couch again without acknowledging the group and exits.*][54]

This nonsensical sequence with entering and exiting lovers trying to make time with the same woman is reminiscent of the Marx Brothers' vaudeville show *I'll Say She Is*. The sex farce of revolving doors coupled with sexually charged dialogue is a significant inspiration for Larry David's comedy as well.

Another point of comparison with Larry David and J. B. Smoove's two-man act to the Marx Brothers' is found in the 1931 film *Monkey Business*. Here is another version of this staple vaudevillian act that can be traced to David's vaudeville aesthetic in *Curb*. Groucho and his brother Chico re-create the two-man act of their early careers with intentional nonsense dialogue that upsets narrative and logic:

GROUCHO: Columbus was sailing along on his vessel—
CHICO: On his what?
GROUCHO: Not on his *what*. On his vessel. Don't you know what vessel is?
CHICO: Sure, I can vessel. [*Chico begins to whistle.*]
GROUCHO: Do you suppose I could buy back my introduction to you? [*Pause.*] Now, one night Columbus's sailors started a mutiny—
CHICO: Nah, no mutinies at night. They're in the afternoon. You know, mutinies—Wednesdays and Saturdays.
GROUCHO: [*An aside to the audience.*] There's my argument. Restrict immigration.[55]

Here the Marx Brothers' display an open mockery of the "discovery" of America by Columbus. They also expose through satire the hostility and disdain toward immigrant European Jews, who in the context of this film are illegal stowaways, played by the brothers themselves. Both "Groucho" and "Larry" use malapropisms and misunderstanding, both intentional and unintended, and feature these characters as frustrated by their seemingly inferior, dependent brothers. The two-man, "nonsense" dialogue deployed by Groucho/Chico opens up a comic derailing of narrative while evaluating societal taboos. The new immigrants with their ethnic roots in the *shtetls* of Eastern Europe embraced the freedom that the vaudeville aesthetic allowed them.

Groucho Marx and Larry David are both secular Jews who often confront the notion of what constitutes "Jewishness" in their work. In the final scene of *Animal Crackers*, Groucho and his brothers come on singing "Our Old Kentucky Home" as a barbershop quartet. When they finish, Groucho remarks in the style of a radio commentator, "This program is coming to you from the House of David."[56] Four Jews singing a Southern Christian homesick homage to Kentucky creates the perfect irony of language that disrupts the simple identification of any specific ethnicity brought to the audience courtesy of descendants of the House of David. With pun intended, this famous Marx Brothers' moment informs the House of Larry David by using the language of Jewish–Christian conflation. Larry and Groucho's "Houses of David" are the originating points for these infamous social assassins.

In *Curb*, Larry David focuses on what comedian Ricky Gervais calls "Jewish humor." In response to Gervais' question, "What is Jewish humor?," David is at first flummoxed but gets to the heart of it:

> LARRY DAVID: There is also a certain rhythm to the way Jews talk that might be funny.
> RICKY GERVAIS: Yiddish is already funny.
> LARRY DAVID: There's like a jazz to it. Like when you listen to Lenny Bruce's albums, there's a jazz to the way he talks. The culture of Jews being funny comes out of—I guess—some kind of oppression. Because oppression would lead to humor, would it not? When you're in a terrible situation, the only thing you could do is to be funny.[57]

The protean ability of the vaudevillians (especially those who grew up as street kids performing to survive) to be "whoever" was invaluable, and not unlike the targets whom David goes after: those who assimilate to get by and fit in to advance a position in society.

In the twenty-first century, the liberal guilt of "passing" and being politically correct is deconstructed in *Curb* through the ethnic-focused stereotype of the vaudeville aesthetic. David uses the notion of being Jewish and how it gets exploited for selfish purposes. The "Ski Lift" episode of *Curb* challenges "Larry" to confront his lack of knowledge about his Jewish ancestry. "Larry" attempts to befriend an Orthodox Jew who is the head of a kidney-transplant consortium (Stuart Pankin), in an effort to get his friend, comedian Richard Lewis, a new kidney. He speaks in gibberish Yiddish, and even pretends to be married to another character who is Jewish (as his own wife is a Gentile) in order to get what he wants. "Larry" agrees to go on a skiing trip in order to impress the man, Ben Heineman, and his daughter, Rachel. "Larry" goes undercover pretending to be an Orthodox Jew as well. Since his wife is a blonde, Christian, woman, he has to ask his friend's Jewish wife, Susie (Susie Essman), to play the role of his Orthodox wife. Asking how he met his wife, "Larry" tells them in a moment of desperate improvisation that he was in a Jewish folk band called "The Hipsters." Ben asks "Larry" what songs he played, and he replies on the fly with, "*Gefilte* Fish Blues," and "My Freakin' Back is Killing Me, and It's Making it Hard to *Kvell*." In the final scene, "Larry" and Ben's unmarried daughter are stuck together after a ski lift breaks down. "Larry" and Rachel are stranded in mid-air as sundown approaches. As Rachel begins to panic, "Larry" is confused as to why:

RACHEL: *Shkee-ah sahumma?.* Sundown. I can't be here alone with you after sundown.

LARRY: Why not?

RACHEL: Because you're a man, and I'm a single woman.

LARRY: So?

RACHEL: So, it's not allowed.

LARRY: Who says so?

RACHEL: The law. The Torah says so. *Hashem* says so.

LARRY: *Hashem?*

RACHEL: Do you know anything?

LARRY: No *Hashem,* I know. But's it's okay, there are extenuating circumstances.

RACHEL: There are no such thing as extenuating circumstances![58]

Larry's clear ignorance of Orthodox Judaism and his continual insults to the rabbi's daughter cause her to jump from the ski lift in order to escape being with a man after sundown in order not to break God's law. Larry has to concede that he is not a practicing Jew, never mind orthodox, and as a result does not get Richard Lewis his kidney. This is one of many episodes in which Larry pretends to be a practicing Jew in order to convince people of what he wants by enlisting their empathy for a fellow Jew.

This kind of ethnic-based humor can be seen early in Groucho's career as well. Also a secular Jew, Groucho and his brothers often included a "Yid" (a stereotypical Hebrew character) in their act, as did many other vaudevillians like Weber and Fields, and Fanny Brice. Gummo and Groucho's early vaudeville acts featured scenes where Groucho as the martinet German-accented schoolmaster, berated Gummo as "Izzy," the Hebrew Boy. A cartoon drawn for a promotional advertisement for a 1911 show at the Lyda Theater in Chicago represents Gummo in an exaggerated Hebrew costume consisting of an ill-fitting black gabardine suit and bowler hat. The cartoon gives a sense of how the stereotype of the weak and whiny Jewish boy, Izzy, was portrayed on stage. Gummo is drawn doubled over and clutching his abdomen, howling, "Someone stuck me in the back of the stomach!"[59] Picking on the weak and bookish "Yid" boy was part of the ethnic humor of the time. Larry David often confronts his own Jewish legacy in his work, both embracing and rejecting it as a comic mask. Ethnic performers in the early twentieth century often traded on satirizing their own heritages.

Coupled with the ethnic mask, for the comedians of Eastern European heritage, the movement from Yiddish, and the language of the *shtetl* with its Anglo-American confrontation, becomes the comic's weapon of choice. Managing the mocking impudence of language in their two-man acts allows

Groucho Marx and Larry David to go on the offensive as humorists. The ethnic component is crucial to the misunderstandings that are perpetuated in the comic language derived from the *shtetl*. Not understanding, and even willfully misunderstanding words and meanings that are communicated both verbally and physically, is the key to this form of comedy represented in the gag. The gag therefore becomes the site of confrontation between two characters that present different sides of perceived stereotypes. These gags were used as subterfuge to comment on the behavior and understanding of ethnic types in order to solicit laughs.

Both Groucho Marx and Larry David engage in this vaudevillian comedy, which embraces confrontation in which Jews and Gentiles are in a complex dance with neither side wanting to admit that there is a third party that is passing for being an authentic American. The attempt at passing for another race or ethnic group is carried over in Larry David's work on *Curb Your Enthusiasm*. Comparing Groucho Marx's ambivalent third party to Larry David's vision of ethnic comedy can be witnessed in season 7, episode 9 of *Curb*, titled "The Table Read." "Larry" tells actor Michael Richards (Kramer on *Seinfeld*), who has been diagnosed with Grote's disease, that he will introduce him to a friend named Danny Duberstein who has "beaten" Grote's. When "Larry" finds out that Duberstein died of Grote's disease, he recruits his roommate Leon to pretend that Leon is Duberstein for Richards's benefit. The following improvised dialogue ensues between "Larry" and Leon using the language of the two-man act:

> LEON: I'll white that shit up! (*Leon speaks in his "white man's" voice.*) "Hello, I'm Danny Duberstein!"
> LARRY: What about Duberstein? It's a Jewish name.
> LEON: Fuck it! Tell him I'm an Ethiopian Jew!

The early vaudeville two-man routines influence the rest of this improvised scene between "Larry" and Leon. Since it is not enough for Leon to sound like a white man, he must also sound like a Jew.

> LARRY: I know! I'll tell him that you were adopted by a Jewish family, the Duberstein's, and you were bar mitzvahed.
> LEON: Yeah, bar mittsfid and all that shit!
> LARRY: Say that again?
> LEON: [*Saying it exactly the same way again.*] Barmitts*fid.*
> LARRY: It's not bar mitz*fid*, it's bar mitz*fud*. [*Over-pronouncing it for Leon.*] Bar mitz*fud*!
> LEON: Barmitts*fid.*

LARRY: *Fud*! Bar Mitz *Fud*! You'd better learn to pronounce this!
LEON: [*Softly under his breath.*] That's what I said. Barmittsfid.

As Larry attempts to make Leon, a black man, first into a white man and then a Jewish man, he insists that he must get the language right. Even if he is not believable in looking like a Jew, getting the words right might just seal the deal. When Leon does show up as Duberstein, he is strangely dressed as Louis Farrakhan, the leader of the Nation of Islam which happens to be—ironically—the "whitest shit I got!" according to Leon. He still says barmitts*fid*, and that he gets "barmitts*fid* once every *thirteen* years" (in order to "recharge the *mitzvah*"), rather than at age thirteen.[60] Combining ethnicity, race, and religious identity (in this case Jew, Gentile, and Muslim), Larry David and J. B. Smoove create a classic two-man act.

Larry David is able to defy the falseness of the liberal political correctness that surrounds him by direct confrontation. An example of the two-man act and the deconstruction of the shibboleth of sensitivity to blacks is seen when "Larry" suggests that Leon, when he is locked out of "Larry's" New York apartment by the doorman because he looks suspicious (in other words, he looks black), wear glasses to make him look more intelligent, since black men in glasses get respect from liberal whites. "Let me give you some advice," says "Larry." "I notice that white people revere black people in glasses. They go out of their way to do stuff for them." Later on in the episode, Leon uses this tactic to get into a sold-out event, vindicating "Larry" and his assessment of the superficiality of the "Caucasian race," when he proclaims, "This is better than anything the civil rights leaders ever came up with!" Leon ends with a paraphrase from Martin Luther King Jr., "I have overcome!"[61] Leon's "overcoming" his blackness through assimilation by wearing glasses can be compared to sociologist John Murray Cuddihy's discussion of rites and rights:

> In my terms: social interaction ritual—i.e. bourgeois-Christian *rites*—were prerequisite to the practice of civil *rights* and, ultimately, a condition of access to them. They were, at once, rites of passage and rites of "passing." But if the Jew's consuming interest was in acculturation, the bourgeois Gentile observed him for the signs of assimilation (social).[62]

Looking back at Groucho Marx's mustache and the reality of his mask of assimilation (in Groucho's case a ludicrous, laugh-inducing disguise of civility that also includes wearing glasses), the connection between the two-man act and the absurd gestures toward passing in Anglo-American society can be observed. The faux-respectability garnered by a character's artificially superior outward appearance is comically contradicted by laughing at this superficiality for what it is—a mask of civility.

Vaudeville historian Robert Snyder describes this need to assimilate without entirely losing the influence of the *shtetl*, saying that "even those who returned to their home streets singing Tin Pan Alley numbers instead of songs of the *shtetl* were not so much abandoning their identity as constructing a new one." Snyder concludes that "[i]n vaudeville, ethnic groups would come to create new American identities out of popular culture."[63] All the characters accept these various ethnic types without question, even though the comedians still essentially sound and look the same as they always have. These vaudevillians convince us of their performed ethnicity because they, and the characters they engage with, want to believe in it. The audience enjoys the comedy of ethnic stereotyping as absurd, and those who believe in its veracity belie their willful ignorance.

This identification with the ethnic other is brought to the comic extreme in an episode from season 8 of *Curb* titled "Palestinian Chicken." Here "Larry" beds a Palestinian woman named Shara (Anne Bedian), who in the middle of sexual intercourse calls out to "Larry" in ecstasy that she will "fuck the Jew out of you!"[64] "Larry's" ambivalence about being a Jew can be seen when he claims his Jewishness only when it serves his needs, in this case, knowing that it will turn Shara on because she is playing out the Palestinian–Israeli conflict through sexual intercourse. The political correctness that Larry David shatters in terms of ethnic identity and its ironic and unintended consequences of bringing Palestinian and Jew together—blissfully, no less—are laughable in the face of the misperception and absurdity that Shara can "fuck the Jew" out of "Larry," and that "Larry" will embrace his Palestinian paramour for her politics rather than merely embracing his desire for her sexually. As "Larry" says to a Jewish friend who shows up after his sexual encounter with Shara, "The penis doesn't care about race, creed, or color." Whereas early twentieth-century immigrants were more focused on hiding their ethnicity to pass as Anglo-American, contemporary comedians portray this false assimilation to explore, exploit, and expose the Anglo-American facade.

The freedom to comment using the vaudeville aesthetic and its resistance to and subversion of American middle-class ideals of proper decorum and social conformity to a rigid notion of self and community, was projected onto the lack of structure and so-called decency that reflected the nature of vaudeville. This produced a variety of impulsive and improvised comic immigrant entertainments that mocked notions of acceptable social interactions. Vaudeville, in its "something for everyone" attitude, meant that all must be treated equally and without regard to class and social status, and what was presumed decent was now subjective according to who was performing and who was enjoying those performances. The derailing of logic and narrative left the door open for the chaos of a "whatever it is, I'm against it" philosophy, and for the audience's upward or downward class mobility, because they had been exposed to such a rule-free variety of popular entertainment.

Groucho Marx and Larry David, both beginning as ethnic outsiders, eventually became assimilated into the land of rich insiders known as Hollywood. Through Jewish-American wealth accrued in the entertainment industry, a new metaphorical *shtetl* was created out of Hollywood comedians. Performers like Groucho Marx and Larry David did (and do) not need to hide or change their Jewishness, but can create a new community where they can fit in and can be themselves through their successful careers in comedy.

In his newfound stardom, Groucho Marx was no longer the outsider nor insider, since he had rejected this part as well. It was this reversal of background/foreground, unseen/seen that ultimately liberated the Marx Brothers and specifically Groucho's act from the insider/outsider binary, leaving space for the destabilizing party of the third part. Vaudeville performers like Groucho Marx could be considered offensive and in defiance of the mores of the new middle class. His vaudeville-inspired performances directly reflected the disjunctive nature of the new cultural values that vaudeville could promote through its independence and social commentary. The new immigrant was a growing influence on Anglo-American culture, and the class system that the United States was chafing under and trying to redefine from its nineteenth-century forebears. As Hollywood films absorbed comic stage performers like Groucho Marx, vaudeville lost its power and significance, and by the end of the 1920s, it was all but obsolete.

The vaudeville aesthetic is represented in the contract scene from *A Night at the Opera*, as mentioned earlier in this chapter, which ends with the following exchange between "Groucho" and Chico:

GROUCHO: Now, I've got something here you're bound to like. You'll be crazy about it.
CHICO: No, I don't like it.
GROUCHO: You don't like what?
CHICO: Whatever it is. I don't like it.
GROUCHO: Well, let's don't break up on old friendship over a thing like that. Ready?

They then proceed to tear the mysterious offending clause out of their contracts. After tearing out several more clauses for seemingly arbitrary reasons and leaving the contract only about one inch long, Groucho then asks Chico to sign the contract that now has no content whatsoever. In response,

Chico says, "I forgot to tell you. I can't write." To which Groucho replies, "That's all right. There's no ink in the pen, anyhow."[65] The characters of "Groucho" and "Larry" remind us that in comedy how we present ourselves socially is contradicted when exposing our undesirable hidden selves through humor. As social assassins, Groucho Marx and Larry David expose the "truthiness" that Stephen Colbert defines as what you want to believe is true based on your "gut," rather than what is actually true. As Larry David tells Ricky Gervais, "We all have the bad thoughts. We just think them and don't say them. But the bad thoughts are funny."[66] Groucho Marx and Larry David embrace living outside of the lines. As evidenced in their stage and screen work, they reinforce the notion that the authority of consensus may have no ink in its pen.

Notes

1 Larry David, "Palestinian Chicken," *Curb Your Enthusiasm*, season 8, episode 3, directed by Robert B. Weide, aired July 24, 2011 (Burbank, CA: Warner Home Video, 2011), DVD.

2 Josh Levine, *Pretty, Pretty, Pretty Good: Larry David and the Making of "Seinfeld" and "Curb Your Enthusiasm"* (Toronto: ECW Press, 2010), 18.

3 John D. Donahue and Richard J. Zeckhauser, "The *Tummler's* Task" (Cambridge, MA: Harvard Kennedy School, Harvard University, March 6, 2012), 118.

4 Paul Klapper, "The Yiddish Music Hall," *University Settlement Studies* 2, no. 4 (1905): 20–21.

5 Kathy Lee Peiss, *Cheap Amusements: Working Women and Leisure in Turn-of-the-Century New York* (Philadelphia, PA: Temple University Press, 1986), 143.

6 Klapper, "The Yiddish Music Hall," 22. For audience responses to the Yiddish theater, see Richard Butsch, *The Making of American Audiences: From Stage to Television, 1750–1990* (Cambridge: Cambridge University Press, 2000), 132–35.

7 John Murray Cuddihy, *The Ordeal of Civility: Freud, Marx, Levi-Strauss, and the Jewish Struggle with Modernity* (New York: Basic Books, 1974), 126.

8 The Marx Brothers, *Horse Feathers* (1932), *Horse Feathers*, DVD (Dir. Norman Z. McLeod. Writ. Bert Kalmar, Harry Ruby, S. J. Perelman, Will B. Johnstone), Paramount Studios: Universal Home Video, Silver Screen Collection, 2004.

9 Ricky Gervais, "Ricky Gervais Meets . . . Larry David," directed by Niall Downing, aired January 5, 2006 (Objective Productions, Channel 4 Television Corporation, UK, 2006), Television Movie.

10 Marx, *Groucho and Me*, 224–25.

11 According to Groucho Marx, the act's name was the Larong Trio. Marx, *Groucho and Me*, 57.

12 Marx, *Groucho and Me*, 57. See also Joe Adamson, *Groucho, Harpo, Chico, and Sometimes Zeppo*, 43–48; Kyle Samuel Crichton, *The Marx Brothers* (Garden City, NY: Doubleday, 1950), 55–77.

13 Marx, *Groucho and Me*, 55.

14 Marx, *Groucho and Me*, 59.

15 Wes D. Gehring, *The Marx Brothers: A Bio-Bibliography* (New York: Greenwood Press, 1987), 60.

16 Gallagher and Shean was a successful act on the first-tier vaudeville circuit as well as Broadway during the 1910s and 1920s. It was a comedy double act starring Edward Gallagher (1873–1929) and Al Shean (born Albert Schoenberg, 1868–1949). Al Shean was the uncle of the Marx Brothers.

17 The Three Nightingales went on to include additional performers, replacing Mabel O'Donnell, like Lou Levy and Janie O'Riley, as the third nightingale. See Gehring, *Marx Brothers: A Bio-Bibliography*, 13–18.

18 Groucho Marx, *The Groucho Phile* (New York: Simon and Schuster, 1977), 32.

19 Anonymous review quoted in Marx, *The Groucho Phile*, 39.

20 Groucho Marx, "Bad Days Are Good Memories," *Saturday Evening Post* (Philadelphia, PA), August 29, 1931.

21 Groucho Marx, "Up from Pantages," *New York Times*, June 10, 1928.

22 Douglas Gilbert, *American Vaudeville: Its Life and Times* (New York: Dover Publications, 1940), 304.

23 *I'll Say She Is* was written with the aid of Tom Johnstone.

24 Gehring, *Marx Brothers: Bio-Bibliography*, 29.

25 Gehring, *Marx Brothers: Bio-Bibliography*, 29–30.

26 Alexander Woollcott, "Hilarious Antics Spread Good Cheer at the Casino," *New York World*, 19 May 1924. Woollcott's review derides Zeppo's importance as the fourth Marx Brother, referring to him as the "property man."

27 Gehring, *Marx Brothers: Bio-Bibliography*, 28.

28 Most of these scripted dialogues were the basis for improvised dialogue during live performances, and therefore the literary narrative was constantly being subverted through ad-libbing.

29 The Marx Brothers and Tom Johnstone, *I'll Say She Is* (from the Library of Congress manuscript, 1923), online at http://www.marx-brothers.org/marxology/home.htm.

30 Marx Brothers and Johnstone, *I'll Say She Is*.

31 *I'll Say She Is* has three versions found in Groucho Marx's papers collected at the Library of Congress, and transcribed by Groucho Marx in *The Groucho Phile* (New York: Simon and Schuster, 1977), as well as on the *Marxology* website at http://www.marx-brothers.org/marxology/story.htm.

32 The "five-year plan" is a reference to Josef Stalin's series of five-year plans for Russia the first of which was to be implemented in 1928. It was designed to enhance the new Soviet government under Stalin militarily, industrially, and economically. This reference also points to the fact that Groucho was well aware of world affairs that informed his comedy throughout his career.

33 Marx Brothers and Johnstone, *I'll Say She Is*.

34 *You Bet Your Life* is discussed in detail in Chapter 1.

35 Marx, "Bad Days," 12.

36 The Marx Brothers, *Duck Soup*, DVD. Dir. Leo McCarey. Writ. Bert Kalmar and Harry Ruby (Paramount Studios, 1933: Universal Home Video, Silver Screen Collection, 2004).

37 Larry David interview, "Seinfeld Reunion," *Curb Your Enthusiasm*, season 7 (New York: Home Box Office, 2010), DVD.

38 Phil Silvers, with Robert Saffron, *This Laugh Is on Me: The Phil Silvers Story* (Englewood Cliffs, NJ: Prentice-Hall, 1973), 31.

39 Silvers, with Saffron, *This Laugh Is on Me*, 46.

40 Silvers, with Saffron, *This Laugh Is on Me*, 50.

41 Silvers, with Saffron, *This Laugh Is on Me*, 51.

42 Silvers, with Saffron, *This Laugh Is on Me*, 52–54.

43 Steve Allen, *The Funny Men* (New York: Simon and Schuster, 1956), 260.

44 Allen, *The Funny Men*, 255.

45 Levine, *Pretty Good*, 81; "Being Larry David," interview by Scott Simon, *Weekend Edition Saturday*, NPR, October 27, 2001, http://www.npr.org/programs/wesat/features/2001/larrydavid/011027.larrydavid.html.

46 Deirdre Dolon, *Curb Your Enthusiasm: The Book* (New York: Gotham Books, 2006), 104–5.

47 Levine, *Pretty Good*, 19.

48 "How It Began," *Seinfeld*, disc 4, season 2 (Culver City, CA: Castle Rock Entertainment, 1991), DVD.

49 "Ricky Gervais Meets . . . Larry David."

50 Dolan, *Curb Your Enthusiasm*, 11.

51 *A Night at the Opera*, directed by Sam Wood (1935; Burbank, CA: Warner Home Video, 2004), DVD.

52 Larry David, "The Anonymous Donor," *Curb Your Enthusiasm*, season 6, episode 2, directed by Robert B. Weide, aired September 16, 2007 (Burbank, CA: Warner Home Video), DVD.

53 The Jess Mack Collection: James R. Dickinson Library, University of Nevada, Las Vegas [as reprinted in Andrew Davis, *Baggy Pants Comedy: Burlesque and the Oral Tradition* (New York: Palgrave Macmillan, 2011), 124–25].

54 *Horse Feathers*, DVD.

55 *Monkey Business*, directed by Norman Z. McLeod (Universal City, CA: Universal Home Video, Silver Screen Collection, 2004), DVD.

56 *Animal Crackers* was staged on Broadway in 1928, and the film version released in 1930. George S. Kaufman, *Animal Crackers*, in *Kaufman & Co.: Broadway Comedies*, ed. Laurence Maslon (New York: Library of the Americas, 2004), 182. Note that the text of *Animal Crackers* found in this anthology is a combination of Sam Harris's 1928 Princeton University archival version and the 1929 version found in the Groucho Marx papers at the Library of Congress. See also *Animal Crackers*, directed by Victor Sheekman (1930; Universal City, CA: Universal Home Video, Silver Screen Collection, 2004), DVD.

57 "Ricky Gervais Meets . . . Larry David."

58 Larry David, "The Ski Lift," *Curb Your Enthusiasm*, episode 8, season 5, directed by Larry Charles, Burbank, CA: Warner Home Video, 2005, DVD.

59 Reproduced in Marx, *Groucho Phile*, 20.

60 Larry David, "The Table Read," *Curb Your Enthusiasm*, season 7, episode 9, directed by Larry Charles, aired November 15, 2009 (Burbank, CA: Warner Home Video, 2009), DVD.

61 Larry David, "Mister Softee," *Curb Your Enthusiasm*, season 8, episode 9, directed by Larry Charles, aired September 4, 2011 (Burbank, CA: Warner Home Video, 2011), DVD.

62 Cuddihy, *Civility*, 127.

63 Robert Snyder, *Vaudeville and Popular Culture in New York* (New York: Oxford University Press, 1989), 63.

64 David, "Palestinian Chicken," *Curb Your Enthusiasm*.

65 *A Night at the Opera*, 1935.

66 "Ricky Gervais Meets . . . Larry David."

3

"The Girlie Show" as the new burlesque

Mae West to Tina Fey

In 1901–2, *Harper's Bazar* featured a series of articles written by Robert J. Burdette and Constant Coquelin titled "Have Women a Sense of Humor?"[1] According to Burdette, women in the late nineteenth century were perceived as having a "more refined" appreciation of humor. They valued, reasoned Burdette, "true humor" and that which is "delicate, sympathetic, refined to the highest culture."[2] In 1909, Boston critic Charles Young condescendingly stated that "[woman] is about as comical as a crutch" and that "real comedy" was unequivocally a "masculine trait."[3]

Vanity Fair raised this question again in 2007–8 with two articles, "Why Women Aren't Funny" by the late Christopher Hitchens and "Who Says Women Aren't Funny?" by *New York Times* television critic Alessandra Stanley. Hitchens contended that women do not need to be funny since they do not have to attract men in the same way that men use humor to attract their female counterparts. Stanley interviewed women humorists including Tina Fey, Amy Poehler, and Kristen Wiig, who insisted that the institutionalization of comedy by men in the twentieth century—particularly in television—attempted to marginalize women as comedians and comic writers in a self-created "boys' club." In Fey's memoir, *Bossypants*, she recalls a story in which fellow *Saturday Night Live* alum Amy Poehler was in a meeting with a predominantly male group of writers and cast members, doing a "dirty and loud and 'unladylike'" comic bit. Jimmy Fallon, the de facto male star of the moment, mocked Poehler for her crudeness saying, "Stop that! It's not cute! I don't like it." According to Fey, "Amy dropped what she was doing, went black in the eyes for a second, and wheeled around on him. 'I don't fucking care if you like it.' Jimmy was visibly startled. Amy went right back to enjoying her ridiculous bit."[4] The notion that men feel threatened by women who are funny, if not even funnier than they are, appears to have been of concern in the late nineteenth century with the advent of the new woman when Kate Sanborn noted in *The Wit of Women*, "No man likes to have his story capped by a better and fresher from a lady's lips. What woman does not risk being called sarcastic and hateful if she throws the merry dart or engages in a little sharp-shooting. No, no, it's dangerous—if not fatal."[5]

* * *

The vaudeville aesthetic came to fruition along with the rise of the new woman during the last decade of the nineteenth century. The new woman represented sexual freedom outside of marriage, with a desire and ability to vote, work, and express herself openly and without censure. She served as a critic of a male-dominated society, and was perceived as a threat to an Anglo-American value system left over from the nineteenth century, reflected in female "comediennes" like Mae West. Feminist cultural critic and humorist Helen Rowland corroborates this notion in her 1911 article "The Emancipation of 'The Rib.'" She remarked that "woman now shares equal honors with man in seeing a joke and sometimes sees it first," and it is this that "has done more to bring about the equality of the sexes and their mutual understanding than any thing else, from coeducation to the suffrage movement."[6] The vaudeville aesthetic in relationship to the new woman was a form of social rebellion that took the emphasis off of the sexuality and perceived promiscuity of female vaudevillians by refocusing on their work as comedians and social commentators through their offensive songs, dances, and comedy writing. Beginning at the turn of the twentieth century, the vaudeville aesthetic enabled the new woman to be forthright when it came to expressing her own sense of humor.

A distinguishing feature of comedy as performed by women beginning in the 1890s was that women like Mae West had begun to create their own material. The legacy and resurgence of the vaudeville aesthetic in female comedians can be traced from early twentieth-century vaudevillian turned film actress Mae West to the revolution, first in radio with Fanny Brice, and then television comedy with Lucille Ball, through the improvisation of live television of Gilda Radner in the 1970s and 1980s, to the twenty-first century with Fey. No single, direct line can be drawn from one funny woman to another, however there is a continuum of female comedians that have created opportunities so that the next generation can exist.

In 1916, entertainment critic and chief editor of *Variety*, Sime Silverman, wrote, "Unless Miss West can tone down her stage presence in every way, she just as well might hop right out of vaudeville into burlesque."[7] The key to this statement is that West needed to "tone down" not her act, but her "stage presence." For any act, stage presence was the meat and potatoes of vaudeville, and without it actors would not be able to put it over. West was in effect being chided for how her body exposed her presumed intentions. Here is a place where Fey's anecdote about Poehler and Fallon and this critique of West come together to expose a fear of female comic insurgency. The notion of women's sociocultural rebellion appeared in an 1891 article for the periodical *Nineteenth Century* titled, "The Wild Women as Social Insurgents."[8] The reaction of the new middle class to comic female vaudeville performers' aggressive behavior signaled a cultural conflict that would not end until vaudeville's popularity began to wane. It was picked up again in the new media formats of radio and television comedy in the 1940s and 1950s. It is still present in the work of Fey and of her contemporaries like Poehler and Sarah Silverman.

The "new" both onstage and off reflected the spirit of the day, and female comics' openly crass and vulgar performances became associated with the new woman. The new woman was subject to the pressures of being considered "a rank lady," as performance historian M. Alison Kibler puts it.[9] While making her fortune from her openly sexual innuendos and choreography, they were not taken seriously as stage artists because their supposed eccentricities defined their acts. The new woman as comic performer embraced the vaudeville aesthetic by engaging in "wild" acts of unique singing and dancing, and by taking the emphasis off the sexuality and perceived promiscuity of female vaudevillians and refocusing on their work as comic performers who, through their humorous acts, moved away from their status as rank ladies. At the turn of the twentieth century, rank ladies were often to be found on the stages of burlesque theaters.

The new women in comedy like West began to caricature gender roles and conflicts between the sexes, and the growing divide between female and male sociocultural expectations on third-tier burlesque stages. The origins of burlesque were, as the name indicates, a satirical form of comedy that mocked legitimate theater and musical revues. The comedians included singers and dancers many of who could not compete with the women who showed their undergarments in "leg shows" because of their girth and unattractiveness. Female comedians like Marie Dressler, May Irwin, Eva Tanguay, Sophie Tucker, and Mae West, all honed their comedy craft in burlesque comic performances that eschewed the roles of the dainty singer, the demure ingénue, and the witty aristocrat. They were part of a now-lost tradition of burlesquing the more dramatic stage fare of the day, including moralistic melodramas, and overblown musical revues that offered little but pretty voices and spectacle. As burlesque moved away from parody of other popular entertainments , female performers became the "joke" acts between the more standard prettier performers who were there to show their legs with the promise of sex. However, as burlesque gave way to the more refined vaudeville stage it reverted to its roots in the mid-nineteenth century barrooms and quasi-brothels known as concert saloons. Burlesque became a platform for buxom women to titillate a mostly male working-class audience. The comedians in burlesque became merely transitional acts between costume changes for the dancers. Many of the burlesque comic female performers attempted to break into vaudeville, but some like Mae West, made the leap from third-tier to first-tier popular entertainments. West's act did not find success in high-class vaudeville until she began working with pianist Harry Richman in 1918. Their act would land them a headline spot on the bill at New York's legendary Palace Theater. West's success at the Palace would capture the attention of United Booking Office head E. F. Albee and garnered West a three-year contract.

The sublime irony of West's career can be observed with her difficulties in finding an audience for her act on the third-tier comic vaudeville stage. Only when she entered the mainstream of Broadway and Hollywood would she outshine many of her contemporaries. While other female vaudevillians like May Irwin, Eva Tanguay, Sophie Tucker, and Kate Elinore found enormous success onstage, they were much less effective in the legitimate world of theater or films. West flew in the face of social propriety and the surface display of modesty and forthrightness, just by being herself onstage: the tough girl born of working-class Brooklyn immigrants who refused to submerge her persona in order to conform to the standards set by commercial producers.

In 1926, West found her place in the most unexpected world of all—not in the popular entertainment of vaudeville but on Broadway, with a play of her own devising, simply and directly titled *Sex*. West's insurgency as a woman, as a comedian, and as a cultural force shattered the boundaries between popular lowbrow entertainments and the bourgeois middlebrow world of the Broadway stage. *Sex*, written by and starring West, was to have three hundred and seventy-five performances before the New York Police Department raided and arrested her company in February 1927. Even though over three hundred and twenty-five thousand people had already seen *Sex*, including members of the police department and their wives, judges of the criminal courts and their wives, and seven members of the District Attorney's staff and *their* wives, West was denounced by reformers and authorities alike. She was subsequently prosecuted and sentenced to ten days in a workhouse on Roosevelt Island— known as Welfare Island—and fined five hundred dollars. The resulting publicity for West only served to increase her public profile and bring her to the attention of Hollywood producers.[10] The very moralizers who were trying to rid American middle-class spectators of acts like West's merely served as a catalyst for her career. Where West faltered as a comic vaudevillian, she thrived as a soon-to-become sound film star, using the same tough-girl act that she had originated over twenty years earlier. Ultimately, it was West's

FIGURE 3.1 *Advertisement for Mae West's Broadway play* Sex *in New York* Graphic *(December 30, 1926).*

Source: Photo by Martha Swope © Billy Rose Theatre Division, The New York Public Library for the Performing Arts, Astor, Lenox, and Tilden Foundations.

creation and performance in her own comic playwriting that launched her career into mainstream comedy culled from her burlesque, then vaudeville, comedy acts.

The reaction of the new middle class to comic female vaudeville performers like Mae West and her so-called offensive onstage behavior signaled a cultural conflict that would not end until the demise of vaudeville in the late 1920s and early 1930s. The subsequent resurgence of the vaudeville aesthetic by female comedians can be traced to the revolution in radio and television comedy especially in the 1940s and 1950s with Fanny Brice and Lucille Ball.

Radio played a significant role for female comedians. Its influence can be seen with the vaudeville comic performer Fanny Brice. Born Fania Borach in New York City in 1891, the future comedy star was the third child of Hungarian-Jewish immigrant saloon owners. Brice dropped out of school in 1908 to join *The Girls from Happy Land*, a burlesque revue. She trained in burlesque comedy, appearing early in the new century with the Hurtig and Seamon Transatlantic Burlesque Troupe, then graduating to Max Spiegel's *College Girls* in 1910 at Manhattan's Columbia Burlesque Theatre. Brice was known for performing comic songs with an exaggerated Yiddish-inflected English and a show-stopping song, "Lovely Joe." Brice's stage work brought her to the attention of producer Florenz Ziegfeld. In two years, she was hired by the Broadway impresario to headline the *Ziegfeld Follies* during the 1910–11 season. She rejoined the *Follies* in 1921 and was featured in two songs that became her signature numbers, "My Man" and "Second Hand Rose." Brice appeared in many Broadway shows, including *Sweet and Low* (1930) and *Billy Rose's Crazy Quilt* (1931), both produced by stage legend Billy Rose. She also starred in films, including *My Man* (1928), *Everybody Sing* (1938, with Judy Garland), and both *The Great Ziegfeld* (1936) and *Ziegfeld Follies* (1946) as herself.

As the humor of the vaudeville stage declined and radio began to dominate comedy in the 1930s, Brice took a character that she created for the *Follies*, Baby Snooks, and transferred her skills to radio. From 1936 until her death in 1951, Brice performed the Baby Snooks character of a bratty child, tormenting her beleaguered father, who would end with a loud "WAAAHHH!" when she did not get her way. The character was so popular that it was produced on various programs like *Ziegfeld Follies on the Air* (1936–38), *Good News* (1938–39), *Maxwell House Coffee Time* (1940–44), and finally in its own incarnation, *The Baby Snooks Show* (1944–51). According to Brice, Baby Snooks was inspired by "baby" characters in vaudeville during the first two decades of the twentieth century.

At that time there was a child called Baby Peggy, and she was very popular. The hair was all curled and bleached, and she was always in pink or blue.

She always looked like an ice-cream soda or something. Then I had talked to people about doing a baby—I thought I could be very funny with it.[11]

Brice impersonated the impish, calculating brat who frustrates her long-suffering and indulgent father (played by Alan Reed). After her Father asks who has made a mess in their living room, Snooks tries to blame it on "Nursie." When Father reminds Snooks that Nursie has left town to visit her sick sister, she says, "I forgot. She done it yesterday." After her father loses patience with this obvious lie, he demands that Snooks confess to breaking a vase. Baby Snooks replies with gravity:

SNOOKS: I had to do it, daddy.
FATHER: You had to? Why?
SNOOKS: On account of the three rattlesnakes. [. . .] Yeah, they came into the parlor and I killed them.
FATHER: Snooks, you know you're not telling the truth.
SNOOKS: Well, maybe it was only two rattlesnakes. . . .[12]

The build up of absurd lies that Snooks tells her Father inevitably ends with his absolute red-in-the-face anger, and Baby Snooks getting her way. The reversal of the power dynamic of children and parents through cunning and deception pointed to the myth of the all-American, middle-class family debunking the authority of the patriarch in the average suburban home.

Brice's influence is seen later in the characters played by Gilda Radner on *SNL*—including a young girl perpetually scared of the bogeyman, and Lisa Loopner, the awkward and childish adolescent in a well-known sketch with comedian Bill Murray. Other *SNL* alumnae like Rachel Dratch and Tina Fey have influences that can be traced back to Brice's character of the "child-woman," both in their live stage work with Second City in Chicago and on *SNL*.

Radio would also give rise to another comedy sensation with Lucille Ball and her subsequent international success through the nascent medium of television. Ball is a significant female comedian through which to understand the power of network television and its production of comedy shows. She, along with her collaborator and husband Desi Arnaz, became one of the most successful of the 1950s comic performer-producers. In 1948, CBS Radio featured an up-and-coming female comedian in a new radio comedy called *My Favorite Husband* (1948–51), about a kooky housewife named Liz Cugat, later renamed Cooper to avoid the ethnic overtones and reinforce the couple's middle-class status that evidently "ethnic" couples could not share, as well as the confusion with Cuban-raised performer Xavier Cugat. The show was a hit, launching Ball's comedy career and leading to the show's development for television. Ball insisted on casting her real-life husband, Desi Arnaz. However, CBS was hesitant to cast Arnaz, since they felt the American audience would not accept a redheaded white beauty queen being married to a Cuban-American bandleader. The irony was that they were already married and had created a successful production company, Desilu. The initial pilot was met with indifference by CBS, so the couple decided to tour their new show in a vaudeville act in which the crazy wife of a Cuban bandleader was perpetually trying to get into her husband's show. The tour proved that American audiences were indeed ready for a mixed ethnic couple and Ball's zany vaudeville-inspired humor. CBS, always ready to cash in on success, put *I Love Lucy* on its 1951 television line-up.

Ball's physical comedy is marvelously demonstrated in the "Lucy Does a TV Commercial" episode from 1952. Lucy, unbeknownst to Ricky, gets herself cast on his show as the "Vitameatavegamin girl," promoting a product with 23 percent alcohol content that she has to drink during the live broadcast. While rehearsing for the commercial spot, Lucy begins to sip the vitamin-meat-vegetable-alcohol supplement, and her physical reactions to the awful-tasting product that "tastes just like candy" are a master lesson in comic timing. As she progresses in the rehearsals, she also gets drunk on the "candy" and begins to enjoy it, then in take after take, begins to lose control of her speech and becomes sloppier and sloppier in her delivery and reaction time.[13] This form of physical comedy, which comments on the false enjoyment and healthiness of commercial products that one must pretend to like in order to get corporate sponsorship, not only is entertaining but also mocks the very driving force of shows like *I Love Lucy*, which depended on sponsors and their exaggerated and deceitful business practices just to stay on the air.

Ball's seriousness as a comic actor in the vaudeville tradition is reflected in her having hired guest stars like former stage comedians Harpo Marx and Phil Silvers; she also went so far as to engage Buster Keaton to teach her his own special brand of vaudeville stage comedy and gags. Lucy and Harpo meticulously re-created the famous mirror scene from *Duck Soup* (1933) as performed by Harpo and Groucho Marx. This classic comedy sequence remains one of the highlights of *I Love Lucy* to this day.[14]

Ball, despite a reputation for being apolitical on her show, actually used show business to comment on the lengths people will go to debase themselves to appear on television, on a wife's necessity to deceive her husband to have the freedom to do as she pleases personally and professionally, on false advertising in television, and on corporate domination of television content and censorship. Moreover, she presented Americans with a mixed ethnic couple whose marital strife is not based on cultural differences but on typical marriage woes that any viewer could relate to. This, combined with

FIGURE 3.2 *Lucille Ball and Harpo Marx in* I Love Lucy *(1955) recreating the "mirror scene" from the Marx Brothers' 1933 film* Duck Soup.
Source: *CBS Photo Archive via Getty Images.*

Ball's status as the successful star and producer of her own show, as well as a producer of other programs in multiple genres—including *Star Trek*, *The Andy Griffith Show*, *The Dick Van Dyke Show*, and *Mission: Impossible*—made her not only a powerful woman in a male-dominated industry but also a subversive force during the 1950s and 1960s. The more she challenged authority and conventions, the more her fame and power increased.

The bridge from the beginning of television comedy to the 1970s and 1980s brought to the fore the comedy of Phyllis Diller, Gilda Radner, and Roseanne Barr. Radner is a prime example of how these "new" humorists took the pain of exclusion of being a woman in comedy and being an overweight and physically awkward teenager, and hid her pain by being funny. *SNL* comedy writer Anne Beatts reminisced about working with Radner in the 1970s: "She once said that she thought comedy originated for her when you're little and you fall down on the ice? And people might laugh at you so you try and make it seem like you fell on purpose? That was the root of her comedy."[15] The female comedians, discussed here, took their pain and masked the hurt with comedy.

Radner's impersonation of poet-cum-rock 'n' roller, Patti Smith, was another contrasting case in point when she portrayed the self-destructive Smith as an angry, frayed, and drugged-out musician, shouting into the microphone, "Gimme Mick! Gimme Mick!," and ending by passing out onstage with a bottle of Jack Daniels bourbon clutched in her hand.[16] The character of the disaffected teen turned rock star turned cautionary tale expressed Radner's internal struggles and served as a source for her comic invention. This legacy led to the work of Paula Poundstone, Sarah Silverman, and Julia Sweeney, who redefined the 1990s and remain driving forces in comedy today.

Sarah Silverman, as a representative of the new generation of women in comedy, came to prominence in the late twentieth century and was recently featured on *Comedians in Cars Getting Coffee*. This web-based comedy phenomenon was created by and stars Jerry Seinfeld. It features, as the title makes amusingly obvious, various comedians chatting with Seinfeld while driving in his vintage cars to go out for coffee. The "webisode" titled "I'm Going to Change Your Life Forever" witnesses the convergence of two generations of contemporary humorists with Silverman (42) and Seinfeld (59). Where the impulse for this humor comes from can be seen when Seinfeld asks Silverman about her upbringing: "I'm really a product of my parents. They were overly honest with their lives when we were kids," says Silverman. "There was never a filter that went 'maybe that's not appropriate for my [eight-year-old] daughter.'"[17] For Silverman, the expression of a filter-free truth guides her worldview in comedy—whether it is appropriate or not.

A prime connection between the generational distance of Mae West, Lucille Ball, and Tina Fey is that they all served as performers, writers, and producers of their own work. Women gaining control over their acts between the turn-of-the-twentieth-century female comedian West and her contemporary correlative Tina Fey, allowed the voices of women to be heard without interference, suppression, or censorship from their male counterparts. They still had to adhere to the marketplace and the economic realities of the popular entertainment industry, but within those confines of the demands of advertisers and executives who watched the numbers very carefully, they had more freedom to pursue their interests in comedy unadulterated.

Tina Fey has distinguished herself from many of her contemporaries both female and male with the creation and performance of her own material in the manner of Mae West. In 1997, Fey was asked by *SNL* producer Lorne Michaels to interview for a writing position on his twenty-plus-year comedy/variety show. Her work in improvisational comedy and sketch writing at Second City in Chicago had attracted Michaels to Fey. In Fey's memoir *Bossypants*, she writes she got the call because the show was diversifying its writing staff. "Only in comedy, by the way, does an obedient white girl from the suburbs count as diversity."[18] Fey went on to become the head writer of *SNL* in 1999—the first woman to do so in the show's history to date—and then to create, produce, and star in her own show, *30 Rock*, a backstage satire of the 30 Rockefeller Center studios where *SNL* is still produced. The show would feature Fey as Liz Lemon, a single, liberal-leaning feminist from suburban Pennsylvania who becomes a writer-producer of *The Girlie Show* (*TGS*). Her boss, an executive at General Electric—the parent company of NBC-TV and the producers of the actual *30 Rock* and *SNL* as well—is run by Jack Donaghy, played by film star Alec Baldwin. Liz hires her former co-comedy performer, Jenna Maroney, as performed by Broadway musical comedy star Jane Krakowski, who, like Amy Poehler, had come up with Lemon/Fey at Second City and *SNL*.

In the initial episode, *SNL* alum Tracy Morgan would play a version of himself as comedy megastar Tracy Jordan, a down-on-his-luck black comedian with a fading film career hired as a "bad boy" to boost ratings and keep the show from being canceled. The trio of Jack, Jenna, and Tracy would serve to create a comedy triangle that resonated with Fey's satirical take on class, gender, and race, with Liz Lemon as the mediator, literally juggling the trials and tribulations of this triumvirate. Lemon represented the single white working woman in a male-dominated workplace run by the ultimate alpha male in Jack Donaghy. The star of *The Girlie Show (TGS) with Tracy Jordan*, played by Tracy Morgan, completes the comedy triangle of Baldwin and Krakowski, as he makes clear in the show's pilot by shouting, "I am the third heat!"[19] Liz Lemon comes into conflict with the "third heat" when, by way of defense that she has been giving special minority treatment to her employees, her producer, Pete Hornberger (Scott Adsit) says, "This is America. None of us are supposed to be here."[20]

Fey uses the outlier notion of the "third heat" of being a minority in comedy and how this affects her characters' perspectives of the world. The development of this worldview can be seen as Fey intentionally creates a television show in *30 Rock* that she describes as follows:

> A triangle between me, Alec Baldwin, and Tracy Morgan felt like it had potential. These three characters would have completely different views about any topic that came up—race, gender, politics, workplace ethics, money, sex, women's basketball—and they would agree and disagree in endless combinations.[21]

Comedy is built on threes according to conventional show business wisdom. The three stars of *30 Rock* were created by Tina Fey to produce the tensions and dynamics of the "third heat" necessary for putting her brand of comedy over to the audience.

Mae West and Tina Fey serve as bookends to the new woman as social critic. An interesting intergenerational connection between these comedians is the portrayal of gender and race in their work. West and Fey use burlesque humor to question middle-class notions of femininity and sexuality. They look at the topics of motherhood and the family and upend the shibboleths of American society. In addition, they take on women's perceived roles in the workplace and their presumed domestic responsibilities. In order to better understand the legacy and continuum of West and Fey, it is essential to look at their stage history and rise through the ranks of comedy and how it affected their acts both as women and as writer/producers of their own material.

Mae West, through her use of burlesque comedy with regard to the new woman, provides insight into the tensions associated with the place of women in American society early in the twentieth century. She was a formidable manipulator of comic innuendo, an infamous social transgressor, as well as a target of censorship. With a wild cavalier attitude and self-possessed toughness of the lower-class outsider, West was the apotheosis of the new woman on the vaudeville stage. Beginning in third-tier burlesque houses, she became a comic insurgent into the middle-class world of the Broadway theater during her twenty-year stage career.

West, now considered a popular and famous cultural touchstone of the female comedic performer, was born in 1893, the daughter of Matilda, an Austrian immigrant, and Jack West, an Irish immigrant who had settled in the Greenpoint section of Brooklyn. Her mother was a "refined" corset model and father a small-time boxer known as Battlin' Jack. Mae was a streetwise "tough girl" who grew up in a part of New York City where the working poor—including a mix of Irish, Italians, Germans, and Poles—were in constant conflict for survival in a new country with limited prospects for immigrants, especially unmarried women. In order to provide for her family after her husband's alcoholism rendered him unemployable, West's mother put Mae on the stage when she was six years old in an attempt to escape their volatile and dangerous Brooklyn neighborhood.[22]

After breaking into popular entertainment at the age of fourteen, West, by the time she reached her early twenties, had progressed from the burlesque houses of Brooklyn to the transitional world of vaudeville at Hammerstein's Victoria Theater in Manhattan. The Victoria was not exactly the big time, but it was well-attended and attracted sensational if not notorious acts. *Variety* commented on West's 1912 act at Hammerstein's Victoria, saying:

> Mae West is a "single" [solo act] now. She has been about everything else, from a chorus girl in the *Follies Bergere* [*sic*] and head of a "three-act" to principal in a Ziegfeld show; that she escaped from the latter evidences some strength of character and this becomes apparent in a way during the act at Hammerstein's.[23]

By 1922, West had tired of touring in vaudeville, and began to set her sights on Broadway. Success on the competitive Great White Way, as it was nicknamed then, was not forthcoming, and from 1922 to her Broadway debut with her original play, *Sex*, in 1926, West was all but unseen, appearing in lackluster musical revues.[24] West's vulgar and sexually aggressive stage persona, developed in her burlesque years, would, however, become the signature of both her commercial stage and film characters propelling her into the lucrative world of Broadway theater, and a major Hollywood career beginning with the early 1930s films *Night After Night* and *She Done Him Wrong* (based on another 1928 stage play, *Diamond Lil*), to *My Little Chickadee*, co-starring with stage and screen legend, W. C. Fields, in 1940.

In sharp contrast to Mae West's upbringing, Elizabeth Stamatina (Tina) Fey was born in Upper Darby, Pennsylvania, just west of Philadelphia, in 1970 to Donald and Jeanne Fey. After studying drama, Tina graduated in 1992 from the University of Virginia. Afterward she moved to Chicago to study at the famed Second City. After about nine months, Fey was admitted to the more intensive Second City Training Center and ultimately spent three years touring before going to the main stage with Second City e.t.c. In 1997, Adam McKay—then head writer at *Saturday Night Live*—recommended Fey as a writer for the show. She admitted to being very nervous about working at the legendary *SNL* and "being a foot shorter than everyone else, younger, and being one of the only female writers at the time."[25] In the end, Fey made history by becoming the first female head writer of *SNL*. She then made her on-camera debut during the 25th season by co-anchoring the "Weekend Update" segment of the show with comedian Jimmy Fallon.

Much like West in her burlesque and vaudeville circuits of the early twentieth century, Fey toured the United States "by van to all kinds of destinations, from upstate New York to St. Paul, Minnesota, to Waco, Texas."[26] These "third-tier" tours with the Second City company doing "best of" sketches were a place to hone her craft in front of a diversity of receptive, as well as hostile, audiences. She also learned—against company policy—to improvise sketches and create characters with her fellow cast members in order to test out new material when the management was not looking. According to Fey, her performance style was influenced by veteran comedy actress Catherine O'Hara from the cast of *Second City Television* (*SCTV*) in sketch writing as well as her portrayal of comic characters.[27]

One of the ironies of working in a field dominated by men came when Fey wanted to use an equal number of male and female performers onstage. As if violating a sacred creed, Fey was told: "'You can't do that. There won't be enough for the girls.' . . . *We were making up the show ourselves. How could there not be enough parts?* [italics in original] . . . what I like to call 'The Myth of Not Enough.'"[28] This double-standard, and being reduced to playing girlfriends or wives in sketches written by men, grated on Fey as she pushed to integrate the cast more equitably with women to write more complex female characters. Fey would spend the next decade fighting for this equality in comedy, ultimately becoming, not unlike West and Lucille Ball before her, the producer, creator, writer, and performer of her own work. *30 Rock* became the primary forum for Fey's comedy. Since her career began, she has won multiple awards for her efforts, including seven Emmy Awards, two Golden Globe Awards, five Screen Actors' Guild Awards, and four Writers' Guild of America Awards, and she was nominated for a Grammy Award as Best Spoken Word Album for her book, *Bossypants*, after five weeks on the *New York Times* Best Seller List. In 2008, Fey's impersonation of then vice-presidential candidate Sarah Palin garnered her the Associated Press Entertainer of the Year Award as a guest performer on *SNL*.

Another compelling connection between West and Fey is the portrayal of gender and race in their work. West used the burlesque humor of normative notions of femininity and sexuality in relation to stereotypical perceptions of women. Fey, in an ironic satire of these same issues, as well as of motherhood, disrupts the values of American society of women in the workplace and their presumed domestic responsibilities.

In big-time vaudeville during the Progressive era, West's conspicuous tough-girl roughness limited her stage success. To appeal to a broader audience who attended the first-tier theaters, West needed a subtler style. As *Variety* saw it, the issue was not West's ability but her open indecency so ingrained in her nature as to be unmaskable. Nothing could detract from her rawness, as a review of a 1916 New York performance by Mae and her sister Beverly, in their short-lived double act, declared:

> Mae West in big-time vaudeville may only be admired for her persistency in believing she is a big-time act and trying to make vaudeville accept her as such. After trying out several brands of turns, Miss West is with us again, this time with a "Sister" tacked onto the billing and the stage. "Sister"'s hair looks very much like Mae's and there the family resemblance ceases in looks as well as work, for "Sister" isn't quite as rough as Mae West can't help but being. . . . This working out new acts, buying new wardrobe and worrying will get to Miss West's nerve in time (but it will probably be a long time).[29]

By 1917, West had indeed ceased in her efforts as a touring vaudevillian and abandoned her aspiration to break into the big time. Her working-class, unruly, and promiscuous persona was seemingly impossible to shake. Expected as a child to make a name for herself in a sensationalized theatrical market, West was constantly being asked to remake herself as a more acceptable female comic performer by taming her lower-class body and voice to accommodate an easily offended—outwardly at least—middle-class public. West flew in the face of social propriety and surface displays of modesty and forthrightness, just by being "herself" onstage: the tough girl born of working-class Brooklyn immigrants who refused to submerge her façade to conform to the standards set by Progressive era moral watchdogs.

After Mae West's breakout stage success writing and starring in *Sex* (1926), her next Broadway venture, *Diamond Lil* (1928), was followed by multiple revivals, including one in 1949 with West still starring at the age of fifty-six. A *New York Times* reviewer attempted to fathom the mystery of West's popularity in this stage vehicle after so many years, writing:

> "Diamond Lil" is a play about the world of sex, but there is very little sex in it. Like an old dime novel, it is full of crime, drink and iniquity. After beating about the bush for two sluggish acts, it settles down hospitably into an old-fashioned vaudeville show in the last act; and Miss West, billowy and swaying at the piano, sings a few sinful ballads in a small voice but with plenty of style. It is performing in the grand manner. . . . After thoughtfully studying her performance twice in a little over two months, this reviewer is still puzzled over one thing. Is Miss West serious or is she kidding?[30]

It could be argued that sex had nothing to do with it. Comedy, as West practiced it, appeared to be mocking the hypocrisy of censors with regard to the proper decorum of women and their relationship to sex on the stage. The point that this reviewer makes about West's play being about sex, but having very little sex in it, is revealing. West's treatment of sexuality could be received both as a serious affront to middle-class reformers, as well as a satire of how this behavior was being viewed as offensive to those middle-class audiences that did not understand her brand of humor.

Critics of the period showed concern for female vaudevillians not demure enough or too raucous and raunchy, considering them to be rough acts that belonged in front of working-class burlesque audiences—West was one of these women. *Variety* more often than not praised the performance of traditional gender roles and also had fervent class biases. Typical of male critics of the era, Sime Silverman in *Variety* favored male stage comics and pretty women who sang sweet and sentimental songs and knew their place. A prime example of the perceived bad influence of the lower-class tough girl comedian can be seen in an early act of West's. As he characterized a 1912 performance:

> [For the song] "Rap, Rap, Rap," Miss West "ragging" this while seated upon a chair, closing the turn without a wait with a "loose dance." There's enough to the act just now for it to pass, if Miss West can be taught how to "get" an audience. She's one of the many freak persons on the vaudeville stage, where freakishness often carries more weight than talent, but Miss West should be coached to derive the full value from her personality.[31]

The "ragging" mentioned in this review was a reference both to the ragtime (early jazz) music and to the suggestive movements that followed along with the song. Also of potential offense, West was seated in a chair, affording audience members a glimpse of her ankles and perhaps more, as her legs moved in "rag" time. The focus of his review, however, is the "many freak persons," as vaudevillians were often characterized, especially female comedians. Silverman, through his megaphone of *Variety*, insisted that first-tier vaudeville and Broadway musicals were the sole domain of discerning popular entertainments that would draw middle- and highbrow patrons, as he tried to suppress the female "freaks" with his critiques.[32]

West focused on sexual innuendo in her stage work, but perhaps not for the reasons that reformers and conservative reviewers had judged her for. The success of an act was relative to how the routine could be interpreted through the body and voice. When these two elements of a comic performance were in conflict it produced the tension needed to create comedy. These comic physical and spoken signals were a double-edged entertainment that had a hint of the salacious, as well as the burlesque mockery of bourgeois prudery.

West and her fellow comic performers returned the voice of the new woman to her body by mocking the self-serious moralizing of cultural reformers, and the middle classes who looked to these socially conservative watchdogs for guidance. West challenged and broke through the boundaries of class and its relationship to gender standards with her performance of the new woman on- and offstage.

In 1928 Mae West's play *Diamond Lil*—about the behind-the-scenes lives of an 1890s concert saloon-cum-brothel (later adapted for film, and retitled *She Done Him Wrong* in 1930)[33]—gave place to what she was known for in her stage and film work from that point on: the funny, sexually suggestive, hidden meanings in her dialogue. As a critic for the *New York Evening Post* put it, "[West] seems to recoil with an almost gun-like precision after each of her more tawdry speeches, and make her own comment upon them, even while she continues to play them seriously."[34] This astute assessment of West's brand of humor was to be associated with camp. Camp, as defined by historian and Mae West biographer Marybeth Hamilton, "was to enact a playful gender inversion as a means of expressing a 'third sex' identity."[35] West's "gun-like" delivery created an ironic distance between what she said and how she said it. A now-famous line from one of her first films, *Night After Night* (1932) exemplifies this idea of doubleness of intention. West, in the first scene when a hatcheck girl exclaims, "Goodness, what beautiful diamonds," wisecracks, "Goodness had nothing to do with it, dearie."[36] The famous line of Mae West's from her autobiography, "It isn't what you do, it's how you do it,"[37] is echoed in an early career vaudeville review from the *New York Telegraph*: "Miss West can't sing a bit but she can dance like George Cohan, and personality just permeates the air every minute she is on stage. In other words, it isn't what Miss West does, but the way she does it that assures her a brilliant career on the stage."[38] Not only was Mae West a purveyor of ribald humor, she knew how to make a name for herself. Instead of censoring her actions and language onstage, she let her behavior create the truth in performance by allowing her body and voice to be interpreted as innocent, obscene, or simply a statement of fact, depending on how the audience member chose to construe her actions.

Mae West's questioning of socially acceptable values—especially with reference to sex and female bodily functions in general—is reflected in Tina Fey's work as well. In stark contrast to West, Fey creates another kind of comedy of sexual tensions in *30 Rock*. As the character of Liz Lemon, Fey plays a woman who is afraid of sex and combats this with an adolescent "ick" factor. Lemon is a woman who wants to focus on her work, and has no time for relationships, especially sexual ones. She rejects the notion that sex is pleasurable and reduces it to an obligation, much like her workaholic character sees all aspects of human interactions. When Liz's boss Jack wants to know how to keep a date platonic, he goes right to Liz, "Lemon, if you want to be helpful, just give me some more advice on how to keep a date asexual."[39] And after catching Jack in his office with a congresswoman he is seeing, named C. C. (Edie Falco), Liz says, "I will leave you to it," and C. C. responds, "*It* being business." Liz comes back nervously with, "Of course! I call the movie *Risky Business* . . . *Risky It*. Because *it* means *business*. [After an awkward pause.] Lemon out." Later on in the episode, Jack explains his relationship with C. C. to Liz:

> JACK: Lemon, that woman you met this morning in my office is not a colleague of mine. We are lovers.
> LIZ: Ew, that word bums me out, unless it's between the words meat and pizza.[40]

Sexual immaturity and how women in the workplace handle their love affairs is a recurring theme on *30 Rock*. Fey reflects the conflicts women have in professional settings. She is also concerned with women being taken seriously as executives and not simply as sexual prospects for male employees.

How women treat each other in the workplace and their social behaviors is very often encountered on *30 Rock*. Season 5, episode 16, titled "Why Does *TGS* Hate Women?," features an opening sequence in which Liz Lemon bemoans the fact that "this started as a show for women starring women. At the very least we should be elevating the way women are perceived in society—Oh! My period! You're all fired!"[41] Liz's "ironic appropriation" of women's issues backfires on her as audiences, writers, and casts alike begin to believe in the stereotype more than the satire. To prove herself right, Liz sets out to hire a "feminist" writer for the show, Abby Flynn (Cristin Milioti), who instead of being a strong female presence portrays the exact type that Liz is so vehemently against: the sexualized girl/woman who seeks men's approval and attention by dressing and acting like a sexy "baby doll." Liz, in an effort to educate Abby that she does not need to be a vapid-talking sexpot, "outs" her as the feminist stand-up comedian who she really is. However, Abby is horrified that her abusive and homicidal ex-husband will discover her whereabouts. She has been using the disguise to escape his notice. Liz's confusion and latent hypocrisy about how women should portray themselves in society is revealed in this exchange:

> LIZ: Abby, I'm trying to help you.
> ABBY: Really? By judging me on my appearance and the way I talk? And what's the difference between me using my sexuality and you using those glasses to look smart?

Instead of taking the easy, politically correct way out, Fey makes the episode more complex as to who has the right to judge women on their behavior and choices—even feminists who claim to have women's best interests in mind. This complexity of female sexuality and gender issues connects West and Fey, in that they both ask the audience to interpret their own assumptions about gender and create rules for social interactions between men and women, as well as women and other women.

Another point of contact between West and Fey is the convergence of race and gender. West's unique comic performance and the use of her body and voice revealed her presumed intentions about how her dialogue was to be received by audiences. West claimed that she was influenced by the sexually suggestive acts of black jazz performers. According to her autobiography, she first saw the "shimmy shawabble" in 1911 in a club for "spades" on Chicago's South Side, and she did the dance the same night in her act calling it a "muscle dance."[42] Performance scholar Sandra Leib noted that West identified with songs associated with black singer-songwriters, which became part of her stage repertoire, like "A Guy What Takes His Time," "Easy Rider," and W. C. Handy's "Memphis Blues," and intentionally equated the black sources of popular entertainment with her musical, dance, and comedy style.[43] Her alignment with black performers, and jazz musicians in particular, painted her as an outsider whose sensual behavior onstage was perceived as a threat to Anglo-American single and married women who aspired to middle-class propriety and decency. An undercurrent of racism accompanied reviews of West's stage style, with pejorative references to black performers and their "wild" behavior. Later in West's career, critic George Jean Nathan in a racially charged rant referred to "the West woman" as a talentless barbarian who knew "absolutely no more about playwriting than the colored piano professor in a bawdy house."[44] West used her sexualized body and voice to expose and mock the hidden desires of the middle and upper classes. The reformers and critics who attacked her supposed immorality were at the same time hypocritically enjoying West's allusions to forbidden pleasures.

Fey, living in a time when subjects of race and gender can be addressed more directly and complexly, confronts issues in her work that are similar to those that West faced in her generation. The need to justify and explain the difficulties of minority status through comedy is often an important part of the storylines for 30 Rock. The unpredictability of how people react in various combinations is achieved on Fey's show through a diversity of perspectives, but not necessarily because of any politically correct interest in being fair to all. In fact, usually the opposite occurs in that the notion of diversity of ethnicity, race, and gender is revealed for being too broad and overly simplistic.

The notion of prejudice and bias can be witnessed in the conflicts between race, class, and gender and is confronted head on in season 3 when Tracy and Jenna get into a battle over who has it "harder" in America—white women or black men. This contest of wills, coming from two overly privileged and wealthy television stars, makes this comparison even more absurd and of course funny. The climactic scene between Tracy and Jenna includes tropes from vaudeville, burlesque, and minstrelsy, as both blackface and whiteface are used in the following scene:

TRACY: [*In whiteface makeup and "blonde" wig.*] Jenna and I are conducting a social experiment.

JENNA: [*In a man's suit and sweater vest with blackface makeup and Afro wig, dances down the hallway singing "Ease on Down the Road" from the all-black musical* The Wiz.]

TOOFER: [*A young black writer talking to a whitefaced "female" Tracy.*] You realize this is incredibly offensive?

LIZ: Yes.

TOOFER: And you realize that blackface makeup reignites racial stereotypes African Americans have worked hundreds of years to overcome?

JACK: [*As if to another white person but to Tracy still in whiteface and wig.*] Here we go.

LIZ: Yeah, it's bad, we get it. Go and get some baby wipes.

JENNA: We are trying to prove who has it hardest in America—women or black men?

JACK: I'll tell you who has it the hardest—white men. We make the unpopular, difficult decisions. The tough choices. We land on the moon and Normandy Beach. Yet they resent us.

KENNETH: Sir, I'm sorry to disagree. But I am also a white man—

JACK: No you're not. Socioeconomically speaking, you are more like an inner-city Latina.[45]

The satire of racial and gender types that get confused and overlap in a mélange of politically correct victimization is overridden by the voice of white male authority in Jack Donaghy, who reduces another white man in Kenneth to a class stereotype that represents neither his race nor his gender.

The setting of Tina Fey's show in 30 Rockefeller Center creates a microcosm of New York City that brings out these conflicts and personal struggles. Its diversity of ethnic groups, sexual orientations, and racial complexities, is interconnected through the diversity of the workplace. The characters, no matter their backgrounds or gender, share the common goal of getting the show on the air, and putting it over to a national audience. When Jack Donaghy wants to search for talent outside of New York City and go to Stone Mountain, Georgia, for a fresh perspective in *30 Rock*'s episode titled "Stone Mountain," Liz resists Jack's oversimplification on what makes people more "real" and down-to-earth, saying:

> You know what? You're the prejudiced one! Sure, some of these people are *simple*, but some are smart like Matlock or wholesome like Ellie May Clampet. But some are skeevy dirtbags like the Dukes of Hazard driving around like maniacs. Children use those roads! My point is, Americans are the *same* everywhere, in that we are all *different*.[46]

The very notion of Americanness itself is a recurring undercurrent of *30 Rock*. The contrast between the elite East Coast intellectual and the rest of America is recognized with the character of Kenneth Parcell (Jack McBrayer), a transplant from the small-town South. This comic sociocultural conflict is brought up in the context of what makes someone "American" in the "Stone Mountain" episode. As Jack asks Liz to find cast members who represent "real America," they go to Kenneth's hometown of Stone Mountain, Georgia, so that Jack can show Liz what he means by "real" in context of the average US citizen. When Liz suggests they look outside of New York to San Francisco for new talent, she has the following exchange with Jack:

JACK: San Francisco? I asked you to find an actor from Middle America, a real person. You are not going to find him in the People's Gay-public of Drug-a-fornia. . . . The television audience doesn't want your elitist, East Coast, alternative, intellectual, left wing—

LIZ: Jack, just say Jewish. This is taking forever.

JACK: Stop trying to amuse *yourself* and start thinking about what makes *actual* human beings laugh. . . . We're going to find the perfect person for the show down here. Someone who represents the real America.

LIZ: Jack, for the eightieth time, no part of America is more American than any other part.

JACK: You are wrong. Small towns are where you see the kindness and goodness and courage of everyday Americans. The folks who are teaching our kids, running our prisons, and growing our cigarettes. People who are still living by core American values.[47]

Liz Lemon's, and conversely Tina Fey's, show—both in its imaginary form as *TGS with Tracy Jordan* and literal one as *30 Rock*—seek to reach their collective audience of Americans, both hypothetical and actual; for Fey "real" and "normal" are subjective at best. Whether people identify as liberal, conservative, or moderate, the idea of "core values" is there to be demythologized from all points of view.

As Tina Fey states in *Bossypants*, "Comedy is about breaking the rules."[48] Simply by being women in comedy, she and Mae West break the rules. *30 Rock* would not be possible without forerunners in West, Fanny Brice, Lucille Ball, and Gilda Radner, but Fey still struggles with the similar issues of what is considered taboo and what is acceptable to American television audiences. To support this notion, regarding the West–Fey connection, *Nineteenth Century*, the aforementioned journal on arts and culture, published a series of editorials in 1891–92 by Mrs. Elizabeth Lynn Linton, an outspoken opponent of women's suffrage. In her attacks on the "Wild Women" of Britain and the United States, Linton claimed that late nineteenth-century Victorian society was being forced into "chaos and topsyturvydom," undermining the values of respectable middle-class citizens.[49] Linton's essays recounted the unruly and unwomanly domestic disorder that was beginning to permeate genteel households, because of "Wild Women of blare and bluster, who are neither man nor woman."[50] Worse yet, women had begun to look and act like men, reducing themselves to "lower forms of ways and works."[51] One of those places that women were reducing themselves to a state of "neither man nor woman" was on the comic vaudeville stage.[52]

In 1916, a *New York Times* reviewer noticed that Mae West was an unknown "with a snappy way of singing and dancing," but *Variety* and other critical periodicals like the *New York Clipper* and *Daily Mirror*, still wondered if the tough girl out of Brooklyn, who danced the Turkey Trot, as well as the Fox Trot, the Monkey Rag, the Grizzly Bear, and the Shimmy, was not "just a bit too coarse for this $2.00 audience."[53] The notion that a female comedian was "a bit too coarse" for an upscale patronage goes along with the idea that women who are funny are very often depicted as "unruly," "oversexed," and somehow repulsive to men—that is, if they are seen as autonomous sexual beings, and potentially dominant relative to sex as well as social standing.

Some critics, middle-class reformers, and audiences of the period considered women in comedy like Mae West to be written off as eccentric and abnormal. The new women, especially from the underclasses, were often characterized and marginalized as rank, wild, or merely crazy. The fear of female comedians comes from not knowing how to control their voices—whether through criticism or reform. It is simpler to label them as strange or bizarre anomalies of normalcy.

Tina Fey, writing about this phenomenon of the crazy female comedian just over one hundred years later, notes:

I have observed that women, at least in comedy, are labeled "crazy" after a certain age. . . . I've known older men in comedy who can barely feed and clean themselves, and they still work. The women, though, they're all "crazy." I have a suspicion—and hear me out, 'cause this is a rough one—I have a suspicion that the definition of "crazy" in show business is a woman who keeps talking even after no one wants to fuck her anymore.[54]

Female humorists at the beginning of the twentieth century were characterized as "eccentric" and "wild" just for not conforming to the "refined" wit women were meant to embody, and this stigma still exists for contemporary female comedians according to Fey.

Tina Fey's connection to live comedy television and its legacy in radio and television of the mid-twentieth century in the work of Fanny Brice and Lucille Ball was evident throughout *30 Rock*'s seven-season history (2006–13). In season 6, *TGS* had its final "live" show and it ended up as a history-of-television comedy from the 1950s, from *The Honeymooners* to *Amos 'n' Andy* to 1960s variety/comedy shows like *Laugh-In* and *SNL* itself. She recalls the golden era of television in a sketch that parodies *The Honeymooners*, called "The Lovebirds." In this scenario, Fey as Alice Kramden patiently awaits her husband, Ralph, played by Alec Baldwin. Ralph threatens Alice, saying, "One of these days [Alice], I'm gonna take a shotgun and BLAM! Blow your face off!" and "You are a real cutup. One of these days, I'm gonna cut you up and feed you to the neighbors' dogs!" The scene ends when Alice, having a heart attack, confesses, "My marriage is a sham. My makeup lady is my lover!"[55] "The Lovebirds" sketch satirizes the nostalgic vision of the television couple for its blatant sexism and misogyny that reinforces the power of situation comedies from the 1950s. The troubles of marriage, the authority of husbands over their wives, and the desperation of women are witnessed through a working-class housewife in a tiny Brooklyn walkup who only has control over herself when she dies. She is mistreated, ignored, and a victim of abuse and neglect. How this vision of comedy in two different eras across sixty-plus years of television comedy history remains in the cultural zeitgeist is evidenced in this show-within-a-show parody.

Another one of Fey's connections to the "golden age" of television, as well as Mae West's work, was a send-up of *Amos 'n' Andy* featuring Tracy Morgan and white actor Jon Hamm. Morgan has, since the show's inception, satirized the real-life rise and fall and rise again of black comedians in the high-pressure and institutionally racist profession of television sitcoms. The episode echoes West's empathy with black entertainers. Here, Morgan plays the "straight man" (Amos) to Hamm's Jim Crow send-up in blackface and country-bumpkin costume (Andy). Morgan tries to be a dignified black character who eschews the malapropisms and foolish buffoonery that characterized *The Amos 'n' Andy Show*, while Hamm riffs on the white actor performing the black comedian as perceived by white audiences. In the sketch, the Tracy Morgan character is forced by contract to perform with the minstrel character as played by Jon Hamm:

HAMM: [*Enters brandishing a fish.*] I's done stole this catfish!
MORGAN: Sir, I am asking you as a human being to please stop talking like that.
HAMM: [*Patting his stomach.*] I's gonna eat it till I'm bellyful!
MORGAN: [*Confronting Hamm with dignity.*] This is debasing to the both of us. I was a Tuskegee Airman.
HAMM: [*Doing a silly tap dance.*] Zippetty-doo-doo!
MORGAN: You may anger me, but I believe nonviolence is the path to change.
HAMM: I believe you can catch a rainbow in your hat!
MORGAN: [*No longer able to take Hamm's effrontery, raises a chair and hits Hamm over the head with it.*] I'll kill you! You ignorant—!
[*The scene is cut off with a "technical difficulties" NBC peacock logo filling the screen.*][56]

Fey's use of television comedy history, satire, and the frustration of performers and writers who had to put up with racism, sexism, and classism to maintain their careers were core tropes illustrating the continuation of the prejudice against the underclass, as witnessed on *30 Rock*. She reinforces the notion that even in the twenty-first century, the prejudicial images of the underclasses are still very much alive.

Male entertainment entrepreneurs of the early twentieth century attempted to remove the comic voice from the body of female performers, thereby creating a dichotomy between the abrasive, humorous female voice and the graceful, statuesque female body, as seen with the Ziegfeld Girls of the 1910s who were meant to "glorify the American Girl." Entertainment impresario Florenz Ziegfeld began the *Ziegfeld Follies* on Broadway in 1907. Using the famous Parisian format of the *Folies Bergère* in combination with an American vaudeville model, the *Follies* consisted of a series of scenes and interludes that featured singers, dancers, and comedians. One of the feature attractions of the *Follies* was the Ziegfeld showgirls who were thought to epitomize the beautiful all-American woman. Conversely, women performers like Mae West were seen as the "rank ladies" who were funny but not feminine. They were clowns not to be taken seriously. The conventionally attractive and dignified female performer was not expected to be heard from, especially in the male province of raucous comedy, but was to remain inscrutable and provocatively sensual. The female burlesque comedian established a place for women that would soon challenge the male-dominated world of stage comedy as they became popular and wealthy stars.

The new women on the comic stage, as represented here by Mae West, resisted and flouted censorship during the first decades of the twentieth century by creating acts that took on the subjects of class, race, and body image, and disturbed preconceived definitions of the feminine. Their comedy came about during an era when the new women began to redefine gender roles and their place in American society. By reinventing the female image onstage through comedy and social commentary, the new female humorists, with their songs, dances, improvisations, and sketches, were able to successfully challenge the Anglo-American middle-class definitions of women's place in the modernist era. By creating characters that defied authorities and reformers alike through their perceived offensive and eccentric performances, comedians like West were able to destabilize the confinement of being labeled "unruly women" and "tough girls," and created a social insurgency on the professional stage. Female comedians worked to reunite the voice and body of the new women performers through their vaudeville acts.

Over a twenty-year period, the rising fame and popularity of women in vaudeville was proof that they had successfully challenged and unseated the attempted control through censorship over their work. Finding themselves in conflict with reformers, authorities, and the press, female comic vaudevillians would create new perceptions of women's voices and bodies in performance for future generations. The dangers of female comedians have been feared since the advent of the new women. As Tina Fey reflects on her training in comedy, "The rules of improvisation appealed to me not only as a way of creating comedy, but as a worldview."[57] The same could be said of Mae West and other interpreters of the new woman through humor in that improvisation is dangerous and cannot be controlled by executives who want to please their advertisers and therefore regulate comedians: what may be coming next is always a surprise for audiences and performers alike. The improvisatory nature of live comedy in addition to women's control over their own material and performances still poses challenges to a male-dominated comedy industry well into the twenty-first century. The legacy of comic insurgents like Mae West, Fanny Brice, and Lucille Ball can be seen in the contemporary acts of Gilda Radner, Roseanne Barr, Ellen Degeneres, Chelsea Handler, Rosie O'Donnell, Bette Midler, Amy Poehler, Julia Sweeney, and Sarah Silverman, and, of course, Tina Fey. These new women of the contemporary comedic stage owe a large debt to their forebears for opening the doors to the "new" new women of the twenty-first century.

Notes

1 *Bazar* was the spelling at the time. Robert J. Burdette, "Have Women a Sense of Humor," *Harper's Bazar*, July 1902: 597–98; Constant Coquelin, "Have Women a Sense of Humor?" *Harper's Bazar*, January 12, 1901: 67.

2 *Harper's Bazar*, January 12, 1901: 67.

3 Charles Young, *Boston Traveler*, January 2, 1909: n.p.

4 Tina Fey, *Bossypants* (New York: Little, Brown and Co, 2011), 143–44.

5 Kate Sanborn, *The Wit of Women*, 4th ed. (1895; New York: Funk & Wagnalls, 2012), 85.

6 Helen Rowland, "The Emancipation of 'The Rib,'" *The Delineator*, March 1911: 176, 231–32.

7 Sime Silverman, "Mae West Double-Act," *Variety*, July 7, 1916, 12.

8 Eliza Lynn Linton, "The Wild Woman as Social Insurgent," *Nineteenth Century*, October 1891, 596.

9 M. Alison Kibler, *Rank Ladies: Gender and Cultural Hierarchy in American Vaudeville* (Chapel Hill: University of North Carolina Press, 1999), 23.

10 Marybeth Hamilton, *"When I'm Bad, I'm Better": Mae West, Sex, and American Entertainment* (Berkeley: University of California Press, 1996), 70–75.

11 Fanny Brice, "Baby Snooks Is 25!" *Radio Life Magazine*, April 7, 1946: 28; Wertheim, *Radio Comedy*, 369.

12 *Ziegfeld Follies of the Air* (January 27, 1936), 5–8; David Freedman Collection, Theatre Arts Library, University of California, Los Angeles. In Wertheim, *Radio Comedy*, 374.

13 Bob Carroll Jr., Jess Oppenheimer, and Madelyn Pugh-Davis, "Lucy Does a TV Commercial," *I Love Lucy*, season 1, episode 30, directed by Marc Daniels (May 5, 1952).

14 Bob Carroll, Jr., Jess Oppenheimer, and Madelyn Pugh-Davis, "Lucy and Harpo Marx," *I Love Lucy*, season 4, episode 27, directed by William Asher (May 9, 1955).

15 Laurence Maslon and Michael Kantor, "Would Ya Hit a Guy with Glasses? Nerds, Jerks, Oddballs, and Slackers," *Make 'Em Laugh: The Funny Business of America* (New York: Twelve, 2008), 238.

16 "Gimme Mick!" refers to *Rolling Stones* front man, Mick Jagger.

17 Jerry Seinfeld with Sarah Silverman, "I'm Going to Change Your Life Forever," *Comedians in Cars Getting Coffee*, created and written by Jerry Seinfeld, directed by Jojo Pennebaker, June 13, 2013, http://comediansincarsgettingcoffee.com/sarah-silverman-i-m-going-to-change-your-life-forever.

18 Fey, *Bossypants*, 119.

19 Tina Fey, "Pilot," *30 Rock*, season 1, episode 1, directed by Adam Bernstein (Universal City, CA: Universal Studios, 2007), DVD.

20 Kay Cannon and Tina Fey, "Lee Marvin vs. Derek Jeter," *30 Rock*, season 4, episode 17, directed by Don Scardino (Universal City, CA: Universal Studios, 2010), DVD.

21 Fey, *Bossypants*, 170–71.

22 For further biographical background on Mae West, see Hamilton, *"When I'm Bad, I'm Better,"* 6–9; Lillian Schlissel, *Three Plays by Mae West: Sex, The Drag, The Pleasure Man* (London: Routledge, 1997), 3; for reminiscences of Mae West in Greenpoint, see the *Daily News* (New York), Brooklyn sec., November 26, 1980, n.p., held in the Mae West file, Brooklyn History Collection, Brooklyn Public Library, New York.

23 Sime Silverman, "Mae West at Hammerstein's Victory," *Variety*, May 25, 1912, 16.

24 Hamilton, *"When I'm Bad, I'm Better,"* 42–45; Jill Watts, *Mae West: An Icon in Black and White* (New York: Oxford University Press, 2001), 70–72.

25 Fey, *Bossypants*, 119.

26 Fey, *Bossypants*, 82.

27 Stuart Levine, "Tina Fey," *Variety*, July 30, 2007, http://variety.com/2007/biz/news/tina-fey-1117969258/

28 Fey, *Bossypants*, 87.

29 Silverman, "Mae West Double-Act," 12.

30 "Mae West in *Diamond Lil*," *New York Times*, February 7, 1949.

31 Silverman, "Mae West at Hammerstein's Victory," 16.

32 Watts, *Mae West*, 36.

33 *She Done Him Wrong* was a box office success and garnered the film an Academy Award nomination for best picture.

34 *New York Evening Post*, March 25, 1933, reprinted in Montrose J. Moses and John Mason Brown, *The American Theatre as Seen by Its Critics* (New York: W. W. Norton, 1934), 305–7.

35 Hamilton, *"When I'm Bad, I'm Better,"* 151.

36 *Night After Night*, released, October 30, 1932, Paramount Pictures, DVD, in *Mae West: The Glamour Collection* (Universal Studios, 2006).

37 West, *Goodness Had Nothing*, 50.

38 Unidentified reviewer, "Mae West," *New York Morning Telegraph* (11 October 1913).

39 Matt Hubbard, "Emmanuelle Goes to Dinosaur Land," *30 Rock*, season 4, episode 21, directed by Beth McCarthy Miller, aired May 13, 2010 (Universal City, CA: Universal Studios, 2010), DVD.

40 Rob Weiner, "Secrets and Lies," *30 Rock*, season 2, episode 8, directed by Michael Engler, aired December 6, 2007 (Universal City, CA: Universal Studios, 2008), DVD.

41 Ron Weiner, "Why Does *TGS* Hate Women?," *30 Rock*, season 5, episode 16, directed by Beth McCarthy Miller, aired February 24, 2011 (Universal City, CA: Universal Studios, 2011), DVD.

42 Mae West, *Goodness Had Nothing to Do with It* (New York: Prentice-Hall, 1959), 64.

43 Sandra Leib, *Mother of the Blues: A Study of Ma Rainey* (Amherst, MA: University of Massachusetts Press, 1981), 133.

44 George Jean Nathan, "Mae West," *American Mercury*, December 1928, 501. For further discussion of West and her relationship to black stage performers, see Hamilton, *"When I'm Bad, I'm Better,"* 153–72.

45 Robert Carlock, "Believe in the Stars," *30 Rock*, season 3, episode 2, directed by Don Scardino, aired November 6, 2008 (Universal City, CA: Universal Studios, 2009), DVD.

46 John Riggi, "Stone Mountain," *30 Rock*, season 4, episode 3, directed by Don Scardino, aired October 29, 2009 (Universal City, CA: Universal Studios, 2010), DVD.

47 Riggi, "Stone Mountain," *30 Rock*.

48 Fey, *Bossypants*, 138.

49 Eliza Lynn Linton, "The Judicial Shock to Marriage," *Nineteenth Century*, May 1891: 691.

50 Linton, "Wild Women as Social Insurgents," 597.

51 Linton, "Wild Women as Social Insurgents," 598.

52 For further discussion of *Nineteenth Century*, see Henry Jenkins, "'Don't Become Too Intimate with That Terrible Woman!': Unruly Wives, Female Comic Performance and *So Long Letty*," *Camera Obscura*, vol. 9 (1–2, 25–26) Duke University Press, January 1, 1991: 203–23.

53 Silverman, "Mae West Double-Act," 12.

54 Fey, *Bossypants*, 270–71.

55 Jack Burditt and Tina Fey, "Live from Studio 6H," *30 Rock*, season 6, episode 19, directed by Mary Beth McCarthy, aired April 26, 2012 (Universal City, CA: Universal Studios Home Entertainment, September 11, 2012), DVD.

56 Burditt and Fey, "Live from Studio 6H," *30 Rock*.

57 Fey, *Bossypants*, 82.

4

Truth and truthiness go to Washington

Will Rogers to Stephen Colbert

The American medicine show was "a hybrid of popular culture and confidence games" which provided entertainment as well as the mystery of remedies in a bottle.[1] Medicine shows and the charlatans who ran them were an amalgamation of "entertainment, sermon, and doctor's house call," and included "[d]og-and-pony shows, magic tricks, pie-eating contests, mediums [spiritualism and séances being a fad of the era], and menageries [freak shows, and human oddities]" all meant to get audiences to purchase bogus cure-alls.[2]

How the seemingly disparate comedians Will Rogers and Stephen Colbert used the techniques of the medicine show—in particular the stump speech and wearing the mask of the fool—to expose charlatans who promise remedies in health, religion, and politics, allows a window into the nature of political satire and critique from the early twentieth century to contemporary comedy. Will Rogers achieves this by playing the "Okie" named "Will" who can tell the truth by simple charm and an unassuming wit that disarms the charlatans of power. Stephen Colbert takes on the character of the charlatan— calling him by his own name of "Stephen Colbert." The character of "Stephen" has a "nation" of followers who are really his television audience, and he seduces them with "truthiness"; a truth that from comes from the gut not from the brain. This truth appears to be seemingly more real because it can be felt and not understood intellectually. To distinguish between the characters that Will Rogers and Stephen Colbert portray, and the actual comedians who play them, I will put their names in quotes as "Will" and "Stephen" when referring to them as their characters.

Will Rogers, through the character of "Will," gets at the truth from giving a seemingly personal opinion of what he "reads in the paper" but actually has gleaned from his background in journalism and talking with experts around the world. "Stephen" performs his bigoted ignorance, while in reality, Stephen Colbert gets his information and ideas from professional experts in their respective fields. How they use the nineteenth-century stump speech and its larger-than-life showmen as sources of their comedy will be the focus of the comparison between Rogers and Colbert. The comedian and social commentator, Fred Allen—through his 1940s radio show *Town Hall Tonight* and an offshoot segment called "Allen's Alley" for the *Texaco Star Theatre*— will be assessed, along with Mort Sahl and Lenny Bruce in the 1950s and 1960s, as the links between "Will" and "Stephen."

The evolution of Will Rogers' stage performances in vaudeville and as a political journalist to Stephen Colbert's twenty-first-century satirical comedian on *The Colbert Report*, as well as live appearances as the characters of "Will" and "Stephen," will serve as a jumping-off point for examining how both humorists enter the real world of United States government as performers and politicized public figures. Examining the evolution of comic performance from Will Rogers to Stephen Colbert serves to reveal comedy as political bellwether, as well as political engagement and its potential influence at the national level on the American government and its representatives. Using the construct of the vaudeville aesthetic found in the stump speech, I look at how Rogers and Colbert create political action through their acts to challenge the authority of national and world leaders, while at the same time reinforcing the critical thinking of the American electorate.

* * *

Comedy exposes fear as a political motivator, letting the audience in on the politicians' game of fearmongering and negative campaigning, and reveals the falsely constructed logic—what Stephen Colbert calls "truthiness"—of the candidates through their stump speeches. The stump speech is a passionate motivating tool that relies on emotion rather than logic or fact-finding, devoid of practical, well-thought-out ideas. The stump speech therefore becomes a series of instigating talking points that appeal to the fearful. Political humorists like Will Rogers and Stephen Colbert perform the charlatan's "come-on" as a stump speech derived from its sideshow sales pitches. The stump speech was a standard vaudeville act of the mid-to-late-nineteenth century, and serves as a lens through which to examine the vaudeville aesthetic and its unique interpreters during times of volatile political and cultural change.

Joe Laurie Jr.'s first-hand account of the history of vaudeville cites a typical stump speech as an act that mocks and insults the politician and preacher as self-determined arbiters of American moral authority who use language to obfuscate their hypocrisy and double standards. A prototypical speech begins, "Brethren and Sistern, I have decided to divide my sermon in three parts. The first part I'll understand and you won't. The second part you will understand and I won't. The third part nobody will understand."[3] The stump speech juxtaposed the narrative clarity of understanding, conventional wisdom, and propriety with the humor of vaudevillians as independent, and potentially threatening to the self-perceptions of the established middle and upper classes of Anglo-Americans.

Will Rogers perfected the stump speech in relationship to political debate. He achieved this beginning in 1925 after spending almost twenty years touring in vaudeville and performing for the *Ziegfeld Follies*. Ultimately, Rogers left the

FIGURE 4.1 *Will Rogers with the cast of the* Ziegfeld Follies *(1925).*
Source: Will Rogers Memorial Museum, Claremore, Oklahoma.

Follies and began touring the country. He ended this tour after eleven weeks on the road and seventy appearances creating his unique humor by culling local political and civic events at various stops throughout the United States. Will Rogers buttonholed anyone he could find to get the latest political news, and then tailored his speeches for the local audience.[4] As he described his process, "I talked with every Editor in each town, all the writers on the papers, Hotel Managers, Ranchmen, Farmers, Politicians, Head Waiters, Barbers, Newsboys, Bootblacks. Everybody I met I would try to get their angle."[5] By identifying with his audience and discussing their concerns directly, Rogers, in the tradition of the nineteenth-century medicine showman, worked in local jokes and names of authorities whom he wished to satirize and expose as fools whom ordinary citizens should not have to suffer.

Rogers focused on how average Americans were being potentially conned by local, legitimized authority, who claimed to be representatives of the people. He spread the word by touring. If a town had a "railroad and a hall," Rogers guaranteed, "we'll be there sooner or later."[6] One of "Will's" earliest stump speeches, as recorded in the New Orleans *Times-Picayune* (1925), witnesses him being introduced to his audience by the mayor of New Orleans and reveals his skill in delivering a seemingly humble yet satirical stump speech:

> I thank you, Mayor Behrman, for your wonderful welcome to New Orleans. I want to thank you with all my heart—if a Comedian has a heart. I don't think ever was a mere Comedian welcomed to a city by full page ads in all your newspapers, and I appreciate it—I appreciate it just as much as if I didn't know that you were using me just as a means of getting someone to tell the benefits of your city to. It was a wonderful thought on the part of the newspapers who had the page and couldn't sell it, but, knowing you had an appropriation to spend on boosting, decided to relieve you of some of it.[7]

"Will" did not stop with pointing out how the mayor and his newspapermen were taking advantage of the public trust by bankrolling their own interests in exploiting his fame. He also pointed out how Louisiana felt superior to Oklahoma (Rogers' birthplace) stating, "You say Oklahoma was 'a part of the Louisiana Purchase'—a part. It was the part they purchased, your end of it was thrown in."[8]

Will Rogers exploited his own Oklahoma heritage by consciously employing his "Okie" dialect (both spoken and written) to appeal to ordinary folks presumably like him. "When I first started out to write," claimed Rogers, "and misspelled a few words, people said I was plain ignorant. But when I got all the words wrong, they declared I was a humorist."[9] In his comedy disrupting the fixed notions of the way things appear and how they actually work begs the questions, why do we assume the system works the way it does, and why do we go along with it? He challenged the binary of the gridlock of authoritative power by creating a third party who cannot be qualified or quantified in the overly simplistic labels of Democrat and Republican.

Disrupting assumed narratives of political power and authority through comedy is the signature of both Will Rogers and Stephen Colbert. By responding to politicians, pundits, and journalists who go along with and reinforce those in charge, they comment and critique authoritarians who claim to "know" by repeating their dishonest pronouncements right back to them. Instead of creating jokes per se, they speak the language of authority and use the devices of political punditry, which assumes an archetypal all-American pose adopting a knowledge that comes from "the gut." Both comedians question normative values and the self-serving logic of influential forthrightness.

Will Rogers, by portraying the image of the cowboy's humble but salt-of-the-earth wisdom, creates a comic mask for his trenchant critique, appearing to be just a regular guy. Stephen Colbert, using the opposite tack, exposes the hypocrisy and abuse of power by political partisans through assuming the persona of an "authority." He embraces the divisive and self-important language and performance of the smug pundit. Rogers' comments expose the hypocrisy of those in power by his own self-deprecation, with his "I only know what I read in the papers" brand of humor, and Colbert with his self-righteous and self-important appeal to his assumed "Colbert Nation" of like-minded followers.

Will Rogers with his trick-roping vaudeville acts and Stephen Colbert as a member of Chicago's Second City comedy group, set out early in their stage careers focusing on live improvisation and creating characters that reflected their quotidian selves. Beginning with Rogers' stage work, the parallels between the humor of the early twentieth century, its mid-century counterpart in the comedy of Fred Allen, and finally its contemporary correlative with Colbert, are examined through the progression of their careers from stage to radio and television, and ultimately into the arena of national American politics. These comedians used the biography of the "ordinary" American in order to communicate their evaluation of the US political system.

Will Rogers began his career in third-tier vaudeville in small towns as far flung as Tuscaloosa, Alabama, and Peoria, Illinois. Here rural audiences demanded their money's worth, or the performers were "given the hook"—literally pulled offstage with a bentwood cane to make way for another act. Rogers and other vaudevillians had only a few minutes to establish their act. He became very adept at reading the audience and tailoring his act in the moment. Moving through the ranks of first-tier vaudeville and ultimately Broadway revues like the *Ziegfeld Follies* was impossible if performers could not get an act to go over, and second chances were rare if nonexistent. The pressure to sell the act, by being able to improvise for any given audience, created a need for performers to hone their craft. Vaudeville acts were traditionally two-a-day performances, sometimes up to ten-a-day, depending on the management's need to exploit the talents on the bill. The pressure to make an immediate impact on the demanding crowds was all-important for keeping a comedy career alive.

Rogers charmed his way into the hearts of audiences all over the country through his cowboy persona and trick-roping act, first seen in Wild West shows at the turn of the twentieth century. However, what really made his act a success was his self-deprecating humor when a trick went wrong. Rogers would quip, "Swinging a rope isn't bad. As long as your head isn't in it."[10] In fact, this humble attitude for the skilled Rogers became a signature of his act, and he began to "throw the tricks" to get to the "mistakes" and the subsequent laugh lines. Audiences responded favorably and Will Rogers kept the mistakes as part of his act.

He moved from a comic vaudevillian to a social commentator as his act evolved. In 1921, a critic for the *Dramatic Mirror* simply known as Rose reported on Rogers' recent shift from trick-roper to comic social critic. "Most of [Rogers'] monologue is political and it certainly was well put over by him," Rose wrote. "Although his rope stunts added greatly to his turn, he could have omitted these for a few moments and just talked, for his dry rural way of delivery had the house roaring after every story he delivered. . . . He has come back stronger than ever, with one of the best talking singles in vaudeville today."[11] Rogers' brand of political humor was beginning to challenge the amorphous definition of what it meant to be an American. He was perceived to reach ordinary folks by embracing his impoverished upbringing in the Oklahoma Territory and his mother's Cherokee heritage. He reinforced the melting-pot notion of American identity and rejected the nationalistic jingoism of assimilationist Anglo-Americans and their Mayflower ancestors.

Eventually Rogers' asides and comments focused less and less on his roping act and, circa 1925, more on what was happening in local, and then national, events. Through his persona as "Will," Rogers would eventually become a cultural critic as he dropped the roping-act entirely and officially became a "humorist" in the tradition of Mark Twain. He would eventually find his way into the US Congress as a serious journalist and spokesman for the "people" during the 1920s and early 1930s. His criticism of the gridlock and petty politicized world of Washington, DC, that ignored the needs of its citizens for self-aggrandizement and enrichment eventually leading to the Great

Depression, gave Rogers something to comment on in his comic stage monologues, and ultimately in print through his newspaper columns. Will Rogers would eventually find himself "stumping" for presidents, especially Franklin Delano Roosevelt, as well as being a reporter and critic on international affairs.

It is of interest to see how the vaudeville aesthetic of the stump speech moved to radio—after Will Rogers' accidental death in a plane accident in 1935—with comedian Fred Allen, and was taken up later with stage performers Mort Sahl and Lenny Bruce in the 1950s and 1960s. Fred Allen was a vaudevillian, not unlike Rogers, who made the successful transition to radio comedy. Rogers had his own radio broadcasts on *The Gulf Headliners* from 1930 to 1935. Like the stage performer turned film writer and actor, W. C. Fields, Allen began with a juggling act that soon was dominated by the comic patter that accompanied it. Raised in Boston's working-class Irish immigrant neighborhoods, Allen tried a variety of stage names, including Freddy James, the World's Worst Juggler. He ultimately went by the last name of his agent, Edgar Allen. After his 1919 engagement at the Palace in New York, Allen began touring with big-time vaudeville acts and starred in a Broadway musical revue, *The Passing Show of 1922*, at the Winter Garden.[12] As vaudeville began its slow demise, Allen, in anticipation of the television sitcom format, proposed an idea to CBS radio in 1932.

> Since the radio comedian really had to depend on the ears of the home audience for his purpose, I thought that a complete story told each week or a series of episodes and comedy situations might be a welcome change. It would enable the listener to flex his imagination, and perhaps make him want to follow the experiences of the characters involved. This, if it worked, would insure the radio comedian a longer life.[13]

The use of the recurring character would take hold in Allen's arguably best period on radio with *Town Hall Tonight* (1935–39) and his most popular segment, "Allen's Alley" (1942–49), which included four recurring characters that are reminiscent of those on *The Colbert Report* more than sixty years later. Riffing from "The March of Trivia," his parody of the popular newsreel *The March of Time* from *The Texaco Star Theatre* (1941–42), Allen, along with writers Nat Hiken (Hiken was soon to be the creator and producer of *The Phil Silvers Show* as well) and Larry Marks, featured interviews with various ordinary "men on the street" (particularly from New York's Chinatown and the Bowery), getting their response to "weekly lowlight[s] from the world of news." As Allen recalled, "I felt that something of this type which would permit me to stroll through a nondescript neighborhood and discuss current events with its denizens would be very amusing."[14] He knocked on the doors of local houses in different neighborhoods to ask questions about popular topics. "Whenever I want to know how America is reacting to an important issue of the day," noted Allen, "I just drop around to Allen's Alley."[15]

Allen's "fake news" interviews, like those used by contemporary comedy shows like *The Colbert Report* and *The Daily Show with Jon Stewart*, involved characters drawn from the ethnic immigrant humor of vaudeville—including Pansy Nussbaum, a Jewish immigrant housewife with an exaggerated Bronx accent, played by Minerva Pious; Ajax Cassidy, a temperamental, heavy-drinking Irish roustabout straight from the variety stage of the nineteenth century, played by Peter Donald; Titus Moody, a New England "country bumpkin" farmer, who appeared as early as the eighteenth century in stage comedies and later became a staple of vaudeville humor, played by Parker Fennelly; and, most famously, the Southern senator Beauregard Claghorn, played by Kenny Delmar, who would become the model for the Warner Bros.' cartoon character Foghorn Leghorn, drawling his ubiquitous "Son, I say, son!"[16] Worth quoting here in comparison to Stephen Colbert's later style of interview is a typical exchange between Allen and Claghorn, as a satirical dialogue of government pomposity and corruption:

ALLEN: Well, Senator, about our question. Do you think advertising has any effect on our manners and customs?
KENNY: [*As Claghorn.*] Ah don't trust advertisin', Son. Especially them ads politicians put in the papers around election time.
ALLEN: Uh-huh.
KENNY: Ah saw an ad last election, it said—Elect this honest fearless, hardworkin' enemy of graft and corruption. I busted out laughin'.
ALLEN: Who was the candidate?
KENNY: Me! So long, Son! So long, that is![17]

Allen's refusal to compromise his comedy for the sake of sponsorship objections, as well as his satirical references to the network, would ultimately cost him his career on radio and make impossible his transition to television. To show how this kind of humor went from insulting to acceptable fifty years later can be seen in Tina Fey's openly mocking the producers and advertisers of her show on *30 Rock*, with NBC, and its parent company General Electric's, approval—something that would have been unfathomable to Allen and other radio and television creator-comedians in the 1940s and 1950s.

Allen, in an open denunciation of how radio was being co-opted by the Madison Avenue admen, called their executives "molehill men." "A molehill man," according to Allen, "is a pseudo-busy executive who comes to work at

9 a.m. and finds a molehill on his desk. He has until 5 p.m. to make this molehill into a mountain. An accomplished molehill man will often have his mountain finished even before lunch."[18] Allen spent seventeen years in radio as a successful satirist of censorship and executive bureaucracy. James Thurber, the celebrated humorist and author, said of Allen, "You can count on the thumb of one hand the American who is at once a comedian, a humorist, a wit, and a satirist, and his name is Fred Allen."[19]

Comic radio's significance as social commentary is still evidenced by a 2012 incident on National Public Radio's successful program *Wait, Wait Don't Tell Me*. NPR correspondent Edward Schumacher-Matos reported, "NPR's 'oddly informative' quiz show *Wait, Wait Don't Tell Me* is intended to entertain, not offend. But more than 100 listeners contacted NPR to complain that a series of jokes about Pope Benedict XVI Saturday crossed the line, *even* for comedy."[20] The idea that comedy should not offend and should not "cross the line" indicates that the vaudeville aesthetic, with its "laughing at and not with" brand of satire, continues despite the efforts of comedy forerunners like Fred Allen. Perhaps because of his verbal brand of comedy and his less than ready-for-television visage, but mainly because of ongoing conflicts with censors, network executives, and sponsors, Allen's television career was not meant to be. As Allen quipped, television was called a "medium, because nothing is well done."[21]

A few comedians found that the stage was a refuge from an era dominated by television advertising and network censorship. When novice comic Mort Sahl put himself on the map in 1954 by commenting that the popular Eisenhower jacket had zippers all over it including "a big zipper here that went all the way across [indicating the heart]," the vaudeville aesthetic entered the post-World War II era with a vengeance. He drove the knife in by continuing to attack the chairman of the House Un-American Activities Committee, Senator Joseph McCarthy: "Ah! They have a new jacket called the *McCarthy* jacket, and it zips up the side, and over the mouth."[22] Sahl took the 1950s stage by storm with his brand of critically charged humor that was revolutionary in a period of Anglo-conformity, irrational fear of communism, and bedroom communities of white-washed American realities. He was direct, abrasive, and not concerned with ingratiating himself with audiences.

Mort Sahl was the self-proclaimed anti-Will Rogers, wisecracking, "I never met a man I didn't like until I met Will Rogers."[23] He took the insult comedy of the *tummler* and combined it with social commentary and the sardonic anti-authoritarian spin of Groucho Marx. Unlike Will Rogers he did not wish to appear to be liked, but appreciated for his forthright rendering of his cultural critique. Sahl summed up the connection between comedy and the vaudevillians' fraught relationship to their inherited homeland saying: "What's really aching Americans is that nobody loves them. If there's no romance, or justice, in your life, life is not worth living."[24] For Mort Sahl the humor demanded a voice for the voiceless and justice in an unjust society. Summing up political history he deconstructs the lies Americans are told about their leaders with this short quip, "George Washington couldn't tell a lie, Nixon couldn't tell the truth, and Reagan couldn't tell the difference."[25] Sahl's credo appears to be, do not believe anyone except yourself, but get the facts first before you form your opinions.

Sahl's defiance was in stark contrast to Will Rogers and Stephen Colbert in that he never performed as a character or in any particular role. He simply commented on his reactions to what he felt were injustices that needed to be discussed openly. Toward the end of his career he was accused of not being funny anymore but more of a scold of American complaisance in the face of corruption and discrimination. However, rather than indulging in pessimism Sahl felt optimistic that by not being afraid to voice your opinions, you are participating in a free and democratic society. In a documentary by Robert B. Weide, Mort Sahl sums up his career by saying, ". . . you can stand up in a society that says, 'Don't rock the boat.' You *can* rock the boat. I'm not afraid to take on anyone. You can have your say in America and really survive. I feel very positive about that. That's the message. Not that you'll get killed for it but that you'll live for it."[26]

Mort Sahl is living proof that it is possible to stand up and be counted and not marginalized through comedy. In 1968 Sahl gave an interview to *Playboy* magazine that gives his perspective on the nature and purpose of social satire saying, "They used to say that no one is above the law. I know a lot of people above the law—and almost everyone is above a lawyer. But I believe no one is above humor. In that sense, my work is never done."[27] One sure way to bring down the powerful and the hypocritical according to Mort Sahl was to be funny. Along with Fred Allen, he serves as a link between Will Rogers and Stephen Colbert as a comic commentator, but unlike them his character was always and forever—himself.

In tandem with Mort Sahl came Lenny Bruce who embraced the jazz vocabulary and improvisational riffing of the humorists of the 1910s and 1920s. Bruce worked the burlesque stage during its nadir. He combined the lewd humor of third-rate burlesque with the trenchant observations of a sociologist. He drew no distinction between Jew, black, or Gentile; for him, satirizing the "straights" crossed all social and cultural boundaries. Bruce, as a Jew himself, carried over the ethnic humor of the *shtetl*. According to Lenny Bruce,

A Jew, in the dictionary, is one who is descended from the ancient tribes of Judea, or one who is regarded as a descendant from that tribe. That's what it says in the dictionary, but you and I know what a Jew is: "One Who Killed Our Lord" . . . there should be a statute of limitations for that crime.[28]

Bruce's observational form of comedy combined the language of minstrelsy with his liberal use of the N-word. He forced the comparison of Jews and blacks as suffering the Anglo-American oppression of racism and anti-Semitism that fed ethnic and class-oriented humorists earlier in the twentieth century.

Fred Allen, Mort Sahl, and Lenny Bruce all used the solo-set-piece in the tradition of the stump speech to make political commentary out of comedy. With the aid of a myriad new media platforms, they believed that Americans had become passive consumers who were subject to fearmongering due to sheer laziness of thought and action. These consumers thereby effectively erased critical reason and expression, according to this new breed of comedians. They are all connected by the use of the vaudeville aesthetic, and in particular, the stump speech as sociocultural observation.

Stephen Colbert takes on the mantle of Rogers, Allen, Sahl, and Bruce. His ordinary background was a perfect template to spin his brand of humor. Colbert, as a self-proclaimed "son of the South," grew up as a Catholic in South Carolina. From there he ventured to Northwestern University and then Chicago's Second City improvisational comedy company. Famous for its ensemble-driven sketch comedy, the Second City comedians were required to reach a tough crowd of late-night and rowdy (oftentimes drunk) audiences who demanded laughs, or performers were given the hook (in this case a metaphor for being fired). Colbert became known for being a team player, as well as a deft improviser. Bringing his act to New York would land him on *The Daily Show* in 1999 as a faux correspondent on the popular "fake news" program. The show's producer and star Jon Stewart was impressed by Colbert's comedic "reporting" and his indignant, if wrong-headed, political commentary inspired by right-leaning political pundits like Bill O'Reilly on legitimate programs like *Fox News*.

Jon Stewart encouraged and helped produce a spinoff to follow the *Daily Show* based on the character of "Stephen Colbert," the self-appointed spokesman of right-wing American ideology. *The Colbert Report*, which premiered in 2005, was an immediate success with audiences, and Colbert was well on his way to creating the persona that would eventually find his way onto congressional committees and into two mock-runs for the presidency of "the United States—of South Carolina."

Stephen Colbert, like Will Rogers before him, found a loyal, national, and international audience, by portraying characters that looked and sounded a lot like themselves but were perfected comic images refined after many years on the road touring American towns and cities—all the while knowing that "the hook" was not far offstage. The stump speech was used by Rogers and reinvented by Colbert as a form of assessment of fraudulent political practices. A 2010 congressional hearing bears witness to how the stump speech was enacted by the character of "Stephen." "Stephen's" faux-conservative indignation over illegal immigration in the United States was encapsulated by the following statement: "My great-grandfather did not travel across four thousand miles of the Atlantic Ocean to see this country overrun by immigrants."[29] His bogus right-wing talk-show host from *The Colbert Report* went public, bringing his satire and social critique directly to the halls of Congress and, later, to the electoral arena as well, with his foray into the Republican primary campaigning for the 2012 presidential election.

Colbert's continuing critique of who constitutes an American and what shapes their values is reflected in his "Colbert Nation." This nation of followers (his audience) is a commentary on the blind allegiance to a right-wing-led nationalism whose ideology parallels the binary of narrow-minded thinking of political demagoguery in a gridlocked battle to determine who is the most American. "Stephen" insists that who is "right" is determined by trusting your instincts. Colbert explains that his character "is not unintelligent, he's just idiotic. It's garbage in, garbage out. He's uninformed, and perfectly happy about that. What's most important to him is what feels right, not what's true."[30] Stephen Colbert uses this logic of the character of "Stephen" to unmask the absurd question of who is in fact the most loyal American.[31]

Eighty years before "Stephen's" confrontation with Congress, Will Rogers was setting the stage for similar confrontations with US representative authorities. Rogers' challenging of what it meant to be an American is illustrated in his 1930 film, *So This Is London*, in which he attempts to get a passport without having the proof of a birth certificate that officially states he is a US citizen. The complexity of defining what characteristics constitute this notion of an American can be witnessed in the following scene:

PASSPORT OFFICIAL: But you are an American citizen?
WILL ROGERS: I think I am. My folks are Indian. Both my mother and father had Cherokee blood in 'em. Born and raised in Indian Territory. Of course, I'm not one of these Americans whose ancestors come over on the Mayflower, but we met 'em at the boat when they landed. And it's always been to the everlasting discredit of the Indian race that we ever let 'em land.[32]

The notion that Will Rogers would have to prove his citizenship in the face of Anglo-usurpers of indigenous Americans is both a source for comedy and the harsh reality of life in the United States at the turn of the twentieth century. Will Rogers' humor stems from the juxtaposition of self-identified "real" Americans whose nationalistic authority is contrasted with Rogers' actual American-Indian roots. That Rogers' authenticity of origin is being questioned by a nation formed and dominated by colonial usurpers, where he is forced to prove his Americanness, lies at the heart of his comedy. Rogers stands as an outsider in his own country who points out the hypocrisy of discrimination and the marginalization of perceived minorities who have to prove themselves as being "as good as" their self-appointed betters.

Stephen Colbert's use of the stump speech is used as direct confrontation where comedy and reality intersect with politics. This was observed in 2006 during the White House Correspondent's Association Dinner, when "Stephen" satirized the George W. Bush presidency in real time. This moment in political history was captured and went viral on *YouTube*. Because neither Bush nor the journalists in attendance knew whether "Stephen" was a real political pundit or merely a celebrity "roasting" the president, he was able to deliver a trenchant critique of the unchecked power of a bankrupt presidency and the news media that perpetuated the myth of a strong and self-righteous American policy, known as the Bush doctrine.

Appearing to agree with "W," "Stephen" pointed out right from the beginning of his soon-to-be-considered offensive stump speech, "Guys like us, we're not nerds on the brainiac patrol. We're not members of the Factinista. We go straight from the gut. Right, sir? That's where the truth lies, right down here in the gut."[33] This showdown was captured and encapsulated when "Stephen," seeming to praise "W" for his unwavering position as the country's self-proclaimed "decider" stated, "the greatest thing about this man is he's steady. You know where he stands. He believes the same thing Wednesday that he believed on Monday, no matter what happened Tuesday. Events can change; this man's beliefs never will."[34] "W." attempted to play along, but his stunned, smirking silence—and that of the crowd of seasoned professional news media correspondents frozen in fear and confusion as the world watched the unvarnished "truthiness" being performed on the world wide web by "Stephen"—spoke volumes. Will Rogers and Stephen Colbert can be seen as changing the national conversation through their comic political commentary by creating new access to knowledge and information that includes all Americans.

In order to put over their characters of "Will" and "Stephen," Rogers and Colbert use what I call "the mask of Arlecchino," donning a comic face that belies their serious intent. As Rogers joked in the mid 1920s, "Everything is changing. . . . People are taking their comedians seriously and the politicians as a joke, when it used to be visa versa."[35] Will Rogers' political punchline has been borne out in his own era, and now in the early twenty-first century through the work of Stephen Colbert. The characters of "Will" and "Stephen" have reached their constituencies by exposing the nonsense couched in conventional wisdom, of those who do not suffer fools gladly, by playing the fool's role.

The influence of the role of the comic fool has its roots in the *commedia dell'arte* and was reasserted in the vaudeville aesthetic in the first two decades of the twentieth century. The Italian sixteenth-century *commedia*'s Arlecchino character is a masked servant who "puts one over" on his master by playing the fool. Arlecchino's seemingly empty-headed servant is able to challenge and expose the brutal totalitarian authority of his master. Through comic role-playing, whether as doctor, lawyer, rich merchant, or policeman, Arlecchino's protean charlatan performances cannot be contained or even defined as "offensive" because of his constant need and skill to improvise in order to survive. How the mask of Arlecchino evolved into the mask of minstrelsy and then to the blackface performances of Bert Williams and Dave Chappelle will be considered in the next chapter. The legacy of portraying a version of oneself connects the vaudeville aesthetic of these humorists across the twentieth century to the current era. How Will Rogers and Stephen Colbert differ in this role-playing is revealed in how they each wear the mask of Arlecchino. Rogers and Colbert have used the mask of Arlecchino to enter the real world as lowbrow comics who give offense by exposing the charlatans who govern, doing so in very distinctive ways.

As the 1920s progressed, the variety of skills developed in vaudeville that Will Rogers sharpened in his early stage shows, especially narrating his roping tricks and the "mistakes" he made, began to evolve into comic commentary on the "errors" and self-important pronouncements from politicians and cultural authorities. Rogers' understated critique was couched in the vaudeville aesthetic, as an editorial in *The Nation* observed. "Mr. Rogers' . . . caustic observations are wrapped in humor," the editorial noted. "If they were delivered without the funny tags, his audience would set the dogs on him."[36] It is his technique, developed from his many years on the vaudeville circuit, that led Will Rogers to relate to his audience as a fellow working-class "employee." He portrayed a servant who could see through the machinations of the "masters" of American society through the comedy of informed observation, masked as the character of "Will."

In 1915, Will Rogers' career moved in a new direction as he appeared before President Woodrow Wilson during the Washington, DC run of the *Ziegfeld Follies*. With Wilson in attendance, Rogers criticized his administration's policies on the American intervention in world politics, particularly with regard to the then nascent World War I. He knew his observations might be dangerous and potentially offensive to the president; however, what he did not bargain for was how the public would receive his satirical act. "How was I to know but what the audience would rise up in mass and resent it," Rogers later wrote. "I had never heard, and I don't think anyone else had ever heard of a president being joked personally in a public theater about the policies of his administration."'[37] Rogers criticized Wilson for entering World War I after having professed an isolationist stance with regard to international conflicts, writing, "It seems we may have to have two more wars to find out who won the last one."[38]

Breaking new ground, Rogers went on to critique Wilson and subsequent presidents, including Calvin Coolidge, Warren G. Harding, Herbert Hoover, and finally Franklin D. Roosevelt in his many stage and radio performances. Rogers was a staunch supporter of FDR, although not without his signature critical humor when Rogers disagreed with the president's policies. Bringing this character of the everyman onstage to confront and challenge the politics of world leaders would be the hallmark and legacy of Rogers' career from this time forward. In an era of staunch nationalism in America, Will Rogers appeared to offend simply by questioning the decisions of the United States government and the values they were meant to represent. Rogers drew the connection between performers and politicians early on in his stage humor. He saw politicians for the charlatans and snake-oil salesmen he had found in medicine shows. Rogers called congressmen who introduced self-serving, unrelated, and irrelevant earmarks to laws "gag men," similar to comedians who introduced sidebar slapstick to their stage acts.[39] The nation's leaders now complained that ordinary citizens were perceiving them as figures to be mocked and dismissed by humorists like Rogers. How, then, was the average American to take their pronouncements seriously if a mere comedian could question their judgment and authority?

In 1924, Rogers, true to his commitment that American citizens should be able to question their government as allowed under the Constitution, openly criticized congressional lawmakers when they decided to sign a naval disarmament treaty. "Who signed such a fool treaty?" Rogers fulminated, "if it's against the treaty which some bonehead signed for us, for the Lord's sake let us quit making treaties."[40] How seriously Rogers' comic evaluation of the nation's lawmakers was taken can be witnessed when Congressman David Kincheloe of Kentucky entered Will Rogers' column "Sinking Battleships" into the *Congressional Record* that year.[41]

In stark contrast to the character of "Will," "Stephen" creates social critique by seeming to condone the very system Stephen Colbert, the comedian, knowingly disagrees with. Colbert performs his coercion and manipulation news journalism through the mask of Arlecchino. Comedians like Colbert, by asking skeptical questions in the guise of purporting to be in agreement with self-proclaimed political and cultural authorities, dons this mask knowingly.

As cultural critic Stephen Duncombe observes, "In doing this [comics like Colbert] hold out the possibility of something else, that is, they create an opening for a discussion on what sort of a political process wouldn't be a joke. In doing this they're setting the stage for a very democratic sort of dialogue: one that asks questions rather than simply asserts the definitive truth."[42] Colbert with his right-wing pundit archetype, who appears to agree with subjects reviled by the political center and left, creates an intimacy with his audience as a way of not simply being a reactionary. "Stephen" confirms what Duncombe contends to be the "identification with the Other [which] is not the banal 'respecting difference' of the multiculturalists: it entails *embracing* difference. It means transforming a distant object into an intimate subject."[43] As Don Corleone said, "Keep your friends close and your enemies closer."[44]

Colbert has steadily transgressed the boundaries between his fictional on-screen character, who is, as his colleague Jon Stewart describes, "this fictional character who is now suddenly interacting in the real world,"[45] not unlike "Will Rogers," the fictional figure of the homespun Okie who became a real-world American everyman. As these characters of "Stephen" and "Will" move back and forth from their stage acts to their real-world presentations of their respective characters, they are neither inside nor outside the cultural mainstream but live in a liminal space, breaking with binary behavior and thinking, through their comedy.

As Jon Stewart sees it, "[Colbert is] able to weave a character in a way that's never been done on television before—rendering this fictional character in 3-D, live, in such a way that he's still able to retain his humanity." The extra dimension, Stewart explains, is the other Stephen, the real one. "The third dimension is him. That's the thing we started to see."[46] The mask of Arlecchino, as worn by the character of "Stephen," has merged with the comedian Stephen Colbert by entering the real world of American politics.

Will Rogers' use of the mask of Arlecchino can be seen with his harsh criticism of the Warren Harding administration. The open corruption during his presidency, which erupted in the infamous Teapot Dome scandal of 1922–23, was criticized by Rogers who cheerfully toyed with the president's tacit permission of fraud. He did this by relating what seemed to be a simple story, but then turned it into a pointed attack on power and authority in the federal government. Referring to a recent fire in the Treasury building, Rogers noted that "the fire started on the roof and burned down and down until it got to the place where the money ought to be and there it stopped. The Harding administration had beat the fire to it. A fire in the Treasury building is nothing to get excited about during a Republican administration."[47] All the while,

Rogers wore a smile on his face, but delivered his message loud and clear that the president's crooked administration was not fooling him or his audience. Harding was said to have been so upset by Rogers' criticizing his presidency that he asked an aide to tell him to desist; suffice it to say, Will Rogers did not.[48]

Stephen Colbert reflects a continuum of comedians who dispel fear and expose the laziness born of the expectation that authorities make life-altering decisions without our questioning their motives and competency in their capabilities. Making light of self-fulfilling fear prophesies through comic satire can potentially dispel unnecessary social anxieties and curb destructive decision-making in the process. Therefore we can look to comedians like Colbert to displace and examine the insecurity of American life by getting audiences to laugh at their own fears and laziness in thought and action, thereby lessening the power of authoritarians who control American sociocultural institutions.

Stephen Colbert as political commentator examines the devaluation of critical thinking through the blind allegiance of his fearful "Colbert Nation," exposing their reliance on intuition and instinctual reactionary opinions, dismissing experts as elitist, and appearing to be sincere and down-to-earth with values that represent a standard moral absolute, meaning that Americans adhere to their unquestioning and uncritical acceptance of those in authority out of terror for the potential loss of personal and material comforts. Colbert, like Rogers before him, gained more and more critical knowledge from traveling the world and conversing with both citizens and influential world leaders, while also developing a keen critical thinking and analysis for his humorous columns and comic monologues.

Colbert criticizes the fearful citizen using a different strategy in his comedy than Will Rogers, Fred Allen, Mort Sahl, and Lenny Bruce. Colbert appears to be the person he is satirizing. "Stephen" as character feels and reacts from the "gut," belying his true, very well-informed punditry, aided by a staff of well-versed researchers and writers, and his discussions with experts and public intellectuals on *The Colbert Report*. Colbert plays the part of the no-nonsense, right-wing, American with cut-and-dried partisan politics and rhetoric.

The character of "Stephen" immerses himself in the world of politics in order to blur the line between comedian and political operative. In an extreme version of exposing the buffoonery of those politicians who believe their own press, Stephen Colbert brought his television character to the 2012 Republican presidential primary in his home state of South Carolina. As quoted in a *New York Times* article, Stephen Hess of the Brookings Institution remarks, "I am much taken by [Colbert's presidential campaign] and can't think of any real parallel in history. Yes, comedians have always told jokes about elections, but this is quite different. This is a funny person being very serious, actually talking about process. What comedian talks about process?"[49] To which I would add, he is forgetting Will Rogers and his foray into the political process in the 1920s.

In the 2010 congressional races, political action committees known as Super PACs spent over $60 million, managing to get their voices heard through what Colbert has described as a "megaphone of cash." In May, Colbert applied for status as a Super PAC with the Federal Elections Commission and was approved in June. "This is 100 percent legal and at least 10 percent ethical," he explained.[50] Colbert had been willing to call the influence of wealth and power out on the table, by simply confronting these corrupting forces and making his Colbert Nation aware of what is going on from the inside. By being perceived as a harmless joke-maker wearing the mask of Arlecchino, Colbert is able to gain access where other serious journalists and experts could not, and cannot.

In the fall of 2007, Colbert announced that he would "try" running in the 2008 presidential primary as a Republican and a Democrat. "That way," he quipped, "I can lose twice."[51] His formal announcement came on October 16. As he later stated on *Meet the Press*, "I don't want to be president. I want to *run* for president. There's a difference. I'd be making the statement that I was able to get on the ballot in South Carolina, and if I can do it, so can you."[52] Almost immediately, the question became who is running for president, Stephen Colbert the person or "Stephen" the character from *The Colbert Report*? Even Colbert himself was not quite sure where the line was being drawn between reality and fiction when he said in an interview, after it became clear that he was not being taken seriously.

Colbert felt that both the Republican and Democrat election committees were lying to him, since both of them had encouraged his potential candidacy at the beginning of the process. Indeed, the "anyone can run for president" notion was directly contradicted by a member of the executive council of elections in South Carolina, Warren Howe, who emphatically stated, "Over my dead body will Colbert's name be on the ballot."[53] Colbert, frustrated by the failure of the democratic process, said, "I came close to believing my own line of crap when I was running for president. Even the *Report* staff was confused, and my publicist asked me, 'Is this a joke or is this real?'"[54] In 2012, Stephen Colbert and "Stephen" entered the Republican primary for the presidency as "President of the United States—of South Carolina." This time he made it clear that it was a satire of the political process that was becoming, just as Will Rogers had predicted, a joke, while the joke was becoming the reality. Because he was not legally registered as a candidate for president, Colbert encouraged his constituency to vote for officially recognized candidate Herman Cain, who had dropped out of the race but was still on the ballot. Cain was more than happy to lend his name to Colbert's faux candidacy, as a vote for Herman Cain was a vote for "Stephen."

Will Rogers, in contrast to Stephen Colbert, never entertained any political aspirations even in jest. He preferred to gain entrance into the world of political process and critique it from the sidelines, as witnessed at the Democratic

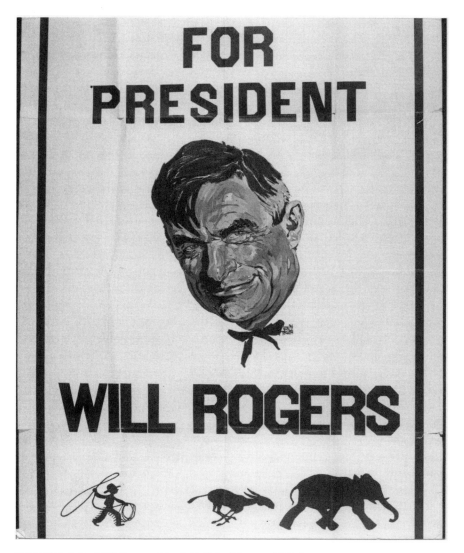

FIGURE 4.2 *Will Rogers Mock Political Poster (1924).*
Source: Will Rogers Memorial Museum, Claremore, Oklahoma.

National Convention in 1924, when two Arizona delegates nominated Will Rogers for president. Rogers's reaction was incredulous at best:

> I was born on election day, but never was able to get elected to anything. I am going to jump out some day and be indefinite enough about everything that they will call me a politician, then run on a platform of question marks, and be elected unanimously, then reach in the treasury and bring back my district a new bridge, or tunnel, or dam, and I will be a statesman.[55]

Even though Rogers never seriously considered a run for any office in the US government, he became a permanent fixture on Capitol Hill as a journalist, watchdog, and humorist. Comedy was where Rogers belonged and his primary way of influencing the political landscape. The comedian as presidential hopeful is a serious prospect with regard to Will Rogers as well. By comparison with Colbert, one of the reasons for Rogers's being considered for the presidency was his understanding of the economic disparity between "the haves and the have nots" in a democratic society. As he forthrightly stated during what he saw as the wasteful extravagance of the wealthy and the government corruption that went hand in hand during the Harding administration, and was to ultimately characterize the Roaring Twenties, "it was not the working classes that brought on the economic crisis, it was the big boys that thought the financial drunk was going to last forever, and over bought, over merged and over capitalized. . . . The difference between our rich and poor grows greater every year."[56] Again, Rogers resonates in the twenty-first century where the disparity between "the rich and the rest of us," as Tavis Smiley and Cornell West note, is of primary concern for the future socioeconomic health of America.[57]

Stephen Colbert too confronts the question of financial disparity by pointing out that wealth controls the narrative about who will potentially be considered for the presidency. "The big boys," as Rogers called them, were now being joined by Colbert when he created a Political Action Committee called "Americans for a Better Tomorrow, Tomorrow."[58] This fundraising organization commented on the influence of money and power over the political election system by becoming party to it. Colbert was mocking the notion of Super PACs by creating one. His committee spent real money on advertising in Iowa and South Carolina in the 2012 Republican primaries, running a "fake" candidate in the Midwest called Rick "Parry" (a riff on then real candidate, Rick Perry), and in the South by running as "Herman Cain," but telling voters through his Super PAC ads that they were actually voting for "Stephen."

Both of these entrances into the real world of politics were meant to focus on the corruption and influence of the "big boys" into a democratic system of government that compromises its values by legalizing, through Supreme

Court rulings like *Citizens United*, the theory that "corporations are people," thereby allowing candidates to solicit unlimited amounts of money from these "people" (corporations as well as extremely wealthy individual donors) without any disclosure as to who these "people" might actually be or who the candidates they support truly are. "Stephen," the character and candidate, is thereby intentionally ridiculing the US system of elections by revealing its corruption by becoming a party to it.

Will Rogers set the stage for contemporary comedians like Stephen Colbert through the excavation of the American political process. Rogers and Colbert, having been trained in front of live audiences in improvisation and reaching people directly on their respective tours, developed their stage-turned-screen personas by refining them in front of "ordinary folks." These comedian-commentators performed the characters of "Will," and his reporting of what he has read in the papers, and "Stephen," whose truthiness comes from the "gut," to live audiences of citizens, politicians, and world leaders, as public figures whose characters interact in the real world.

By creating the comic persona of the self-deprecating humorist as with "Will," or the overbearing, self-righteous conservative of "Stephen," they each create comic characters that allay the fears that authoritative majorities try to instill in its citizenry. Progressive-era journalist and social commentator H. L. Mencken noted that "the old categories of true and false disappear from the American metaphysic, and in place of them there are only categories of right and wrong."[59] This is where Rogers and Colbert use the humor as a site for reflecting on the absurdity and lack of self-awareness of those in authority by pointing out that their self-assured confidence of what is "right and wrong" is sorely lacking in critical thought and imagination. Will Rogers and Stephen Colbert do this by simply questioning Mencken's acknowledged "old categories of true and false."

Both Rogers and Colbert, using the vaudeville aesthetic of the stump speech as comic and critical monologue, by inserting their characters of "Will" and "Stephen" into the political process, have consequently entered the halls of United States democracy wearing the mask of Arlecchino. That both humorists were considered qualified to become president because of their analysis of the pitfalls and achievements of America, as well as their offering advice and solutions on how to avoid political gridlock in order to return the focus to the needs of the citizens, shows that their work as comedians goes beyond popular entertainment into an active sociocultural discourse. By providing the critical thinking and dialectic necessary to gain valuable knowledge and awareness of America's strengths and weaknesses, Rogers and Colbert have shown that healthy debate through the vaudeville aesthetic is the key to a progressive agenda with forward thinking and political action.

Will Rogers' and Stephen Colbert's popularity with diverse audiences of working, middle, and upper classes shows that their comedy can work on multiple levels and be universal. Comedy can also put it over on the power elites of American politics, as in Colbert's 2006 address to the White House Correspondents' Dinner. With George W. Bush at Colbert's elbow, as well as White House journalists of all stripes sitting right in front of him, Colbert uses "Stephen" to critique the sitting president of the United States and the reporters who collude with his agenda. Did the president "get it" when "Stephen," referring to "W.," said, "We're not so different, he and I. We both get it."[60] Whether or not he did, Colbert's audience got it, and in the great tradition of the stump speech, "Stephen," like "Will" before him, exposed the "truthiness" of the presidency and the abuses of power in the United States through the comic portrayal of self through comedy.

The intersection between popular comic entertainment and sociocultural analysis was examined in a *New York Times* op-ed from August 2010. Journalist Alexander Nehamas asks a compelling question about the nature of popular culture and entertainment as informed by Plato's analysis of classical constructs of entertainment and culture in *The Republic*. Nehamas asks students of Plato, "Are we passive consumers or active participants" in our interaction with popular entertainment? And "do we [as audience], as Plato thought, move immediately from representation to reality?"[61] Has popular entertainment in the form of reality television, the twenty-four-hour news cycle, and television situation comedy become the site of how we view reality? Is the quotidian becoming viewed as a sitcom and ultimately as infotainment, indistinguishable from the world of comic entertainment?

Contemporary fears and anxieties fueled via the twenty-four-hour media cycle are offered perspective and analysis in the form of popular comic actor-writers like Jon Stewart and Stephen Colbert. As Colbert states, mocking right-wing conservative pundits and journalists in a 2010 episode of *The Colbert Report*, "I know you watch this show to keep abreast of what to be scared and/or angry about."[62] Colbert comments on the unquestioning trust we place in contemporary charlatans as performed on "news" programs on Fox, CNN, and MSNBC, creating a "truthiness": something like truth as informed by unvetted public opinion and popular entertainment.

Most recently Stephen Colbert used the guise of his right-wing pundit, "Stephen," to call out the racism of institutionalized journalism. "Stephen" compared himself to the conservative pundit, Bill O'Reilly, from the *O'Reilly Factor* show on *Fox News*—O'Reilly being the inspiration whom Colbert claims to have modeled his character on—when he responded on *The Colbert Report* with a segment titled, "Colbert Agrees With Bill O'Reilly: 'Black People Are Scary.'" Colbert begins by showing O'Reilly and other *Fox News* "opinionators" claiming that black people are responsible for the majority of violent crime that is perpetrated in the United States. "Stephen" then uses the statistics provided by these fearmongers and shows that the end result is that in reality only ".009%" of black Americans commit these crimes. Using the mask of Arlecchino to appear to agree with his adversaries, Stephen Colbert is able to reveal their racism. Ultimately, he exposes the "serious journalism" of Bill O'Reilly and *Fox News* for the charlatanism that it is.

A link between the medicine show fraud's stump speech and the mask of Arlecchino discussed in this chapter can be connected to the blackface masks of minstrelsy to be discussed in the next chapter with Bert Williams and Dave Chappelle. Bert Williams' legacy of the blackface mask, and the reverse-racial whiteface masking of Dave Chappelle, sheds further light on how these comic masks can expose racial prejudice and dispel "truthiness" as a false construct through the vaudeville aesthetic.[63]

Notes

1 Ann Anderson, *Snake Oil, Hustlers, and Hambones: The American Medicine Show* (Jefferson, NC: McFarland, 2000), 1.

2 Anderson, *Snake Oil, Hustlers, and Hambones*, 1.

3 Joe Laurie, Jr., *Vaudeville: From the Honky-Tonks to the Palace*, New York: Henry Holt, 1953, 438.

4 Richard D. White, Jr., *Will Rogers: A Political Life* (Lubbock, TX: Texas Tech University Press, 2011), 75.

5 "Interview with Will Rogers," *Tulsa Daily World*, December 13, 1925; Betty Rogers, *Will Rogers* (Norman, OK: University of Oklahoma Press, 1979), 186.

6 Rogers, *Will Rogers*, 185.

7 Will Rogers, *The Papers of Will Rogers*, ed. Steven K. Gragert and M. Jane Johansson, vol. 4, *From the Broadway Stage to the National Stage: September 1915–July 1928* (Norman, OK: University of Oklahoma Press, 2005), 395.

8 Interview with Will Rogers, *Times-Picayune* (New Orleans), November 11, 1925.

9 James M. Smallwood and Steven K. Gragert, eds, *Will Rogers' Weekly Articles*, vol. 1, *The Harding/Coolidge Years: 1922–1925* (Stillwater, OK: Oklahoma State University Press, 1980).

10 P. J. O'Brien, *Will Rogers: Ambassador of Good Will, Prince of Wit and Wisdom* (Chicago: John C. Winston, 1935), 268.

11 Rose, "Review of Will Rogers," *Dramatic Mirror*, November 19, 1921, 743.

12 The source material used here on Fred Allen comes from Alan Havig, *Fred Allen's Radio Comedy* (Philadelphia: Temple University Press, 1990), and Wertheim, *Radio Comedy*.

13 Fred Allen, *Treadmill to Oblivion: My Days in Radio* (Boston, MA: Little, Brown, 1954), 5.

14 Allen, *Treadmill to Oblivion*, 179.

15 Fred Allen, *Texaco Star Theatre*, December 16, 1942, Lawrence G. Blochman Collection, Division of Rare Books and Special Collections, William Robertson Coe Library, University of Wyoming, Laramie.

16 Allen, *Treadmill to Oblivion*, 192.

17 *The Fred Allen Show*, May 15, 1949, 4–6, Blochman Collection.

18 Allen, *Treadmill to Oblivion*, 27.

19 Joe McCarthy, introduction, *Fred Allen's Letters* (Garden City, NY: Doubleday, 1965), ix.

20 Edward Schumacher-Matos, "Does Roasting the Pope as a Gay Icon Cross the Line?," National Public Radio, March 22, 2012, http://www.npr.org/blogs/ombudsman/2012/03/22/149175809/roasting-the-pope-as-a-gay-icon-civilized-or-crossing-the-line.

21 Fred Allen, "The Life and Death of Vaudeville," quoted in Laurence Senelick, ed., *The American Stage: Writing on Theater from Washington Irving to Tony Kushner* (New York: Library of America, 2010), 567.

22 Laurence Maslon and Michael Kantor, "The Groundbreakers," *Make 'Em Laugh: The Funny Business of America* (New York: Twelve, 2008), 334.

23 Maslon and Kantor, "The Groundbreakers," *Make 'Em Laugh*, 334.

24 Gerald Nachman, *Seriously Funny: The Rebel Comedians of the 1950s and 1960s* (New York: Pantheon Books, 2003), 85.

25 Mort Sahl, quoted in Nachman, *Seriously Funny*, 98.

26 Robert B. Weide written and directed, *Mort Sahl: The Loyal Opposition*, American Masters Series, Season 4, Episode 7, PBS Home Video, first aired September 18, 1989.

27 Nat Lehrman, "Playboy Interview: Mort Sahl," *Playboy*, February 1969, 60.

28 Lenny Bruce, *Lenny Bruce Without Tears*, written by Barbara Baker, Fred Baker, and John Parson, directed by Fred Baker (New York: Fred Baker Films, 1972), http://www.amazon.com/gp/product/B00DFYF8SC/ref=atv_feed_catalog?tag=imdb-amazonvideo-20.

29 "Immigrant Farm Workers," House Committee on Immigration, Citizenship and Border Security, 111th Cong., C-SPAN 3, September 24, 2010, http://www.c-spanvideo.org/program/295639-1.

30 Stephen Colbert, interview with *Daily Variety*, April 25, 2006, in Lisa Rogak, *And Nothing but the Truthiness: The Rise (and Further Rise) of Stephen Colbert* (New York: St. Martin's Press, 2011), 114.

31 Throughout the chapter, "Will" and "Stephen" will refer to the characters that the eponymous performers respectively portray.

32 *The Story of Will Rogers*, directed by Donald B. Hyatt (Newton: NJ: Shanachie Entertainment, 2003), DVD, originally released by NBC *News Presents*, 1961.

33 Reprinted in Stephen Colbert, Richard Dahm, Paul Dinello, and Allison Silverman, *I Am America (And So Can You!)* (New York: Grand Central Publishing, 2007), 221; "Colbert Roasts Bush—2006 White House Correspondents' Dinner," YouTube video, 24:11, from White House Correspondents' Association Dinner, televised by C-SPAN on April 29, 2006, posted by "Ocular Politics," December 15, 2010, http://www.youtube.com/watch?v=U7FTF4Oz4dI.

34 Colbert et al., *I Am America*, 224.

35 Will Rogers, "Weekly Column," *New York Times*, November 23, 1932.

36 Rogers, *Will Rogers*, 157.

37 Will Rogers, "Weekly Column," *New York Times*, February 17, 1924; *Will Rogers' Weekly Articles*, vol. 1, 192.

38 Will Rogers, "Weekly Column," *New York Times*, January 21, 1923.

39 Will Rogers, *The Illiterate Digest* (New York: A. L. Burt Company, 1924), 323.

40 Will Rogers, "Interview with Will Rogers," *Tulsa Daily World*, February 1, 1925.

41 66 Congressional Record, n.p. (Dec. 18, 1924); *Washington Post*, December 7, 1924.

42 Henry Jenkins, "Manufacturing Dissent: An Interview with Stephen Duncombe," *Confessions of an Aca-Fan* (blog), July 23, 2007, http://henryjenkins.org/2007/07/manufacturing_dissent_an_inter.html.

43 Stephen Duncombe, *Dream: Re-imagining Progressive Politics in an Age of Fantasy* (New York: New Press, 2007), 59.

44 *The Godfather*, directed by Francis Ford Coppola (Hollywood: CA: Paramount Pictures Home Entertainment, 2008), DVD.

45 Jon Stewart, interview by Charles McGrath, "How Many Stephen Colberts Are There?" *New York Times Magazine*, January 8, 2012: 22.

46 McGrath, "How Many Colberts?," 24.

47 Will Rogers, *Will Rogers at the Ziegfeld Follies*, ed. Arthur Frank Wertheim (Norman, OK: University of Oklahoma Press, 1992), 150.

48 Rogers, *Will Rogers at the Ziegfeld Follies*, 150.

49 McGrath, "How Many Colberts?," 22.

50 Stephen Colbert, "Colbert Super PAC Treasure Hunt Solution," *The Colbert Report*, June 28, 2012, http://www.colbertnation.com/colbert-superpac.

51 Stephen Colbert, interview with *Beaufort Gazette*, October 17, 2007.

52 Reprinted in Lisa Rogak, *And Nothing but the Truthiness: The Rise (and Further Rise) of Stephen Colbert* (New York: Thomas Dunne, 2011), 213; Stephen Colbert, interview by Tim Russert, *Meet the Press*, NBC, October 21, 2007.

53 Rogak, *And Nothing but the Truthiness*, 214–15; Warren Howe, interview with CNN, October 31, 2007.

54 Stephen Colbert, interview by *Stand Up with Pete Dominick*, Sirius XM, March 13, 2008.

55 Will Rogers, "Weekly Column," *New York Times*, March 12, 1933.

56 Will Rogers, Columbia Network, November 11, 1934, in O'Brien, *Will Rogers*, 147–50.

57 Tavis Smiley and Cornell West, *The Rich and the Rest of Us: A Poverty Manifesto* (New York: Smiley Books, 2012).

58 Stephen Colbert, "Colbert Super PAC—Irresponsible Advertising," *The Colbert Report*, June 29, 2011, http://www.colbertnation.com/the-colbert-report-videos/391013/june-29-2011/colbert-super-pac---making-a-better-tomorrow--tomorrow.

59 H. L. Mencken, *Mencken's America*, ed. S. T. Joshi (Athens, OH: Ohio University Press, 2004), 189–90.

60 Reprinted in Colbert et al., *I Am America*, 221.

61 Alexander Nehamas, "Plato's Pop Culture," *New York Times*, August 29, 2010: 4.

62 Stephen Colbert, "The Word—Docu-Drama," *The Colbert Report*, April 26, 2010, http://www.colbertnation.com/the-colbert-report-videos/308060/april-26-2010/the-word---docu-drama.

63 Stephen Colbert, "The Word—Color-Bind," *The Colbert Report*, Episode #09127 (July 23, 2013), http://www.colbertnation.com/the-colbert-report-videos/428008/july-23-2013/the-word---color-bind.

5

The mask of minstrelsy
Bert Williams to Dave Chappelle

Bert Williams mastered the performance of the stump speech that characterized Will Rogers and Stephen Colbert's vaudeville aesthetic. Williams created a recurring preacher character in Elder Eatmore. The following excerpt is from "Elder Eatmore's Sermon on Generosity," one of his most successful vaudeville routines:

> The Lord loveth a cheerful giver. Tonight, my friends, you can omit the cheerful. The truth is the light, and here is the truth: y'all is way back in my salary and something has got to be done here this evening. . . . Because if something ain't done, your shepherd is gone. That's all. THAT IS ALL. I admit that times is tight because when there used to be a ham coming here and a fowl or two there from different members of this flock, I managed to make out fair to middlin'. They all comes to he who waits. But you all done learnt me that self-preservation is the first law of he who gets it. And the Lord helps they who helps their selves. . . . And my friends I need, I *need* . . . T'ain't no use talkin' about what I need I needs everything, from my hat *down*, and from my overcoat *in*.[1]

Like Rogers and Colbert, Bert Williams is able to attack institutionalized greed and deception through the mask of the counterfeit minister, shedding light on the hypocrisy of authority—in this case religious authority—and those that allow themselves to be duped by it. Dave Chappelle inherits this vaudeville mask bringing social commentary to contemporary comedy. These comedians are united through the vaudeville aesthetic of the mask of minstrelsy coupled with the stump speech.

Ralph Ellison—novelist, critic, and scholar—wrote that in a nation founded by colonials and populated by immigrants and former slaves, "the Declaration of an American identity meant the taking on of a mask," since "the discipline of national self-consciousness . . . gave Americans an ironic awareness of the joke that always lies between appearance and reality. . . . The darky act makes brothers of us all."[2] Ellison points out that blackface comedy—from its popularity in nineteenth-century minstrelsy to its reappropriation in twenty-first-century humor—depicts our collective national racism, because it cannot be hidden. The racial stereotyping that makes audiences laugh is out in the open for all to see with the burnt-cork black mask.

* * *

The vaudevillian-turned-*Ziegfeld Follies* star Bert Williams was one of the first comedians to introduce the notion of black comedy for black audiences. White audiences could laugh without knowing that they were being criticized for their misperceptions and bigotry, while black audiences enjoyed the double meanings of Williams' humor. Beginning with the stage career of Bert Williams, this paradox of white audiences admiring black performers in comedy for their theatrical skills, yet still considering them inferior, will be considered against the white performance of black characters in *The Amos 'n' Andy Show* as well as the stand-up, television, and film performances of Richard Pryor, and ending with the complex ongoing stage and screen career of Dave Chappelle.

The legacy of the blackface mask in this study moves from the ambivalence of comedy legend Bert Williams to the sociocultural examination of racism and bigotry in Dave Chappelle's work. It is the ability to recognize the continuum of the comedic black mask of minstrelsy from the early twentieth-century perspective of Bert Williams that allows Chappelle to enter the conversation of blackface versus whiteface masking on *Chappelle's Show*. Observing and evaluating the links between Bert Williams and Dave Chappelle makes a unique case for the continued use of blackface minstrelsy in contemporary comedy.

First, it is necessary to be aware of the roots of the comic black performer beginning in the marketplace of the early-to-mid-nineteenth century in the United States, with its sideshow presentation of hawkers and medicine men with dubious wares. This style of performance required larger-than-life characterizations to draw in, convince, or fool potential customers into parting with what little money they had. From illusionists and religious fanatics declaring "the end of the world" to the sideshow hucksters with their exotic miracle cure-alls and promises of contact with a mythical Far East, the marketplace-cum-medicine show was littered with salesmen as performers

FIGURE 5.1 *Bert Williams (ca. 1911).*

Source: Photographs and Prints Division, Schomburg Center for Research in Black Culture, The New York Public Library, Astor, Lenox, and Tilden Foundations.

wearing the masks of charlatans. The combination of American entertainment and commerce at the turn of the twentieth century used a mask that promised racial and ethnic authenticity, and required a continuous balance between appearances and realities.

The minstrel show, according to theater historian Laurence Senelick, "was one of the few truly indigenous American entertainments and made a profound impression worldwide." Senelick goes on to note that: "Its influence can be traced in much American popular music and theater, and many outstanding performers, including Eddie Cantor, Al Jolson, and Bert Williams, owed a great deal to its traditions."[3] Comic acts like Bert Williams presented a fractured vision of the "American" through the lens of class, ethnicity, and race.

The blacking-up by performers, beginning with Irish immigrants and then Jews from Eastern Europe, dominated minstrelsy in the mid-to-late-nineteenth century. As a product of the medicine shows of the antebellum period, the wearing of burnt cork as a performance mask by the white-working-immigrant class, was not only a form of popular entertainment but, according to performance scholar Michael Rogin, a reflection of the "Americanizing" of ethnicity, intentionally separating ethnic immigrants by racial subjugation.[4] To assimilate, impoverished immigrants added themselves to the American melting pot by excluding blacks through racial denigration and the reinforcing of stereotypes.

White vaudevillians, by imitating and mocking what they considered the inferiority of blacks as lazy and ignorant "darkies," performed their assumed superiority for comic effect in blackface. Minstrelsy provided the forum for this display of ethnicity versus race in the integration of Americans at the turn of the twentieth century. A dark skin could not be assimilated, as could a lighter skin, which became the ultimate definition of the "real" American in the burgeoning nation. This form of popular entertainment successfully reduced blacks to crude types that provided justification for discrimination through the rejection of the darker races as being unworthy of serious consideration.

In the world of stage comedy this distinction of color was achieved by the burnt-cork mask as worn by white performers. However, as this performance tradition continued, blacks themselves were at first required to black-up to add further "authenticity" to their acts. Ultimately, certain black performers, such as Bert Williams, chose to wear blackface, debunking the myth of the "darky" as having any relationship to the reality of African, Caribbean, and South American immigrants and former slaves. Bert Williams was able to achieve his success wearing the burnt-cork mask of minstrelsy and ghosting the legacy of the black mask of the indentured servant, *Arlecchino*.

The blackface mask in comic performance can be seen as far back as the sixteenth century in Western Europe with the *commedia dell'arte* and its comedic character types. Some background needs to be provided as to the nature and evolution of the *Arlecchino* mask in order to better understand how this form of masking affected comedy into the early twentieth century in vaudeville. First and foremost, *Arlecchino's* leather, flesh-like, half-mask represented a black face. The denigrating image of blackened faces that supposedly depicted lazy, foolish, ignorant, slaves, and servants whose scheming (as much as their ignorance would permit) allowed them to survive in the world of their "betters" can be witnessed in the literal mask of *Arlecchino* and its inheritance in the burnt-cork mask of minstrelsy's endmen (who literally stood on either end of the stage)—Tambo and Bones. Comedy scholar James Phillips refers to the historical inference of why *Arlecchino* was represented by a black leather mask.

> *Arlecchino* . . . was influenced by the Roman theater's characterization of African slaves. The *lenones* of the Roman theater were the portrayers of African slaves, and similarities exist between their black mask and the black half-mask of the early *Arlecchino*. As an innocent fool, *Arlecchino* juxtaposed extreme stupidity with wisdom and grace and was a master of physical comedy and acrobatics.[5]

The tradition of the comic mask from the *commedia dell'arte*, as observed with Will Rogers and Stephen Colbert and in this chapter with Bert Williams and Dave Chappelle, points to a need on the part of comedians to hide the satirical intent of their performances. In Rogers and Colbert's case they perform a comic version of themselves as white men who are a bit foolish— one humble and the other self-important. Williams and Chappelle perform the black-male stereotype of the fool—again one self-deprecating and the other flamboyantly outrageous—through the blackface mask.

By masking critical commentary, comic performers throughout comedy history were able to obscure their intent and attempt to escape the scrutiny of the upper classes and authoritarians. Comic performers in the late nineteenth century hid under the veil of the "darky" whose rebellion against their masters would be perceived as a joke. In a similar vein, *commedia* servants would be able to trick their masters since the comic mask concealed their intelligence, strength, and insurgency. Black performers in blackface like Bert Williams worked under the radar of white authority in a similar fashion in vaudeville as informed by minstrelsy.

As minstrel shows progressed into the 1880s their format became more and more standardized. The author of "Dixie" and white minstrel performer Dan Emmett is credited with formulating its three-part structure, including sketches, songs, dances, and slapstick comedy performed in a stereotyped black vernacular.[6] The first part of the minstrel act was performed in a semicircle of nine people, with one member on each end playing the tambourine or the castanet-like "bones" (literally animal bones). Brudder Tambo and Brudder Bones, as the endmen were called, told absurd jokes and performed foolish gags in between songs and dances. Tambo would be characterized as the skinny and fast-talking Zip Coon, and Bones was to become the overweight, slow, malapropism-spouting darky, Jim Crow. The character of Mr. Interlocutor was a white master of ceremonies who performed from the middle of the semicircle. His dignified and haughty manner contrasted with that of the rambunctious, inarticulate endmen. The next section, known as the olio, consisted of novelty acts including acrobats, singers, dancers, magicians, and comic sketches—that gave way later in the century to vaudeville acts. The second half of the show featured a stump speech in which a "learned" lecture or religious sermon was parodied. The blackface performer of the stump speech wished to possess and disseminate great intellectual prowess but reduced himself to an insipid and nonsensical ignoramus. A short play served as the third part of the program and typically represented the lives of "simple and carefree Negroes" who laughed and sang about their presumably joyful plantation existence.[7]

Minstrelsy informed Bert Williams' work throughout his stage career. He first met and worked with his soon-to-be-partner, George Walker, in 1893, when he landed a job with Martin and Selig's Mastodon Minstrels in San Francisco as an endman.[8] After touring, the troupe returned to San Francisco, this time landing on the infamous Barbary Coast at the Midway Plaisance. The Midway was the lowest and hardest of the venues to play. It featured "hootchy-kootchy" dancers and was located near dance halls, saloons, and brothels. It was here that the duo would become Williams and Walker. During the 1896–97 season, the team would perform for thirty-six weeks at Koster and Bial's vaudeville house. They also performed in blackface, billing themselves as "Two Real Coons" to distinguish themselves from the other white performers in blackface acts.[9]

By 1903, Williams and Walker created a show that would make Broadway history at the New York Theatre. They would headline in "the first full-length musical written and played by blacks to be performed at a major Broadway house,"[10] with In Dahomey. This was Williams and Walker's ambitious effort to "explore the African background onstage."[11] The musical included elements of the medicine and minstrel shows, beginning with a barker pitching cure-alls. The "doctor's" stump speech was an intentional parody of the nineteenth-century performance stereotype of the lazy, foolish, and ignorant black that Williams had been expected to portray earlier in his career.[12] Now that he had control of the production elements, he and Walker could comment on black types for black audiences who would be in on the jokes, while white audiences remained in the dark.

Black audiences responded by making *In Dahomey* a Broadway hit. The satire appreciated by black audiences was derived from characters like the Medicine Man, who presented his "cure" to "turn colored folks white" in the opening stump speech. The mockery performed by the comic portrayal of the blackface mask allowed black audiences to knowingly understand the absurd and offensive notion that donning the whiteface mask of Anglo-Americans could easily cure black folks. The irony of black audiences being forced to sit in "nigger heaven" (the upper balconies furthest from the stage) reinforced the onstage comic critique. A *New York Times* review reflects the black spectator's reaction: "At intervals one heard a shrill *kiyi* of applause from above or a mellow bass roar that betokened the seventh heaven of delight."[13] The "double consciousness" of a performance using the blackface mask—meaning one thing for a black audience and another for a white one—was a term that the Harlem Renaissance poet and activist W. E. B. Du Bois would coin in his seminal book, *The Souls of Black Folk* (1903), was lost on the white critic however.[14]

The performance traditions of minstrelsy masking and its insistence on the stereotypes of blacks for comic effect can be seen in the following exchange between Williams and Walker, in which the slick and wily Walker tries to convince the seemingly foolish and gullible Williams of his deceptive plot:

WALKER: All you have to do is fill the satchel [with money]; I'll get the satchel—you won't have nothing to bother about—that's 'cause you're a friend of mine, see?

WILLIAMS: And what do I do with this satchel?

WALKER: All you got to do is bring it to me at a place where I tell you.

WILLIAMS: When they come to count up the cash and find it short, then what?

WALKER: By that time we'll be far away—where the birds are singing sweetly and the flowers are in bloom.

WILLIAMS: [*With doleful reflection.*] And if they catch us they'll put us so far, far away we never will hear no birds singin'. And everybody know you can't smell no flowers through a stone wall.[15]

In the hands of Williams, the reversal of the slow and witless darky contradicts its perceived stereotype by exposing Walker's manipulative trickery and get-rich-quick schemes; in this medicine show redux, the country rube outwits the citified charlatan.

The black mask of minstrelsy had myriad implications both on- and offstage. According to Williams, blackface was at first a curse, but ultimately he took charge of its power by intentionally using it in his comic acts. In an interview from 1921, he is quoted as saying,

The real Bert Williams is crouched deep down inside the coon who sings and tells stories. . . . I'd like a piece that would give me the opportunity to express the whole of the negro's character. The laughter I have caused is only on the surface. Now I'd like to go much deeper and to show our depths that few understand yet. . . . If I could interpret in the theatre [an] underlying tragedy of race, I feel that we would be better known and better understood.[16]

As Williams states here, his desire to be "better known and better understood" led him to embrace the burnt cork of minstrelsy in order to communicate with black and white audiences in different ways. This could be construed by both audiences as offensive—for blacks, it reinforced nineteenth-century racist stereotypes of the "slow, shuffling, negro"; whites might be offended if they caught on to the "upstart" nature of a smart and talented black performer who was in control of his art form.[17] However, white audiences might also be forced to acknowledge the absurdity of the comic actor as a false representative of a "real" black man onstage.

Williams was able to negotiate this double consciousness to become one of the most successful black comic vaudevillians of the 1910s and 1920s in one of the most popular of entertainments that show business had to offer for white audiences—the *Ziegfeld Follies*. The comfortable familiarity and theatrical effect of blackface reinforced Williams' intent in playing a stereotype of the darky expected of him by white audiences. He wore this crude, offensive, and racist mask to undermine the comic implications of his act—speaking to two very different audiences simultaneously.

Bert Williams' double life also revealed his ambivalence toward his work and his stage persona. As his signature song, originally written for the 1905 musical *Abyssinia*, "Nobody," reflects:

I ain't never done nothin' to nobody,
I ain't never got nothin' from nobody, no time!
And until I get somethin' from somebody, sometime,
I don't intend to do nothin' for nobody, no time!
I ain't never done nothin' to nobody . . .[18]

The thoughtful, ironic lyrics and delivery bear witness to an erasure of Williams as a performer that followed him offstage, all in the name of comic entertainment. The literal obliteration of his facial features from the burnt-cork mask that he willingly wore was a perpetual reminder of the negation of his race, reinforcing an erroneous stereotype of an African that belied his true identity as a Bahamian and an American, rendering him a "nobody." Ironically, this song would be in demand throughout his career, haunting Williams at the same time that it made him a star. "For seven whole years I had to sing it," Williams was quoted as saying. "Month after month I tried to drop it and sing something new, but I could get nothing to replace it, and the audiences seemed to want nothing else."[19]

The legacy of minstrelsy and its positioning in the early 1910s and 1920s is seen in a sketch by Bert Williams and fellow *Ziegfeld Follies* comedian Eddie Cantor. It was first performed in the 1919 edition of the *Follies* in which Cantor plays a recent college graduate and the son of a railway porter wearing white horn-rimmed glasses, affecting a mincing walk, and wearing blackface. The porter is played by Williams who also wears the burnt cork of the minstrel show. The hardened father is angry that his son has not turned into a football hero while away at school, and is about to strike him when Cantor exclaims in a high-pitched whine, "Remember, Daddy, I have a temper," to which Williams replies, "I'll show you where you got it from!" The sketch ends with Williams placing his porter's cap on his son's head, saying, "Pick up them bags! This is my graduation and your commencement."[20] Several tropes from the vaudeville stage are at work in this two-man blackface act between seeming comic opposites. Comedic acts like Williams and Cantor presented a fractured vision of the American-born vaudeville aesthetic through the lens of class, ethnicity, race, and even gender roles. The distinction between a working-class father and his college-educated son; the macho patriarch and his effete, feminized progeny; ethnic comedy and interracial casting via blackface; the pragmatic, common-sense older generation versus the intellectual and impractical younger generation—all are reflected in this conflict as performed by these vaudevillians. This sketch, as it grew out of the minstrel show, juxtaposes opposite types and shatters them through comic satire as it re-envisions and complicates what it meant to be working and middle class, masculine and feminine, black and Jewish.

Bert Williams continued to use blackface, long after it was expected of black comedians to do so. According to Williams himself, he felt "great protection" wearing the comic mask that he had made his trademark since his medicine-show barker days. "A black face," claimed Williams, "run-down shoes and elbow-out make-up give me a place to hide."[21] Williams wore blackface for most of his professional career, from his act with partner George Walker to the *Ziegfeld Follies* to his few silent film shorts that still survive.

As Williams expressed in a 1917 interview, "It was not until I was able to see myself as another person that my sense of humor developed."[22] Williams would later say that he did not believe in such a thing as "innate humor." "It has to be developed by hard work and study, just as every other human quality," he said.[23] His decision to perform in blackface was made for a booking at Detroit's Wonderland theater. He blackened his face and wrote his first song to perform,

"Oh! I Don't Know, You're Not So Warm!" Simply stated, Williams said of the experience that "I began to find myself."[24] The protection of the comic mask of burnt cork was liberating and helpful in his characterizations as, "I shuffle onto the stage, not as myself, but as a lazy, slow-going negro."[25] This transformation through the black mask distanced the performer from the character. For Bert Williams it was a relief, and for the audience it could be considered offensive and alternatively entertaining, perhaps simultaneously, as well as a commentary on race and its perception. Aida Overton Walker, herself a successful performer and wife of Williams' partner, George Walker, affirms that comic offense was not necessarily felt by black audiences while black performers "alone know how easy it is for a colored show to offend a white audience."[26] As her statement implies, the importance of black performers not appearing to offend white audiences was the key to survival in the racist world of modernist-era American popular entertainment. Bert Williams learned this lesson as his lucrative career in front of white audiences attests.

Minstrelsy's legacy in vaudeville depicts black performers in blackface as the ultimate outsiders. These vaudevillians, because of their social masks, could never be on the inside, unlike ethnic immigrants whose "passing" was made less complex by virtue of skin color. Blackface performer Bert Williams, although a major star with the *Ziegfeld Follies*, relates a telling story of not being informed of an Actors' Equity strike in 1919—although W. C. Fields and Eddie Cantor both claimed to have been close to Williams and praised his stage work as influencing their own stage successes, they did not inform him of the walkout. As Williams described the incident later to Fields: "I went to the theater as usual, made up and dressed. Then I came out of my dressing room and found the big auditorium empty and the strike on. I knew nothing of it: I had not been told. You see, I just didn't belong."[27] In a profession that admired and capitalized on his comic genius, Bert Williams remained removed from the mainstream of white comedians who were able to break through into radio and television. The virulence of racism ensured that minstrelsy was carried over into radio and television not by black vaudevillians but by white ones.

How radio and television used the vaudeville aesthetic allows an examination of the changes and crossovers of blackface (albeit white) vaudevillians and their acts to the new media of radio and television. The fraught relationship to race and comedy in these new media was witnessed with the sixty-year history—beginning first with radio (1928), then television (1951)—of *The Amos 'n' Andy Show*.[28] Using the techniques of vaudeville, and more specifically of minstrelsy, through the caricatures of Jim Crow and Zip Coon, *Amos 'n' Andy* would highlight the strange appeal and rejection of black comedians in their own profession. The simple fact that *Amos 'n' Andy* was created and performed on radio[29] by white performers Freeman Gosden and Charles Correll exemplifies this complex relationship to race and comedy in mid-twentieth-century America.

Radio provided for a focus on the voices and nuances of the characters and how they expressed themselves. It gave the listener an auditory image that was directly related to the vocal patterns and rhythms of the characters. It also gave an excellent perception of how the two-man act was predicated on timing, intonation, and inflection of dialogue. A scene from *The Amos 'n' Andy Radio Show*, called "The Locked Trunk's Secret," begins with the description of the characters from a script written and performed by Gosden and Correll in the central and secondary roles of Amos, Andy, Kingfish, and Lightening. This opening depicts the reinforcement of stereotypes of the lazy, ignorant, black male who is easily duped as he tries to figure out a scheme to make money without having a job. The narrator in a full stentorian voice of white authority begins the scene by describing the current misadventure of Amos and Andy saying, "To a lot of people an auction sale is a very serious business, but to Andy, it is just another excuse to keep himself occupied to avoid that distasteful thing known as work." Right away Andy is signaled to the audience as being lazy just by attending an auction, which "for a lot of people" is "serious business." Why it is not serious business for Andy as well seems to have to do with his avoidance of work; his blackness is coded in his assumed indolence. The scene continues with Andy describing his experience at the auction:

AMOS: So you been at one of them auctions ain't you, son?

ANDY: Yeah, but this time I done bought something.

AMOS: What did you buy, Brother Andy?

ANDY: I don't know, but I paid five dollars for it.

AMOS: Five dollars? How come you pay five dollars for something you don't know what 'tis?

ANDY: Well Amos, you know how's they works it at deez auctions? You bids by nodding yer head. Well, the auctioneer man put this thing up just as I was dozing off, and he say, who'll bid five dollars. My head kinda dropped down, and he say, "you got it!"

AMOS: You done dozed yourself out of five dollars!

ANDY: Yeah.[30]

Not only does Andy go to the auction to get out of working, he also falls asleep, which gets him deeper into trouble. He loses five dollars (a fair amount of money for the times) just through his laziness. Andy is tricked out of his money by not being sharp enough to take this business seriously. The "Negro" dialect used by these white actors indicates their ignorance and foolishness, particularly in contrast to the white narrator whose vocal authority and vocabulary is in direct opposition to these doltish, black characters.

Melvin Patrick Ely's comprehensive study of *The Amos 'n' Andy Show* covers the thirty-five-year career of Gosden and Correll and its significance in the history of radio and television. He notes that by 1960, they were an anomaly—white men portraying, then writing, black stereotypes formed from the legacy of minstrelsy. Minstrelsy had been a century in the making when Gosden and Correll began their radio show in the late 1920s. For several generations whites had created the perception of blacks on the comic stage, and for many Anglo-Americans, this was their only contact with blacks. As Ely puts it,

> The wonder is not that America in the 1960s had no place for Gosden and Correll, but rather that, during thirty-five years of profound social change, a radio and television series with roots in nineteenth-century minstrel shows had given Americans their most popular, pervasive, sustained picture of what purported to be black life and personality. *Amos 'n' Andy*'s popularity crossed boundaries of region, social standing, age, ethnic origin, and even race.[31]

The legacy of the Gosden and Correll characterizations of black men was rejected by the next generation of black comedians in the 1960s and 1970s—with Dick Gregory and especially Richard Pryor.

Richard Pryor was born in Peoria, Illinois, in harsh poverty. He grew up in his grandmother's brothel where his mother worked as a prostitute. After a two-year junket in the US Army—spent mostly in the brig—he moved to New York City in 1963 to work the Greenwich Village stand-up comedy clubs. Pryor would play these clubs and tour until an apocryphal 1967 gig in Las Vegas. At this point, Pryor wanted to get off the mainstream comedy circuit and decided to move to San Francisco. He became part of the counterculture alongside such activists as Huey P. Newton co-founder of the black empowerment organization, the Black Panther Party. Pryor's work would become politically and socially conscious during this period, and would influence his act from that point onward. Pryor made many successful comedy albums, especially his third record, *That Nigger's Crazy* (1974), from his stand-up acts, which were not unlike the forerunners of radio comedy. After guest hosting *SNL* and having a brief run with his own *The Richard Pryor Show* (co-written with comedian Paul Mooney), Pryor was cast in conventional movies, like *Car Wash, Stir Crazy*, and *Harlem Nights*. However, his unique brand of comedy was witnessed in the concert films *Richard Pryor: Live In Concert* (1979), and *Richard Pryor: Live on the Sunset Strip* (1982)—after his tragic self-immolation during a bout of drug-induced psychosis. His honesty about the seemingly insurmountable hardships of childhood abuses, racism, and dealing with celebrity, were all openly discussed in these stage performances.

Pryor's critical vision of white America is captured in a 1976 stand-up routine where he uses the stump speech in order to appear to celebrate US independence while actually condemning the whitewashing of the harsh realities of slavery. Speaking with the accent of Fred Allen's corrupt preacher/politician, Senator Claghorn, complete with malapropisms and the "truthiness" of disinformation, Pryor offered up a "bicentennial prayer" for the nation's two-hundredth birthday:

> We are gathered here today to celebrate this year of bicentenniality. In hope of freedom and dignity. We are celebratin' two hundred years of white folks kickin' ass. Now white folks have had the essence of disunderstanding on their side for quite a while. How elsen ever we offer this prayer. And the prayer is, how long will this bullshit go on! How long?! How long?! How long will this bullshit go on?! That is the eternal question. Man has always asked, how long?![32]

As if in answer to the question of "how long?" both Richard Pryor, and later Dave Chappelle, dropped out of extremely successful and lucrative careers in comedy and left for Africa. With this literal return to the continent from which their ancestors were captured and enslaved, audiences, particularly white ones, saw these black celebrities as "crazy" for abandoning their wealth and fame, while Pryor and Chappelle saw this as an escape back to a homeland where they were treated like regular people.

Pryor was inspired to drop the N-word from his act since there were no "niggers" in Africa and therefore there should be none in America: "So I went to the motherland it was so beautiful just seeing black people in charge of everything. I'm talking about from the wino to the president. It was black. Blue black. The original black."[33] Chappelle, feeling infected with the disease of Hollywood, wanted to cleanse himself of the sickness that was destroying him and his fellow humorists in America; in Africa, he could be treated as a human being rather than a black commodity.

Chappelle would hire Richard Pryor's friend and co-writer Paul Mooney for *Chappelle's Show*. Mooney appeared in sketches such as "Negrodamus," a riff on the prophet Nostradamus, who offered often controversial and unflinching observations on race in America. In a segment called "Ask a Black Dude," Mooney, responds to questions which presumably only a "black dude" can answer. One of his quips reflects what white audiences respond to in black comedy: "Everybody want to be a nigger, but nobody want to *be* a nigger." The camera cuts back to Dave in front of a live studio audience saying,

"I'm gonna get canceled for sure," alluding to the fact that his show is owned and funded primarily by the white producers and advertisers of Comedy Central.[34] Chappelle recognizes the legacy and paradox of black Americans having been simultaneously denigrated and admired in comedy. He creates humor out of the pain of racism and bigotry, commenting on this complex contradiction throughout the extremely troubled history of race in post-Civil War America.

Like Bert Williams and Richard Pryor, Dave Chappelle would learn his craft on the stage grappling with the image of black men and their struggles with equality with regard to race and manhood. Chappelle came up in the comedy clubs of Washington, DC. Beginning even earlier in life than Williams, Chappelle performed his first stand-up gig at fourteen. Shuttled back and forth between his divorced parents, from urban DC to the small college town of Yellow Springs, Ohio, Chappelle was introduced to the extremes of human behavior. From the big city crack epidemic of the 1980s to the mellower marijuana-smoking hippies of rural Ohio, Chappelle saw both the good and bad effects of drugs, white and black race relations, and the city and country denizens who populate his comedy.

After achieving celebrity with an HBO special, *Killin' Them Softly* (2000), he was rewarded at the relatively young age of 30 with his own Comedy Central vehicle, aptly named *Chappelle's Show*. The show's influence is exceptional given that it taped only two seasons, plus a few "lost episodes" from an aborted third season. Chappelle created a stir when he walked away from his third-season contract of $50 million and disappeared, only to resurface in South Africa. He has not returned to the show since.

Chappelle's perceived meltdown should have been less surprising. In a June 2004 stand-up performance in Sacramento, California, he walked off the stage after berating his audience for incessantly shouting, "I'm Rick James, bitch!," which had become a catchphrase from Chappelle's well-known satire of the funk musician. After a few minutes, Chappelle returned to the stage and continued his rant at the audience, saying, "The show is ruining my life." He let them know that he was not happy working "twenty hours a day" and that the popularity of the show was making it difficult for him to continue his stand-up career, which was "the most important thing" to him. Chappelle ended the performance by saying, "You know why my show is good? Because the network officials say you're not smart enough to get what I'm doing, and every day I fight for you. I tell them how smart you are. Turns out, I was wrong. You people are stupid." Season 3 was scheduled to air on May 31, 2005, but it never materialized.[35]

For Dave Chappelle, the commentary on America's relationship to its inherent racism is born of two major events in US history: ethnic immigration and slavery. Chappelle is also interested in comedy as a way of delving into Americans' relationship to their own history of prejudice and anger toward others unlike themselves. Chappelle reinforces that it is not just white, Anglo-American racism alone that is the problem. Pointing to the direction that his future work will take as early as 1998 in an HBO stand-up special that he finished by saying,

> You can't help it. If you an American, you a racist. We are brought up from the beginning to think in generalizations. We never look at the individual. I'm a racist. I know I'm a racist. You know how I know? The other day I caught myself being racist *against* myself. There's so much shit going on, I got mixed up. Forgot whose team I was on and shit.[36]

To this end, Chappelle takes on the infamous N-word to attack institutionalized racism in the United States.

Much like Sid Caesar and Tina Fey with their satire of middle-class American family sitcoms, Chappelle uses the vaudeville aesthetic to deal with race and class conflicts. "Let's see how offensive [the N-] word sounds now," he says, when it's the last name of a white family. A sketch depicting an Ozzie and Harriet Nelson-type white family from 1950s television has all the hallmarks of this idealized tribe with one distinction: their surname is Niggar. Chappelle plays Clifton, "the colored milkman" (also a parody of the white-bread, milk-drinking folks and their "darky" servant) who relishes saying, "Morning, Niggars!" and "It's my favorite family to deliver milk to! The Niggars!" Later in the scene, when Clifton and his wife are denied a table at a restaurant and they see the Niggars' son with his white date getting their table with no problem, Chappelle as Clifton says, "This racism is killing me inside!" and explodes into pain-felt laughter.[37]

However we choose to view the use of blackface in vaudeville comedy of the early twentieth century from the sociological distance of the early twenty-first century, Chappelle has doubled and reversed the offensiveness of blackface today. Right from the beginning of *Chappelle's Show*, he intended to offend. As he stated quite clearly during the show's second episode, "Welcome back to *Chappelle's Show*. America's number one source for offensive comedy." Chappelle went on to say, "I am a genetic dissenter," then showed the history of his black ancestors' dissent in reverse from 2004 (the first season of his show) to the beginnings of African slavery.[38]

Chappelle came right out of the gate on his new show in 2004 with a sketch that was sure to provoke controversy and confirm that he was indeed "America's number one source for offensive comedy." In the sketch, styled as a faux-news story in a bogus version of a documentary-style investigation,

Chappelle portrays Clayton Bigsby, "a *black* white supremacist." This bizarre contradiction is made possible because Clayton is blind and no one is willing to tell him that he is actually black. He grows up in a racist environment that embraces the Ku Klux Klan and cheers the notion of "white power." The bizarre irony of Clayton's black-to-white supremacist is captured in a moment when Chappelle as Bigsby pulls up next to a car that is blasting rap music. He shouts from the passenger seat for the presumably black passengers of the car next to him to turn that "jungle bunny music off!," as he is driven away by his white friend, Jasper, yelling at the top of his lungs, "I hate niggers!" The camera cuts to the car Clayton has been shouting at, and three white teenagers are revealed high-fiving each other and reveling in having been called "niggers"— by a black man, no less.[39]

Chappelle works to confront racism by exposing its arbitrary and capricious nature, born of willful ignorance and ingrained hatred from America's resistance to dealing with its legacy of slavery and its complex relationship with immigration and colonization. This confrontation of difficult subject matter through comedy uses the mask of minstrelsy (both white and black, in this case), role reversal, and the defiance of expectations, creating comic tension and encouraging the audience to laugh—even if it is just out of disbelief.

Chappelle offends to open up a discussion. For instance, Clayton Bigsby, at the book signing of his bluntly titled *Nigger Book*, yells, "Open up your hearts and let your hate out!" Getting the hate out is what Chappelle wants his audience to do in order to get the discourse on racism into the open. According to Chappelle, one of the primary reasons that 150 years of race hatred has been condoned in America is that meaningful and honest conversation about this complex subject and its reality has been suppressed. As he told James Lipton in an interview for *Inside the Actor's Studio*,

I think that America needs an honest discourse with itself. . . . Because it needs to be talked about. It's like the elephant in the room that nobody wants to talk about. . . . The truth is permanent, and everything else falls by the wayside. . . . I just want to be on the right side of history.[40]

In a 2004 interview, Chappelle addressed his confrontational style and its necessity in comedy, saying:

[Racism] is so ingrained in our culture; it's got such deep roots in American life. And the thing is that it's always kind of under-recognized; we don't like to deal with these things in our past. But if America was a dude, the best thing to do would be to confront your problems and admit that you have these problems, and that's how you get past them.[41]

Chappelle clearly sees the connection of confronting one's own history (whether black or white), to get at the larger issues in American society and to move forward to, at the very least, an awareness of how we all arrived here in the first place. In this, he echoes George Santayana's famous quote, "Those who cannot remember the past are condemned to repeat it."[42] Chappelle, in order to confront the past of racial injustice, and significantly white-America's legacy of slavery, uses comedy in order to view the trauma of history through the lens of comedy.

Dave Chappelle's connection to the vaudeville aesthetic of Bert Williams' era can be seen in two interviews in 2006, one with Anderson Cooper and the other with Oprah Winfrey. Chappelle felt some of his sketches that were planned for the never to be completed third season of *Chappelle's Show* were "socially irresponsible."[43] He pointed to the "pixie sketch," in which magical pixies appear to people and encourage them to reinforce stereotypes of their respective races. In this sketch, Chappelle is wearing blackface and dressed as a minstrel performer direct from the nineteenth century. According to Chappelle, during the filming of this sketch, a white crew member was laughing in a way that made him uncomfortable, forcing him to rethink the show. "It was the first time I felt that someone was not laughing with me but laughing at me."[44] In 1900 Edward Harrigan, a playwright and librettist of popular musical revues, feared that the new humor of Eastern European immigrant vaudevillians was "laughing *at* and not *with*" American audiences. Dave Chappelle's comment echoes Harrigan's admonition and brings the question of racially offensive comedy and its legacy to the forefront of his work. A look into how Chappelle ended up giving these interviews with Cooper and Winfrey is related to his astonishingly sudden rise to celebrity and fortune.

Chappelle's fame was not simply a flash in the pan, as the endurance of *Chappelle's Show* reveals (the DVD sales for the first two seasons are some of the highest on record). With its appeal to black, white, Latino, and Asian audiences, both male and female, Chappelle hit a nerve in the early twenty-first century that had arguably not been seen since the rise, fall, and resurrection of Richard Pryor in the late 1970s and early 1980s. In Chappelle's comedy, being offensive becomes necessary to create meaningful conversations that cannot happen otherwise. His interview with Lipton concludes with "I'm a comedian, man. That's how I look at the world. . . . The only way to know where the line is, is to cross it. What is life if nobody's crossing the line?"[45]

In an effort to cross the line of comedy, Chappelle confronts the history of minstrelsy by pointing out black celebrities who are hired to perform a form of minstrel buffoonery especially in the music industry. Chappelle's satire of the

1990's funk star Rick James and more recent rapper Lil Jon are comic targets for his understanding of why racial stereotypes are reinforced even with contemporary black performers. In stark contrast to Bert Williams' performance of the song *Nobody*, Chappelle portrays Rick James with a famous tag line that he would come to be identified with, shouting, "I'm Rick James bitch!" Complete with gold capped teeth, hair extensions, and an abusive attitude toward hangers-on and women, Chappelle would comment on musicians like James who promoted the stereotypes of black dress and behavior that reinforced the racial stereotyping found in minstrel shows of the past.

This can be witnessed when Chappelle portrays Lil Jon, as he pretends not to hear or comprehend what is being asked of him, "Ahhhhhhwhaaaaaat?" and also when he is in agreement with something that benefits him, saying, "Yeeeeaaaaahhhhh!." Chappelle then has the character contradict these minstrel-like responses by speaking in a sophisticated and thoughtful way without the affectation of dialect or ignorance. Chappelle comments on the act that is performed by this musician to sell his image and his records of an uneducated, "keeping it real" homeboy. In a sketch titled, "A Moment in the Life of Lil Jon," a doctor who is helping to set his arm fracture asks Lil Jon if he has any proof of insurance. He repeats over and over, "HAWHAAAAAAT?," in avoidance of the question, but when asked about drug use he replies, "It depends upon what you mean by drug use." In a *60 Minutes* television news-style interview, a middle-aged white female interviewer asks Lil Jon about his painful history:

INTERVIEWER: In my research I found out that you had been beaten brutally by two white police officers under mistaken identity. Is that correct?

LIL JON: [*In a serious overly articulated voice.*] Yes, that's true. That was the first time in my life that I that ever experienced any type of racial discrimination. I made up my mind then and there that I would transcend these social constraints. See madam, so often black youth are cast aside by a society that is too afraid of them to recognize their humanity. [*He pretends to cry.*]

INTERVIEWER: That must have been very painful for you?

LIL JON: YEEEEEEAHHHHHHHH![46]

The double standard of how black celebrities are viewed by their public and how they behave like black stereotypes in order to create an image of the street-wise, ghetto, homey, is consciously exploited and revealed on Chappelle's Show for what it is: a black mask of minstrelsy. Blacks in the early twentieth century, like Bert Williams, could only perform this image of black men as simple, foolhardy, buffoons. But beneath this racial mask they were able to signal to their more discerning audiences that the truth was hidden beneath the surface. Chappelle uses the legacy of minstrel shows to remember that the history of racial discrimination is still very much with us in the twenty-first century.

Dave Chappelle is able to go much further than Bert Williams. He chooses to wear both the mask of blackface minstrelsy and the relatively newer mask of whiteface to confront racial divides in his comedy in order to speak to multiracial audiences simultaneously. In the first episode of season 2 of *Chappelle's Show*, he again comes right out without holding back in his confrontation of race through the vaudeville aesthetic. In a sketch called "The Racial Draft," Chappelle sets up a scenario in which black, white, Latino, Jewish, and Asian "delegations" are asked to draft (as in professional sports franchises) racially ambiguous celebrities and public figures like Tiger Woods (half black/half Asian); Lenny Kravitz (half black/half Jewish); Colin Powell (all black but looks white); and the Wu Tang Clan (black musicians with an Asian-sounding band name—but not really Asian at all) into racially "pure" teams. First off is the black delegation represented by musician and actor Mos Def in a Jheri-curled version of a blaxploitation character direct from 1970s cinema. His first pick is Tiger Woods to become officially all-black. As played by Chappelle in the first of three protean performances in the sketch, Woods accepts his new place on the all-black team by saying, "So long, fried rice. Hello, fried chicken!" Tackling black and Asian stereotypes with the guise of Tiger Woods, who moves from being considered a half-breed to a full-blood, is made comical by the fact that Woods' appearance and his dark skin can never eradicate his Asian heritage simply through a declaration of racial drafting.

Chappelle takes on blackface minstrelsy in a reversal of this trope by wearing whiteface makeup when he plays the leader of the white delegation. In his "white man's parlance," stiff body movements, and uptight demeanor, Chappelle declares, "Will you cut the malarkey! There's a white man talking here!," when the audience openly boos him. After he drafts Colin Powell into the white delegation, Chappelle, now in the guise of a sports commentator, remarks that "last he heard," Powell was not white at all, being in fact "100 percent black." To top it off, the black delegation, to agree with this deal, gives away former Secretary of State Condoleezza Rice to the whites, as the ecstatic black delegation loudly cheers.[47]

The elusiveness and outright absurdity of these racial divisions points to how the United States cannot seem to come to terms with its concerns surrounding race and ethnicity. The promise of a post-Civil War melting-pot nation that embraces immigrants and former enslaved blacks as part of its citizenry may have come a long way since the turn of the twentieth century, but still has much further to go in reconciling its racial past with the unrest and confusion of its conflicted present. To conclude this bizarre and ever-complicated ethnic identification game, the Asian delegation chooses to draft the Wu Tang Clan, two black hip-hop artists, whose band name is enough to make them Asians. As the duo accepts their new team-Asia nomination, the sketch ends with Wu Tang's joyful declaration of "*Konichiwa*, bitches!," comically fusing Japanese with black argot.

As the "Racial Draft" reveals, Dave Chappelle's performance of Tiger Woods, the leader of the white delegation, and a black sports commentator, displays the virtuosity of the protean comic performer, coupled with the whiteface/blackface masks of minstrelsy and the legacy of the vaudeville stage in the early twenty-first century. However, this racial humor would later backfire on Chappelle in the third season of *Chappelle's Show* with the now-infamous pixie sketch. This episode would ultimately force Chappelle to reconsider his multi-million dollar contract from Comedy Central and more importantly reconsider his future as a comic artist. The pixie sketch features Chappelle in blackface wearing the burnt cork and servant costume appropriated from minstrelsy. The pixie first appears as the conscience of a middle-class black man who does not want to choose chicken over fish as an airplane meal, since it will play into the racist stereotype of blacks craving fried chicken. The minstrel pixie tap-dances and encourages Chappelle to choose the chicken. The sketch looks at these racist connotations as they affect the day-to-day existence of blacks who have to consistently resist oversimplified images of their culture.

Later the pixie is confronted by two rappers called the Yin Yang Twins—in another pseudo-Asian, rap-group naming—who appear on a reality show called *Cribs*. The musicians wear the gold chains and sport gear of the ghetto-born stereotyped musicians who suddenly become rich, and show off their expensive and ostentatious high-end cars, clothes, and houses. The sketch ends with the rappers, without a hint of irony, howling happily like crazed monkeys. Chappelle as the blackface-minstrel pixie is horrified, talking directly to the audience saying, "Never thought I'd say this, but *I'm* embarrassed!"[48]

After Dave Chappelle's third season walkout and getaway to Africa, a *Time* magazine interviewer wrote that Chappelle was concerned "if the new season of the show had gone from sending up stereotypes to reinforcing them."[49] As interviewer John Farley notes, "The crux of [Chappelle's] crisis seems to boil down to his almost obsessive need to 'check my intentions.' He uses the phrase a few times during the interview and explains that it means really making sure that he's doing what he's doing for the right reasons." Chappelle points to his inner circle, as well as his own trust issues, as he began to believe that he was not being laughed *with* (particularly by non-blacks) but rather laughed *at*. As witnessed with the white teens who enjoy being called "niggers" in the black-white supremacist sketch, Chappelle worries that the racial stereotyping is being reinforced and laughed at for reasons unrelated to his intentions.

Chappelle's fear of working against his own interests and creating a modern-day minstrel show forced him to reevaluate his work and to do so he went to Africa to get some perspective. As Chappelle explained in an interview with James Lipton, going to Africa "reminded me, I'm a real person," not just a celebrity, not just a commodity.[50] Chappelle's insight extends to how creativity is exploited in Hollywood to the point where strong and creative people are driven to extreme, damaging actions. Chappelle, while discussing friend and fellow comedian Martin Lawrence, asked the *Actor's Studio* audience, "So, let me ask you this. What is happening in Hollywood that a guy that tough [Lawrence] will be on the street waving a gun screaming, 'They are trying to kill me!'? What's going on? Why is Dave Chappelle going to Africa?" Chappelle concludes with the notion that perhaps it is not the presumed craziness of artists that is the issue. "Maybe that environment [of Hollywood] is a little sick," he states.[51]

It was not until Dave Chappelle wore actual blackface in the pixie sketch that his concerns became paramount as to where the line of offensive comedy could be crossed. As he said to Oprah Winfrey, blackface is "the visual personification of the N-word."[52] Donning the whiteface mask and portraying black stereotypes in clothing and physical expression have always been Chappelle's way into conversations about race, but the actual use of burnt cork appears to have confronted Chappelle with a legacy that may have been just too painful to deal with. The question that he faced about being laughed at rather than with is the key to understanding how this vaudeville aesthetic works.

Bert Williams chose to wear blackface in a time when making that choice meant using a performance mask to hide behind in order to confront racist images in his comedy. But in the twenty-first century, Chappelle—even though the choice may appear less fraught, and even though he had portrayed any and all stereotypes of race required for his comedy to be funny as well as meaningful—never actually wore the blackface mask until the pixie sketch. Had Chappelle, as the self-proclaimed "source for offensive comedy," gone too far over the line, even for him?

In an interview after the pixie sketch was shown by collaborators Charlie Murphy and Donnell Rawlings to a live audience in Chappelle's absence, the overriding sentiment was that Chappelle had achieved his goal of creating a much-needed racial discourse that could be had only through laughing *with* as well as *at* the pixie sketch simultaneously. As one black female audience member noted, "I thought it was funny. I thought it was intelligent. It was uncomfortable and I think that's the point of it. It's supposed to draw attention to people's stereotypes, and talk about it and make it funny. That's why the show's successful. I think that's the joint."[53] Chappelle appeared to concur when, in yet another moment of candor during his interview with Lipton, he described the journey he is on in his own work:

> I don't know how the whole Dave Chappelle thing is gonna end. But I feel like I'm gonna be like some kind of parable. By either what you're supposed to do, or you're not supposed to do. I'm gonna be either a legend or just some tragic fuckin' story, but I'm goin' full throttle. I'm goin' all the way. I'm eager to find out how this is gonna resolve itself.[54]

As James Lipton relates during the interview, Richard Pryor felt he had "passed the torch" of comedy to Dave Chappelle. The evolution from Bert Williams to Richard Pryor to Chappelle is the legacy of the comic mask, as it comments on race and American society while hiding in plain sight through comic performance. Along with the recognition of their artistry, these comedians were plagued by the notoriety that came along with their success. Chappelle's anxiety about the cost of fame can be seen as early as 1998, in his first HBO special, which he ends by saying, "I hope this shit don't make me famous!" Here we can see that he is already worried about how his inner circle and his fans will begin to treat him differently. And perhaps this is the point, that in the end the pressures placed on artists from Williams to Pryor to Chappelle become greater and greater as their success mounts. Money and influence breed a sickness that leaves the comic artist with a dilemma of how to be true to his craft while at the same time producing acts that have to hew to an economic reality that may not feed their work and ultimately works against them. Dave Chappelle made his choice to walk away from tens of millions of dollars, and that road less traveled by has made all the difference.

Bert Williams and Dave Chappelle, like other blackface performers before them, trouble the notion of how blackface was and is simply a "theatrical device," not unlike clowns' white makeup, and the fraught racial stereotyping that comes along with this racial masking ultimately transforms their comedy into something they had not intended. Robert C. Toll, popular entertainment historian, writes that when,

> Audiences could believe minstrels' caricatures of blacks, they could also, on another level, understand that the minstrel show was an unthreatening white man's charade. The blackface mask allowed performers, and perhaps

also their patrons, to cast off their inhibitions and to play out their fantasies of themselves in their stereotypes of blacks.[55]

Williams, like Chappelle being asked repeatedly to perform the Rick James character in concert, was consistently asked to perform the song "Nobody" throughout his theatrical career, a song about erasing one's own personal identity. This master of pantomime, song and dance, and the comic sketch, could never shake off the image of the burnt-cork mask. Even at the height of his popularity, Bert Williams remained a solitary figure who was an outsider both on- and offstage, as his experience with the Actor's Equity Strike of 1919 made clear.

Beginning with Clayton Bigsby in season 1 of *Chappelle's Show* and moving to the "Racial Draft" in season 2, and finally the pixie sketch of season 3, Chappelle has managed to increase the stakes in his need to express offensive comedy that has meaning beyond just the jokes. How blackface/whiteface masks have influenced Chappelle's comedy is clear from the success of how it is used by him in each of his show's successive seasons and in his stand-up work. It also alienated him from his colleagues and audiences in the end. As Williams and Walker's musical successes with *In Dahomey*, *Abyssinia*, and *Shuffle Along* showed through W. E. B. Dubois' notion of double consciousness, the black audience was in on the joke, even if the white audience was not; however, the black audience was still relegated to "nigger heaven," segregated from the orchestra seating of whites.

Blackface minstrelsy's history from Bert Williams' impressive twenty-nine-year stage career, to the phenomenal success of the radio and television comedy *Amos 'n' Andy*, to Richard Pryor's breakthrough of race-consciousness comedy in the 1970s, to the rapid rise and fall of *Chappelle's Show*, reveals the powerful and troubled legacy of racial stereotyping in comedy, and the ambivalent effect on black and white audiences into the early twenty-first century. As reported in the *New York Times* as of August 2013, Chappelle is considering touring with an original stand-up act again. How the legacy of the vaudeville aesthetic with regard to black masking, minstrelsy, and medicine show stump speeches moves into the future, will be interesting to observe through the next generation of comedians coming-up alongside Dave Chappelle.[56]

Notes

1 Bert Williams, "Elder Eatmore's Sermon on Generosity," recorded on *Bert Williams, The Remaining Titles: 1915–1921*. Document Records (DOCD-5661), 1999.

2 Ralph Ellison, "Change the Joke and Slip the Yoke," in *Shadow and Act* (New York: Random House, 1964), 53–55.

3 Laurence Senelick, "Minstrel Shows," in *The Cambridge Guide to American Theatre*, 2nd ed., ed. Don B. Wilmeth (Cambridge: Cambridge University Press, 2007), 447.

4 Michael Rogin, *Blackface, White Noise: Jewish Immigrants in the Hollywood Melting Pot* (Berkeley, CA: University of California Press, 1996), 53.

5 James Phillips, "Zanni," in *Fools and Jesters in Literature, Art, and History: Bio-Bibliographical Sourcebook*, ed. Vicki K. Janik (Westport, CT: Greenwood Press, 1998), 510.

6 Edward Christy is credited for refining the format from Emmett's original. See "People & Events: Edward P. Christy, 1815–1862," *American Experience* website, http://www.pbs.org/wgbh/amex/foster/peopleevents/p_christy.html.

7 Robert C. Toll, *Blacking Up: The Minstrel Show in Nineteenth-Century America* (New York: Oxford University Press, 1974), 52, 55, 56.

8 Bert Williams, "Bert Williams Tells of Walker," *Indianapolis Freeman*, January 14, 1911: 5.

9 Edmond Gagey, *The San Francisco Stage: A History* (1950; second printing, New York: Columbia University Press, 1970), 6–7, 13.

10 Camille F. Forbes, *Introducing Bert Williams: Burnt Cork, Broadway, and the Story of America's First Black Star* (New York: Basic Civitas Books, 2008),100.

11 Eric Ledell Smith, *Bert Williams: A Biography of the Pioneer Black Comedian* (Jefferson, NC: McFarland, 1992), 50.

12 Will Marion Cook, *The Music and Scripts of "In Dahomey": Music of the United States*, vol. 25 (New York: A-R Editions, 1996), xxiv.

13 "*Dahomey* on Broadway," *New York Times*, February 19, 1903: 9.

14 W. E. B. Du Bois, *The Souls of Black Folks*, 5th ed. (Chicago: A. C. McClurg, 1903; Mineola, NY: Dover reprint, 1994), 9–24.

15 Douglas Gilbert, *American Vaudeville: Its Life and Times* (New York: Dover, 1940), 285–86 (see introduction, n. 5).

16 Unidentified clipping, "Bert Williams a Real Optimist," February 6, 1921, Bert Williams file, Harvard Theatre Collection, Houghton Library.

17 Unidentified clipping, "Bert Williams a Real Optimist," February 6, 1921, Bert Williams file, Harvard Theatre Collection, Houghton Library.

18 Lyrics Alex Rogers, Music Bert Williams, "Nobody," from *Abyssinia*, 1905.

19 Lester A. Walton, "Bert Williams, Philosopher," *New York Age*, December 29, 1917: 6.

20 Anthony Slide, ed., *The Encyclopedia of Vaudeville* (Westport, CT: Greenwood Press, 1994), 84; Forbes, *Introducing Bert Williams*, 273.

21 "Bert Williams a Real Optimist," Bert Williams file, Harvard Theatre Collection, Houghton Library.

22 Walton, "Bert Williams, Philosopher," 6.

23 Walton, "Bert Williams, Philosopher," 6.

24 Bert Williams, "The Comic Side of Trouble," *American Magazine*, January 1918, 60.

25 "Bert Williams a Real Optimist," Bert Williams file, Harvard Theatre Collection, Houghton Library.

26 Aida Overton Walker, "Interview," *Pittsburgh Leader*, May 11, 1906.

27 Bert Williams quoted in Forbes, *Introducing Bert Williams*, 297.

28 See also *The Amos 'n' Andy Show* in Chapter 1.

29 Gosden and Correll would be replaced by black performers Alvin Childress and Spencer Williams for the television series.

30 Frank Gosden and Charles Correll, "The Locked Trunk's Secret," *The Amos 'n' Andy Radio Show*, original broadcast date, November 5, 1943, http://www.radiolovers.com/shows/A/amosandy/1943/AMOSANDY43110532-22-mono25m51s_TheLockedTrunksSecret_.mp3.

31 Melvin Patrick Ely, *The Adventures of Amos 'n' Andy: A Social History of an American Phenomenon* (Richmond, VA: University of Virginia Press, 2001), 9.

32 Richard Pryor, "Bicentennial Prayer," *Richard Pryor: The Anthology, 1968–1992*, recordings produced by Robert Marchese, Richard Pryor, David Banks, and Biff Dawes (Los Angeles, CA: Rhino Entertainment Company, Warner Archives, 2001).

33 Pryor, "Africa," *Richard Pryor: The Anthology*.

34 Paul Mooney, "Ask a Black Dude," *Chappelle's Show*, season 1, episode 5, aired February 19, 2003 (Hollywood, CA and Paramount Pictures Home Entertainment, 2004), DVD.

35 Jim Carnes, "Dave Chappelle Lets Rude Crowd Have It, Sticks Up for Cosby's Comment," *Sacramento Bee*, June 18, 2004, http://www.freerepublic.com/focus/news/1156342/posts.

36 Dave Chappelle, *HBO Comedy Half-Hour: Dave Chappelle*, directed by Troy Miller (North Hollywood, CA: Dakota Pictures, 1998), HBO TV.

37 Dave Chappelle and Neal Brennen, "The Niggar Family," *Chappelle's Show*, season 2, episode 2, aired January 28, 2004 (Hollywood, CA: Paramount Pictures Home Entertainment, 2005), DVD.

38 Dave Chappelle and Neal Brennen, "Genetic Dissenter," *Chappelle's Show*, season 1, episode 2, aired January 29, 2003 (Hollywood, CA: Paramount Pictures Home Entertainment, 2004), DVD.

39 Dave Chappelle and Neal Brennen, "Frontline: Clayton Bigsby," *Chappelle's Show*, season 1, episode 1, aired January 22, 2003 (Hollywood, CA: Paramount Pictures Home Entertainment, 2004), DVD.

40 Dave Chappelle, interview by James Lipton, *Inside the Actor's Studio: Dave Chappelle* (New York, NY: Sony/BMG Music Entertainment, 2006), DVD.

41 Dave Chappelle, interview by David Katz, "What's So Funny about Race?," in *The "High Times" Reader*, eds., Annie Nocenti and Ruth Baldwin (New York: Nation Books, 2004), 432.

42 George Santayana, *Reason in Common Sense*, vol. 1 of *The Life of Reason* (New York: Charles Scribner's Sons, 1905), 284.

43 Dave Chappelle, interview by Anderson Cooper, *Anderson Cooper 360*, CNN, July 7, 2006, http://transcripts.cnn.com/TRANSCRIPTS/0607/07/acd.01.html.

44 Dave Chappelle, interview by Oprah Winfrey, "Chappelle's Story: Dave's Moral Dilemma," *The Oprah Winfrey Show*, February 3, 2006, www.oprah.com/oprahshow/Chappelles-Story/.

45 Lipton, *Inside the Actor's Studio: Dave Chappelle*.

46 Dave Chappelle and Neal Brennen, "A Moment in the Life of Lil Jon," *Chappelle's Show*, season 2, episode 6, aired February 25, 2004 (Hollywood, CA: Paramount Pictures Home Entertainment, 2005), DVD.

47 Dave Chappelle and Neal Brennen, "The Racial Draft," *Chappelle's Show*, season 2, episode 1, aired January 21, 2004 (Hollywood, CA: Paramount Pictures Home Entertainment, January 2004), DVD.

48 Dave Chappelle and Neal Brennen, "The Lost Episodes," *Chappelle's Show*, season 3, episode 2, aired July 16, 2006 (Hollywood, CA: Paramount Pictures Home Entertainment, 2006), DVD.

49 Dave Chappelle, interview by John Farley, "On the Beach with Dave Chappelle," *Time*, May 15, 2005, http://www.time.com/time/arts/article/0,8599,1061415,00.html

50 Lipton, *Inside the Actor's Studio: Dave Chappelle*.

51 Lipton, *Inside the Actor's Studio: Dave Chappelle*.

52 Chappelle, interview by Winfrey, "Chappelle's Story."

53 Chappelle and Brennen, "The Lost Episodes," *Chappelle's Show*.

54 Lipton, *Inside the Actor's Studio: Dave Chappelle*.

55 Robert C. Toll, "Show Biz in Blackface: The Evolution of the Minstrel Show as a Theatrical Form," in *American Popular Entertainment: Papers and Proceedings of the Conference on the History of American Popular Entertainment*, ed. Myron Matlaw (Westport, CT: Greenwood Press, 1977), 23.

56 Jason Zinoman, "A Comic Quits Quitting," *New York Times*, August 15, 2013, http://www.nytimes.com/2013/08/18/arts/dave-chappelle-returns-to-stand-up-with-stories-to-tell.html?pagewanted=all&_r=0.

Epilogue

The rule is henceforth the molecular, the random. As for the real,
for meaning and for truth, they are the exceptions—that is to say,
a mystery.

PASSWORDS, JEAN BAUDRILLARD

Comedy in America over the past one hundred and twenty plus years has questioned the conventional wisdom and "truth" of institutional thinking. Vaudeville acts during the first two decades of the twentieth century depicted a modernist industrialized nation at a time of one of its most intensive paradigm shifts. Vaudeville comedy with its short, sharp, shocks used the two-man act, burlesque, the stump speech, and the art of the *tummler* in order to confront fixed notions of class, ethnicity, gender, and race. Characters derived from minstrelsy, medicine shows, and the ethnic humor of early twentieth century immigrants, commented on longstanding truths troubled by the popular comic entertainers examined here.

As confirmation of this notion, Stephen Colbert claims that one of the essential issues of our time is that Americans have replaced truth with "truthiness." When coining the term in 2005 on *The Colbert Report* he announced:

> Face it folks. We are a divided nation. Not between democrats and republicans, or conservatives and liberals, or tops and bottoms. No. We are divided by those who think with their head, and those who know with their heart. . . . The "truthiness" is anyone can read the news to you. I promise to feel the news *at* you.[1]

The search for truthiness in comedy is derived from these humorists' attacks on absolutists who claim to have the truth exclusively on their side.

Between the poles of Groucho Marx and Larry David, radio and television created a place for comic vaudevillians. From the blackface act of Bert Williams to the whiteface performance of Dave Chappelle, the truthiness of identity was confronted and challenged during this period of comedy history. From Baby Snooks and Allen's Alley to The Hinkenloopers and Sergeant Bilko, a host of innovators drew their inspiration from this comic form, including Mort Sahl and Lenny Bruce. Characters like Lisa Loopner, Mudbone, and Tracy "I-am-the-third-heat!" Jordan, became iconic representations of contemporary vaudeville by Gilda Radner, Richard Pryor, and Tracy Morgan respectively.

In the first season of *Saturday Night Live* (1975) for instance, Richard Pryor hosted and performed a sketch with cast member Chevy Chase. In order to apply for a job, the white employer (Chase) engaged the black applicant (Pryor) in a word association test:

CHASE: Spear-chucker.
PRYOR: White trash.
CHASE: Jungle bunny!
PRYOR: Honky.
CHASE: Spade.
PRYOR: Honky-honky.
CHASE: Nigger.
PRYOR: *Dead* honky.[2]

It was the first time in the history of a nationally televised comedy routine that a white man would address a black using the N-word. For Pryor this sketch was standard fare for exposing the hostility that had followed him his whole life, but for many white audience members it was a revelation that racism could be so entrenched in American culture. This is also an instance where comedy in America connected Bert Williams and Richard Pryor with the anger of the casual but systemic racism that whites had expressed since the post-Civil War era without overtly acknowledging it. Williams expressed his anger from the stage by threatening his blackface "son" played by Eddie Cantor in the porter sketch, and chastising W. C. Fields for his exclusion from the actors' union strike. Pryor also expressed this normalized racism through a form of comedy that embraced the tropes of minstrelsy and infused it with a barely suppressed virulent rage that came from many years of humiliation and discrimination. Dave Chappelle took this even further, staging a walk-out from celebrity and fortune.

Since its beginnings in the late nineteenth century, American comedy continues to reinforce, as Larry David reminds us, that "the bad thoughts are funny."[3] The bad thoughts are the substance of the vaudeville aesthetic. This stage practice sprung from the pain and struggle of the bigotry leveled at ethnic immigrants, the sexism shown toward marginalized women, and the legacy of slavery and Jim Crow racism that has haunted black Americans into the twenty-first century. It embraces the notion that we are complex beings with contradictory notions of sociocultural values and behaviors. As contemporary cultural theorist Stephen Duncombe notes with regard to Anglo-political moral systems:

> It does no good to condemn these feelings insisting that people must not think bad thoughts. This way leads to hypocrisy and self-deception and a politics obsessed with purity and authenticity. . . . We have to make peace with our desires—violent, racist, and sexist as they may be—and find safe expression for them.[4]

One of the places for this expression of suppressed desire and anger is found in comedy formed from the vaudeville aesthetic.

New media theorists David Thorburn and Henry Jenkins comment in *Rethinking Media Change*, that "contemporary experiments in story-telling are crossing and combining several media, exploiting computer games or web-based environments that offer immersive and interactive experiences that mobilize our familiarity with traditional narrative genres drawn from books, movies, and television."[5] As if in response to this theory, comedian Jerry Seinfeld—co-creator of the television phenomenon, *Seinfeld*—has produced a new web series of ten- to twenty-minute comedy segments that feature a simple two-person act called *Comedians in Cars Getting Coffee*. This latest incarnation of the vaudeville aesthetic features various comedians chatting with Seinfeld while driving in vintage cars as they go out for coffee. It combines the variety, non-narrative, talk show format of Groucho Marx and *You Bet Your Life* and Dave Chappelle's casual interactions with guests and audiences on *Chappelle's Show* for the digitalized age.

As new media evolves into the twenty-first century, internet platforms like *YouTube* incorporate the vaudeville aesthetic with the short form of homemade videos that anyone can create and disseminate. This new form of vaudeville comedy requires only having an act with no other criteria save that it is short, self-contained, and reaches its audience with an immediacy that is sustained in the concise form that traditional vaudeville used to provide audiences with "something for everyone." Literally *YouTube*, *Facebook*, and *Twitter* are forums that have become an unlimited and uncensored form of entertainment and social commentary where any "act"—video or written text—is accepted and "followed" by whoever can get the viewer's attention. The internet is readily accessible to creators of content and audiences alike. The list of acts on *YouTube* is surprisingly familiar, including videos of funny songs, dances, comic sketches and characters, and eccentric anthropomorphic animal acts. It emulates its predecessor of the turn-of-the-twentieth-century vaudeville stage with its multiplicity of amateur and professional performances. The internet represents the next wave of the vaudeville aesthetic.

Like vaudeville, some of the acts found there are inspiring and genuinely engaging, most are average, and some are terrible, but the opportunity exists to innovate and create with the freedom and experimentation that was created through the vaudeville aesthetic. Larry David, Tina Fey, Stephen Colbert, and Dave Chappelle have moved vaudeville comedy into a new century with new media forms. These "new" vaudevillians are continuing to laugh at, as well as with, audiences that are racially, ethnically, and economically complex, crossing borders defined by normative notions of sociocultural behaviors. The comedy born of Groucho Marx as Jewish-insult-provocateur-*tummler*, Mae West as the insurgent new woman, Will Rogers as half-breed Native American everyman, and Bert Williams as the double-conscious "negro" minstrel, challenged these over-simplified and stereotyped identifications. Formerly submerged and inferred, these stereotypes are now explicitly exposed as patently false by David, Fey, Colbert, and Chappelle.

Vaudeville comedy and its successor in contemporary comedy is one of the few forums in current media that gets at the truth through purposefully offensive performances. Nobel laureate economist Paul Krugman's recent *New York Times* article, titled "Moment of Truthiness," provides a summation of America's present circumstances: "We have an ill-informed or misinformed electorate, politicians who gleefully add to the misinformation, and watchdogs who are afraid to bark."[6] The "new" comic vaudevillians of the early twenty-first century—like their fellows of the early twentieth century— are the watchdogs that are *not* afraid to bark.

Notes

1 Stephen Colbert, "Truthiness," *The Colbert Report*, 2005–present. Created by Stephen Colbert. New York: Comedy Central, www.colbertnation.com, webcast. Airdates, October 17, 2005 to present.

2 Paul Mooney, "Job Interview with Richard Pryor and Chevy Chase," *Saturday Night Live*, season 1, episode 7. Airdate December 13, 1975, DVD streamed via Netflix.

3 Ricky Gervais, "Ricky Gervais Meets . . . Larry David." Dir. Niall Downing. Objective Productions, Channel 4 Television Corporation, UK. Airdate January 5, 2006, Television Movie.

4 Stephen Duncombe, *Dream: Re-Imagining Progressive Politics in an Age of Fantasy* (New York: The New Press, 2007), 76.

5 David Thorburn and Henry Jenkins, eds, *Rethinking Media Change: The Aesthetics of Transition* (Cambridge, MA: The MIT Press, 2003), 3.

6 Paul Krugman, "Moment of Truthiness," *New York Times*, August 15, 2013, http://www.nytimes.com/2013/08/16/opinion/krugman-moment-of-truthiness.html?_r=0.

Bibliography

Videography and CD recordings

Fred Allen

Town Hall Tonight. Lawrence G. Blochman Collection, Division of Rare Books and Special Collections, William Robertson Coe Library, University of Wyoming, Laramie. (1935–1939).

Texaco Star Theatre. Lawrence G. Blochman Collection, Division of Rare Books and Special Collections, William Robertson Coe Library, University of * Wyoming, Laramie. (1941–1944).

Lucille Ball

Lucille Ball: Finding Lucy. American Masters Series, PBS. Writ. Thomas Wagner. Dir. Pamela Mason Wagner. Airdate, December 3, 2000.

I Love Lucy: The Complete Series, seasons 1–7. Created by Lucille Ball and Desi Arnaz. Hollywood, CA: Paramount Pictures Home Entertainment, 2007. Airdates, October 15, 1951 to May 6, 1957, DVD.

Lenny Bruce

Lenny Bruce Without Tears, written by Barbara Baker, Fred Baker, and John Parson, directed by Fred Baker. New York: Fred Baker Films, 1972.

Dave Chappelle

Dave Chappelle: Killin' Em Softly. Writ. Dave Chappelle. Dir. Stan Lathan. (New York: Home Box Office, 2000), HBO-TV.

Dave Chappelle Live at the Fillmore: For What It's Worth. Writ. Dave Chappelle. Dir. Stan Lathan. (Culver City, CA: Sony Picture Home Entertainment, 2004), DVD.

Chappelle's Show, seasons 1–2 and "Lost Episodes (season 3)" Created by Dave Chappelle and Neal Brennen (Hollywood, CA: Paramount Pictures Home Entertainment, 2004), DVD.

HBO Comedy Half-Hour: Dave Chappelle. Writ. Dave Chappelle. Dir. Troy Miller (North Hollywood, CA: Dakota Pictures, 1998), HBO TV.

Inside the Actor's Studio: Dave Chappelle. Created by James Lipton (New York, NY: Sony/BMG Music Entertainment, 2006), DVD.

Stephen Colbert

The Colbert Report, 2005–present. Created by Stephen Colbert. New York: Comedy Central, www.colbertnation.com, webcast. Airdates, October 17, 2005 to present.

"Colbert Roasts Bush—2006 White House Correspondents' Dinner," from White House Correspondents' Association Dinner, televised by C-SPAN on April 29, 2006, posted by "Ocular Politics," December 15, 2010, YouTube.

Larry David

Curb Your Enthusiasm, seasons 1–7. Created by Larry David (New York: Home Box Office, 2010), DVD.

Curb Your Enthusiasm, season 8. Created by Larry David (New York: Home Box Office, 2011), HBO-TV.

Tina Fey

30 Rock, seasons 1–7. Created by Tina Fey. Universal City, CA: Universal Studios Home Entertainment, DVD. Airdates, October 11, 2006 to January 31, 2013, DVD.

The Women of SNL – Tina Fey, Amy Poehler, Maya Rudolph, Molly Shannon, and Kristen Wiig. Writ. Tina Fey. Created by Lorne Michaels. Universal City, CA: Universal Studios Home Entertainment, 2012, DVD.

W. C. Fields

W. C. Fields, Straight Up. Writ. Joe Adamson and Ronald J. Fields. Dir. Joe Adamson. Prod. Robert B. Weide and Whyaduck Productions. Santa Monica, CA: Direct Cinema Limited, 1986, DVD.

Buster Keaton

Buster Keaton: A Hard Act to Follow. American Masters Series, PBS. Writ. and Dir. David Gill and Kevin Brownlow. Airdate, September 30, 1987.

The Buster Keaton Collection (Includes: *The Playhouse, Steamboat Bill Jr., The General*, and several other shorts) Montreal, Canada: St. Clair Vision, 2007, DVD.

The Buster Keaton MGM Collection: The Cameraman, Spite Marriage, Free and Easy. Burbank, CA: Warner Home Video, 2004, DVD.

Buster Keaton: The Short Films Collection, 1920–1923 (Includes: *The Haunted House, One Week, The Goat, The Playhouse, Cops, The Balloonatic*, and several other shorts). New York: Kino International, 2011, DVD.

Make 'Em Laugh: The Funny Business of America. Writ. Michael Kantor and Laurence Maslon. Dir. Michael Kantor (New York: Rhino Entertainment, 2008), DVD.

Groucho and The Marx Brothers

Groucho Marx: You Bet Your Life – The Best Episodes. Los Angeles, CA: Shout! Factory, 2004, DVD.

The Marx Brothers Collection (Includes: *The Cocoanuts, Animal Crackers, Monkey Business, Horse Feathers, Duck Soup*), Paramount Studios: Universal Home Video, Silver Screen Collection, 2004, DVD.

The Marx Brothers in a Nutshell. Writ. Joe Adamson and Robert B. Weide. Dir. Richard Patterson. Prod. Robert B. Weide and Whyaduck Productions. Stamford, CT: Vestron Video, 1982, DVD.

In Living Color

In Living Color, Seasons 1–5. Created by Keenan Ivory and Damon Wayans. Los Angeles, CA: 20th Century Fox Home Entertainment. Airdates, April 15, 1990 – May 19, 1994, DVD.

Richard Pryor

Richard Pryor: The Anthology, 1968–1992, recordings produced by Robert Marchese, Richard Pryor, David Banks, and Biff Dawes (Los Angeles, CA: Rhino Entertainment Company, Warner Archives, 2001), CD.

Richard Pryor: Live at the Sunset Strip. Writ. Richard Pryor. Dir. Joe Layton. Culver City, CA: Columbia Tristar, 1982, DVD.

Will Rogers

Will Rogers: Rediscovering Will Rogers American Masters Series, PBS. Writ. and
   Dir. Stephan Chodorov. Airdate, November 30, 1994.
The Story of Will Rogers. Writ. Richard Hanser and Rod Reed. Dir. Donald B.
   Hyatt (Newton: NJ: Shanachie Entertainment, 2003), DVD, originally released
   by NBC *News Presents,* 1961.

Mort Sahl

Mort Sahl: The Loyal Opposition. Writ. and Dir. Robert B. Weide. Prod. Robert B.
   Weide and Whyaduck Productions and PBS American Masters Series. Airdate,
   September 18, 1989.

SCTV

Second City Television Network – SCTV: Second City Television Network –
   (Volumes 1–3) Los Angeles, CA: Shout Factory Theatre. Airdates, September
   21, 1976 – July 17, 1984, DVD.

SNL

Saturday Night Live – The Complete First Four Seasons (Seasons 1–4), 1975–
   1979. Created by Lorne Michaels. Universal City, CA: Universal Studios Home
   Entertainment. Airdates, October 11, 1975 to May 26, 1979, DVD.

Jerry Seinfeld and Larry David

Seinfeld, seasons 1–9. Created by Larry David and Jerry Seinfeld. Culver City,
   CA: Sony Pictures Home Entertainment, 2004, Airdates, July 5, 1989 to May
   14, 1998, DVD.
Comedian. Writ. Jerry Seinfeld. Dir. Christian Charles. (Burbank, CA: Buena Vista
   Productions, 2002), DVD.
Comedians in Cars Getting Coffee. Created by Jerry Seinfeld,
   (comediansincarsgettingcoffee.com, June 13, 2013), Web Series.

Phil Silvers

Sgt. Bilko: The Phil Silvers Show—50th Anniversary Edition, seasons 1–4. Created
   by Nat Hiken and Phil Silvers. (Hollywood, CA: Paramount Pictures Home
   Entertainment, 2006). Airdates, September 20, 1955 – June 19, 1959, DVD.

American Vaudeville

Vaudeville. American Masters Series, PBS. Written and Conceived by Greg
   Palmer. New York: Fox Lorber Home Video, 1997, DVD.

Bert Williams

"Elder Eatmore's Sermon on Generosity," recorded on *Bert Williams, The
   Remaining Titles: 1915–1921.* Document Records (DOCD-5661), 1999.

Manuscripts and archives

Brooklyn History Collection, Brooklyn Public Library, Brooklyn, New York: *Mae
   West clippings file.*
Harvard Theatre Collection, The Houghton Library, Harvard University, Cambridge,
   MA.
Lawrence G. Blochman Collection, Division of Rare Books and Special
   Collections, William Robertson Coe Library, University of Wyoming, Laramie,
   WY: *Fred Allen special collection.*

Library of Congress, Rare Book and Manuscript Division, Washington, DC:
    Groucho Marx papers and manuscripts special collection.
New York Public Library Rare Book and Manuscript Division, New York City.
Robinson Locke Collection of Theatrical Scrapbooks, Billy Rose Theatre
    Collection, New York Public Library for the Performing Arts, New York City:
    Eddie Cantor clippings file.
    W.C. Fields clippings file.
    Buster Keaton clippings file.
    The Marx Brothers clippings file.
    Will Rogers, clippings file.
    Mae West clippings file.
    Bert Williams clippings file.
University of Iowa Library, Special Collections Department, Iowa City, IA:
    Keith/Albee collection.
University of Southern California, Department of Special Collections, Doheny
    Library, Los Angeles, CA: *Gosden and Correll collection, 1928–1960.*
Will Rogers Memorial Museums, Claremore, OK.

Primary sources and recordings

Albee, Edward F. "Twenty Years of Vaudeville." *Variety* 72, no. 3, September 6,
    1923: 18.
Allen, Fred. *Treadmill to Oblivion: My Days in Radio*. Boston, MA: Little, Brown,
    1954.
Allen, Steve. *The Funny Men*. New York: Simon and Schuster, 1956.
Baker, Barbara, Fred Baker, and John Parson, directed by Fred Baker. *Lenny Bruce
    Without Tears*. New York: Fred Baker Films, 1972.
Brice, Fanny. "Baby Snooks Is 25!" *Radio Life Magazine*, April 7, 1946: 28.
Caesar, Sid with Eddy Friedfeld. *Caesar's Hours: My Life in Comedy with Love
    and Laughter*. New York: Public Affairs Books, 2005.
Cannon, Kay, and Tina Fey. "Lee Marvin vs. Derek Jeter," *30 Rock*, season 4.
    Universal City, CA: Universal Studios, 2010.
Cantor, Eddie. *World's Book of Best Jokes*. Cleveland: World Publishing, 1943.
Cantor, Eddie, with Jane Kesner Ardmore. *Take My Life*. Garden City, NY:
    Doubleday, 1957.
Cantor, Eddie and David Freedman. *Ziegfeld: The Great Glorifier*. New York: Alfred
    H. King, 1934.
Chaplin, Charles. *My Autobiography*. New York: Simon and Schuster, 1964.
Christy, Edward P. "People Events: Edward P. Christy, 1815–1862." *American
    Experience* website, http://www.pbs.org/wgbh/amex/foster/peopleevents/p_
    christy.html.
"Colbert Roasts Bush—2006 White House Correspondents' Dinner," YouTube
    video, 24:11, from White House Correspondents' Association Dinner, televised
    by C-SPAN on April 29, 2006, posted by "Ocular Politics," December 15, 2010,
    http://www.youtube.com/watch?v=U7FTF4Oz4dI.

Colbert, Stephen. "Colbert Super PAC—Irresponsible Advertising." *The Colbert Report* (June 29, 2011), http://www.colbertnation.com/the-colbert-report-videos/391013/june-29-2011/colbert-super-pac—making-a-better-tomorrow—tomorrow.

—— "Colbert Super PAC Treasure Hunt Solution." *The Colbert Report* (June 28, 2012), http://www.colbertnation.com/colbert-superpac.

—— "Interview by *Stand Up with Pete Dominick*," Sirius XM (March 13, 2008).

—— "Interview" with *Beaufort Gazette* (October 17, 2007).

—— "Interview by Tim Russert." *Meet the Press*, NBC (October 21, 2007).

—— "The Word—Color-Bind." *The Colbert Report* (July 23, 2013), http://www.colbertnation.com/the-colbert-report-videos/428008/july-23-2013/the-word-color-bind.

—— "The Word—Docu-Drama." *The Colbert Report* (April 26, 2010), http://www.colbertnation.com/the-colbert-report-videos/308060/april-26-2010/the-word—docu-drama.

Colbert, Stephen, Dahm, Richard, Dinello, Paul, and Silverman, Allison. *I Am America (And So Can You!)*. New York: Grand Central Publishing, 2007.

David, Larry. "Being Larry David," interview by Scott Simon. *Weekend Edition Saturday*, NPR, October 27, 2001, http://www.npr.org/programs/wesat/features/2001/larrydavid/011027.larrydavid.html.

Day, Donald, ed. *The Autobiography of Will Rogers*. New York: Avon Books, 1975.

Fey, Tina. *Bossypants*. New York: Little, Brown, 2011.

Fields, Ronald J., ed. *W.C. Fields by Himself: His Intended Autobiography with Hitherto Unpublished Letters, Notes, Scripts and Articles*. Englewood Cliffs, NJ: Prentice-Hall, 1973.

Freud, Sigmund. *Jokes and Their Relation to the Unconscious*. Trans. James Strachey. London: W. W. Norton, 1960.

Gervais, Ricky. "Ricky Gervais Meets . . . Larry David." Dir. Niall Downing. Objective Productions, Channel 4 Television Corporation, UK. Airdate, January 5, 2006, Television Movie.

Gosden, Freeman and Charles Correll. "The Locked Trunk's Secret." *The Amos 'n' Andy Radio Show*, original broadcast date, November 5, 1943, http://www.radiolovers.com/shows/A/amosandy/1943/AMOSANDY43110532-22-mono25m51s_TheLockedTrunksSecret_.mp3.

Gragert, Steven K., ed. *Radio Broadcasts of Will Rogers*. Stillwater, OK: Oklahoma State University Press, 1983.

—— and M. Jane Johansson, eds. *The Papers of Will Rogers: From the Broadway Stage to the National Stage, Volume Four, September 1915 – July 1928*. Norman, OK: University of Oklahoma Press, 2005.

Howe, Warren. "Interview with CNN." (October 31, 2007).

"Immigrant Farm Workers," House Committee on Immigration, Citizenship and Border Security, 111th Cong., C-SPAN 3, September 24, 2010, http://www.c-spanvideo.org/program/295639-1.

Kaufman, George S. *Animal Crackers* in *Kaufman Co.: Broadway Comedies*, ed., Laurence Maslon. New York: Library of the Americas, 2004.

Keaton, Buster. *The Playhouse*, directed by Buster Keaton, in the *Buster Keaton Collection* (1921; Montreal, Canada: St. Clair Vision, 2007), DVD.

Keaton, Buster, with Charles Samuels. *My Wonderful World of Slapstick*. New
    York: Da Capo Press, 1960/1982.
Keith, Benjamin Franklin. "The Vogue of Vaudeville." *American Vaudeville As Seen
    by Its Contemporaries*, ed., Charles W. Stein, 15. New York: Alfred A. Knopf,
    1984.
Laurie, Jr., Joe. *Vaudeville: From the Honky-Tonks to the Palace*, New York: Henry
    Holt, 1953.
Lehrman, Nat. "Playboy Interview: Mort Sahl." *Playboy*, (February 1969): 60.
Lenny Bruce Without Tears, written by Barbara Baker, Fred Baker, and John
    Parson, directed by Fred Baker (New York: Fred Baker Films, 1972), http://
    www.amazon.com/gp/product/B00DFYF8SC/ref=atv_feed_catalog?tag=imdb-
    amazonvideo-20.
Lewis, Robert M., ed. *From Traveling Show to Vaudeville: Theatrical Spectacle
    in America, 1830–1910*. Baltimore, MD: Johns Hopkins University Press,
    2003.
Marinetti, F. T. *Critical Writings*, ed., Gunter Berghaus, trans., Doug Thompson.
    New York: Farrar, Straus, Giroux, 2006.
Marx Brothers. *Fun In Hi Skule* (from the Library of Congress manuscript, 1921)
    online at "Marxology" website. http://www.marx-brothers.org/marxology/
    balcony.htm.
Marx Brothers, and Tom Johnstone. *I'll Say She Is* (from the Library of Congress
    manuscript, 1923), online at "Marxology" website. http://www.marx-brothers.
    org/marxology/home.htm.
Marx, Groucho. "Bad Days Are Good Memories." *Saturday Evening Post*,
    Philadelphia, PA, August 29, 1931.
—— *Groucho and Me*. New York: Bernard Geis Associates, 1959.
—— *The Groucho Phile*. New York: Simon and Schuster, 1977.
Marx, Groucho, and Richard J. Anobile. *The Marx Bros. Scrapbook*. New York:
    Darien House, 1973.
Marx, Harpo. *Harpo Speaks!* New York: Limelight Editions, 2008; New York:
    Bernard Geis Associates, 1961.
Mooney, Paul. *Black Is the New White*. New York: Gallery Books, 2009.
Mort Sahl: The Loyal Opposition, American Masters Series, Season 4, Episode 7,
    written and directed by Robert B. Weide. Airdate, September 18, 1989. PBS
    Home Video, DVD.
Pryor, Richard. *Richard Pryor: The Anthology, 1968–1992*. Recordings produced
    by Robert Marchese, Richard Pryor, David Banks, and Biff Dawes. Los
    Angeles, CA: Rhino Entertainment, Warner Archives, 2001.
Rogers, Betty. *Will Rogers*. Norman, OK: University of Oklahoma Press,
    1979.
Rogers, Will. *The Illiterate Digest*. New York: A. L. Burt, 1924.
—— *The Papers of Will Rogers*, Vol. 4, *From the Broadway Stage to the National
    Stage: September 1915–July 1928*, eds., Steven K. Gragert and M. Jane
    Johansson. Norman, OK: University of Oklahoma Press, 2005.
—— "The Pilgrims" (14 April 1935), in *Radio Broadcasts of Will Rogers*, ed.,
    Steven K. Gragert. Stillwater, OK: Oklahoma State University Press, 1983.
—— *Will Rogers at the Ziegfeld Follies*, ed. Arthur Frank Wertheim. Norman, OK:
    University of Oklahoma Press, 1992.

Ruby, Harry, and Bert Kalmar. *Horse Feathers*, Tentative Script, 11 February 1932, Groucho Marx papers and manuscripts special collection, Library of Congress Library of Congress, Rare Book and Manuscript Division, Washington, DC.

Schlissel, Lillian. *Three Plays by Mae West: Sex, The Drag, The Pleasure Man.* New York: Routledge, 1997.

Seinfeld, Jerry with Sarah Silverman. "I'm Going to Change Your Life Forever," *Comedians in Cars Getting Coffee.* Writ. Jerry Seinfeld. Dir. Jojo Pennebaker (http://comediansincarsgettingcoffee.com/sarah-silverman-i-m-going-to-change-your-life-forever, June 13, 2013), Web Series.

Sennett, Mack with Cameron Shipp. *King of Comedy.* Garden City, NY: Doubleday, 1954.

Silvers, Phil with Robert Saffron, *This Laugh Is on Me: The Phil Silvers Story.* Englewood Cliffs, NJ: Prentice-Hall, 1973.

Smallwood, James M., and Steven K. Gragert, eds. *Will Rogers' Weekly Articles*, Vol. 1, *The Harding/Coolidge Years: 1922–1925*. Stillwater, OK: Oklahoma State University Press, 1980.

—— eds. *Will Rogers' Daily Telegrams*, Vol. 3, *The Hoover Years: 1931–1933*. Stillwater, OK: Oklahoma State University Press, 1979.

Smith, Harry B., book and lyrics; music, Gustav Kerker, "I Don't Care!" from the musical *The Sambo Girl*, Broadway premiere, 16 October 1905.

Stein, Charles W., ed. *American Vaudeville As Seen by Its Contemporaries.* New York: Alfred A. Knopf, 1984.

Stewart, Jon, interview by Charles McGrath. "How Many Stephen Colberts Are There?" *New York Times Magazine* (January 8, 2012): 22.

Walker, Aida Overton. "Interview." *Pittsburgh Leader* (May 11, 1906).

West, Mae. *Goodness Had Nothing To Do With It.* New York: Prentice-Hall, 1959.

Williams, Bert. "Bert Williams Tells of Walker." *Indianapolis Freeman* (January 14, 1911): 5.

—— "The Comic Side of Trouble." *American Magazine* (January 1918): 60.

—— "Elder Eatmore's Sermon on Generosity," recorded on *Bert Williams, The Remaining Titles: 1915–1921*. Document Records (DOCD-5661), 1999.

Secondary sources

Adamson, Joe. *Groucho, Harpo, Chico, and Sometimes Zeppo: A History of the Marx Brothers and a Satire on the Rest of the World.* New York: Simon and Schuster, 1983.

Allen, Frederick Lewis. *Only Yesterday: An Informal History of the 1920s.* New York: Harper and Brothers, 1931.

Anderson, Ann. *Snake Oil, Hustlers, and Hambones: The American Medicine Show.* Jefferson, NC: McFarland, 2000.

Apkon, Stephen. *The Age of the Image: Redefining Literacy in a World of Screens.* New York: Farrar, Straus and Giroux, 2013.

Auslander, Philip. *Liveness.* New York: Routledge, 1999.

Brioux, Bill. *Truth and Rumors: The Reality Behind TV's Most Famous Myths.* Westport, CT: Greenwood Publishing, 2008.

Burger, Hans. "Through the Television Camera." *Theatre Arts*, March 1, 1940: 209.

Butsch, Richard. *The Making of American Audiences: From Stage to Television, 1750–1990*. Cambridge, UK and New York: Cambridge University Press, 2000.

Cantril, Hadley and Gordon W. Allport. *The Psychology of Radio*. New York: Harper and Brothers, 1935.

Carnes, Jim. "Dave Chappelle Lets Rude Crowd Have It, Sticks Up for Cosby's Comment." *Sacramento Bee* (June18, 2004), http://www.freerepublic.com/focus/news/1156342/posts.

Chandler, Charlotte. *Hello, I Must Be Going*. New York: Doubleday, 1978.

Cook, Will Marion. *The Music and Scripts of "In Dahomey": Music of the United States*, vol. 25. New York: A-R Editions, 1996.

Cooper, Anderson. "Dave Chappelle Interview." *Anderson Cooper 360*. CNN, July 7, 2006, http://transcripts.cnn.com/TRANSCRIPTS/0607/07/acd.01.html.

Coquelin, Constant. "Have Women a Sense of Humor?" *Harper's Bazaar* (January 1901): 67.

Critchley, Simon. *On Humour*. London: Routledge, 2002.

Crichton, Kyle Samuel. *The Marx Brothers*. Garden City, NY: Doubleday, 1950.

Cuddihy, John Murray. *The Ordeal of Civility: Freud, Marx, Levi-Strauss, and the Jewish Struggle with Modernity*. New York: Basic Books, 1974.

Cullen, Frank with Florence Hackman and Donald McNeilly, eds. *Vaudeville Old New: An Encyclopedia of Variety Performers in America*, vols. 1 and 2. New York: Routledge, 2007.

Czitrom, Daniel J. *Media and the American Mind: From Morse to McLuhan*. Chapel Hill, NC: University of North Carolina Press, 1982.

Dale, Alan. *Comedy is a Man in Trouble: Slapstick in American Movies*. Minneapolis, MN: University of Minnesota Press, 2000.

Davis, Andrew. *Baggy Pants Comedy: Burlesque and the Oral Tradition*. New York: Palgrave Macmillan, 2011.

Day, Donald. *Will Rogers: A Biography*. New York: David McKay, 1962.

Dickstein, Morris. *Dancing in the Dark: A Cultural History of the Great Depression*. New York: W. W. Norton, 2009.

Dimeglio, John E. *Vaudeville U.S.A.* Bowling Green, OH: Bowling Green University Popular Press, 1973.

Dolon, Deirdre. *Curb Your Enthusiasm: The Book*. New York: Gotham Books, 2006.

Donahue, John D., and Richard Zeckhauser. "The Tummler's Task: A Collaborative Conception of Port Protection." *Ports in a Storm: Public Management in a Turbulent World*, ed. John D. Donahue and Mark H. Moore. Washington, DC: Brookings Institution Press, 2012: 116–32.

Du Bois, W. E. B. *The Souls of Black Folks*, 5th edn Chicago: A. C. McClurg, 1903; Mineola, NY: Dover, reprint, 1994.

Duncombe, Stephen. *Dream: Re-Imagining Progressive Politics in an Age of Fantasy*. New York: The New Press, 2007.

Dunning, John ed. *On the Air: The Encyclopedia of Old-Time Radio*. New York: Oxford University Press, 1998.

Ellison, Ralph. *Shadow and Act*. New York: Random House, 1964.

Ely, Melvin Patrick. *The Adventures of Amos 'n' Andy: A Social History of an American Phenomenon*. Richmond, VA: University of Virginia Press, 2001.

Erdman, Andrew L. *Blue Vaudeville: Sex, Morals and the Mass Marketing of Amusement, 1895–1915*. Jefferson, NC: McFarland, 2004.

—— *Queen of Vaudeville: The Story of Eva Tanguay*. Ithaca, NY: Cornell University Press, 2012.

Erdman, Harley. *Staging the Jew: The Performance of an American Ethnicity, 1860–1920*. New Brunswick, NJ: Rutgers University Press, 1997.

Erenberg, Lewis. *Steppin' Out: New York Nightlife and the Transformation of American Culture, 1890–1930*. Westport, CT: Greenwood Press, 1981.

Eyles, Allen. *The Marx Brothers Their World of Comedy*. New York: A. S. Barnes, 1969.

Farley, John. "On the Beach with Dave Chappelle." *Time* (May 15, 2005), http://www.time.com/time/arts/article/0,8599,1061415,00.html.

Forbes, Camille F. *Introducing Bert Williams: Burnt Cork, Broadway, and the Story of America's First Black Star*. New York: Basic Civitas Books, 2008.

Gagey, Edward. *The San Francisco Stage: A History*, second printing. New York: Columbia University Press, 1950/1970.

Gehring, Wes D. *The Marx Brothers: A Bio-Bibliography*. New York: Greenwood Press, 1987.

Gilbert, Douglas. *American Vaudeville: Its Life and Times*. New York: Dover, 1940.

Goldman, Herbert G. *Banjo Eyes: Eddie Cantor and the Birth of Modern Stardom*. New York: Oxford University Press, 1997.

Gunning, Tom. "Mechanisms of Laughter" *Slapstick Comedy*, eds., Tom Paulus and Rob King, 137–151. New York and London: Routledge, 2010.

Hamilton, Marybeth. *"When I'm Bad, I'm Better": Mae West, Sex, and American Entertainment*. Berkeley, CA: University of California Press, 1996.

Havig, Alan. *Fred Allen's Radio Comedy*. Philadelphia, PA: Temple University Press, 1990.

Hilmes, Michelle. *Radio Voices: American Broadcasting, 1922–1952*. Minneapolis, MN: University of Minnesota Press, 1997.

"In Vaudeville: A Short History of This Popular Character of Amusement." *Midway* 1 (October 1905): 27.

Janik, Vicki K., ed. *Fools and Jesters in Literature, Art, and History: Bio-Bibliographical Sourcebook*. Westport, CT: Greenwood Press, 1998.

Jenkins, Henry. "'Don't Become Too Intimate with That Terrible Woman!': Unruly Wives, Female Comic Performance and *So Long Letty*." *Camera Obscura*, vol. 9 (1–2, 25–26) Duke University Press, January 1, 1991: 203–23.

—— "Manufacturing Dissent: An Interview with Stephen Duncombe," *Confessions of an Aca-Fan* (blog), July 23, 2007, http://henryjenkins.org/2007/07/manufacturing_dissent_an_inter.html.

—— *What Made Pistachio Nuts?: Early Sound Comedy and the Vaudeville Aesthetic*. New York: Columbia University Press, 1992.

Karnick, Kristine Brunovska. "Commitment and Reaffirmation in Hollywood Romantic Comedy" in Kristine Brunovska Karnick and Henry Jenkins, eds. *Classical Hollywood Comedy*. New York: Routledge, 1995.

Katz, David. "What's So Funny about Race?," in *The "High Times" Reader*, eds. Annie Nocenti and Ruth Baldwin. New York: Nation Books, 2004.

Kibler, M. Alison. *Rank Ladies: Gender and Cultural Hierarchy in American Vaudeville*. Chapel Hill, NC: University of North Carolina Press, 1999.

King, Rob. *The Fun Factory: The Keystone Film Company and the Emergence of Mass Culture*. Berkeley, CA: University of California Press, 2009.

King, Rob, and Tom Paulus, eds. *Slapstick Comedy*. New York and London: Routledge, 2010.

Klapper, Paul. "The Yiddish Music Hall." *University Settlement Studies* 2, no. 4 (1905): 20–1.

Knopf, Robert. *The Theater and Cinema of Buster Keaton*. Princeton, NJ: Princeton University Press, 1999.

Krugman, Paul. "Moment of Truthiness." *New York Times* (August 15, 2013), http://www.nytimes.com/2013/08/16/opinion/krugman-moment-of-truthiness.html?_r=0.

Levine, Josh. *Pretty, Pretty, Pretty Good: Larry David and the Making of* Seinfeld *and* Curb Your Enthusiasm. Toronto: EWC Press, 2010.

Levine, Lawrence W. *Highbrow/Lowbrow: The Emergence of Cultural Hierarchy in America*. Cambridge, MA: Harvard University Press, 1988.

Levine, Stuart. "Tina Fey." *Variety* (July 30, 2007): http://variety.com/2007/biz/news/tina-fey-1117969258/.

Leib, Sandra. *Mother of the Blues: A Study of Ma Rainey*. Amherst, MA: University of Massachusetts Press, 1981.

Lindenbaum, Isidore. "Film on the Marx." *Television Magazine* (August 1952): 31.

Linton, Eliza Lynn. "The Judicial Shock to Marriage." *Nineteenth Century* (May 1891): 691.

—— "The Wild Woman as Social Insurgent." *Nineteenth Century* (October 1891): 596.

Lott, Eric. *Love and Theft: Blackface Minstrelsy and the American Working Class*. New York: Oxford University Press, 1995.

Make 'Em Laugh: The Funny Business of America, Episode Three: The Knockabouts. Public Broadcasting Service, DVD, Ghost Light Films; Thirteen/WNET.org; Rhino Entertainment, 2008.

Marc, David. *Comic Visions: Television Comedy and American Culture*, 2nd edn. Malden, MA: Blackwell, 1997.

Maslon, Laurence and Kantor, Michael, *Make 'Em Laugh: The Funny Business of America*. New York: Twelve, 2008.

May, Lary. *The Big Tomorrow: Hollywood and the Politics of the American Way*. Chicago: The University of Chicago Press, 2000.

—— *Screening Out the Past: The Birth of Mass Culture and the Motion Picture Industry*. Chicago: University of Chicago Press, 1983.

McCarthy, Joe, ed. *Fred Allen's Letters*. Garden City, NY: Doubleday, 1965.

McLean, Jr., Albert F. *American Vaudeville as Ritual*. Frankfort, KY: University of Kentucky Press, 1965.

McLeod, Elizabeth. *The Original Amos 'n' Andy: Freeman Gosden, Charles Correll and the 1928–1943 Radio Serial*. Jefferson, NC: McFarland, 2005.

McPherson, Edward. *Buster Keaton: Tempest in a Flat Hat*. New York: Faber and Faber, 2007.

Mencken, H. L. *Mencken's America*, ed. S. T. Joshi. Athens, OH: Ohio University Press, 2004.

Mordden, Ethan. *Ziegfeld: The Man Who Invented Show Business*. New York: St. Martin's Press, 2008.

Moses, Montrose J., and John Mason Brown. *The American Theatre as Seen by Its Critics*. New York: W. W. Norton, 1934.

Nachman, Gerald. *Seriously Funny: The Rebel Comedians of the 1950s and 1960s*. New York: Pantheon Books, 2003.

Nasaw, David. *Going Out: The Rise and Fall of Public Amusements*. New York: Basic Books, 1990.

Nathan, George Jean. "Mae West." *American Mercury* 15 (December 1928): 501.

Nehamas, Alexander. "Plato's Pop Culture." *New York Times* (August 29, 2010): 4.

O'Brien, P. J. *Will Rogers: Ambassador of Good Will, Prince of Wit and Wisdom*. Chicago: John C. Winston, 1935.

Peiss, Kathy Lee. *Cheap Amusements: Working Women and Leisure in Turn-of-the-Century New York*. Philadelphia, PA: Temple University Press, 1986.

Riis, Thomas. *Just Before Jazz: Musical Theater in New York, 1890–1915*. Washington, DC: Smithsonian Institution Press, 1989.

Rogak, Lisa. *And Nothing but the Truthiness: The Rise (and Further Rise) of Stephen Colbert*. New York: Thomas Dunne Books, 2011.

Rogin, Michael. *Blackface, White Noise: Jewish Immigrants in the Hollywood Melting Pot*. Berkeley, CA: University of California Press, 1996.

Rowland, Helen. "The Emancipation of 'The Rib,'" *The Delineator* (March 1911): 231–32.

Royle, Edwin Milton. "The Vaudeville Theatre." *Scribner's Magazine* 26 (October 1899): 489.

Schumacher-Matos, Edward. "Does Roasting the Pope as a Gay Icon Cross the Line?" National Public Radio, March 22, 2012. http://www.npr.org/blogs/ombudsman/2012/03/22/149175809/roasting-the-pope-as-a-gay-icon-civilized-or-crossing-the-line.

Sanborn, Kate. *The Wit of Women*, 4th edn, 1895; New York: Funk Wagnalls, 2012.

Santayana, George. *Reason in Common Sense*, vol. 1 of *The Life of Reason*. New York: Charles Scribner's Sons, 1905.

Savran, David. *Highbrow/Lowdown: Theater, Jazz, and the Making of the New Middle Class*. Ann Arbor, MI: University of Michigan Press, 2009.

Schechter, Joel, ed. *Popular Theatre: A Sourcebook*. London and New York: Routledge, 2003.

Schlissel, Lillian. *Three Plays by Mae West: Sex, The Drag, The Pleasure Man*. London: Routledge, 1997.

Seldes, Gilbert. *The 7 Lively Arts*. New York: Sagamore Press, 1957.

—— *The Public Arts*. New York: Appleton-Century-Crofts, 1958.

Senelick, Laurence, ed. *The American Stage: Writing on Theater from Washington Irving to Tony Kushner*. New York: Library of America, 2010.

Simon, Scott. "Being Larry David." *Weekend Edition Saturday*, NPR, October 27, 2001, http://www.npr.org/programs/wesat/features/2001/larrydavid/011027.larrydavid.html.

Slide, Anthony, ed. *The Encyclopedia of Vaudeville*, Westport, CT: Greenwood Press, 1994.

—— ed. *Selected Vaudeville Criticism*. Metuchen, NJ: The Scarecrow Press, 1988.

Smiley, Tavis and West, Cornell. *The Rich and the Rest of Us: A Poverty Manifesto*. New York: Smiley Books, 2012.

Smith, Eric Ledell. *Bert Williams: A Biography of the Pioneer Black Comedian*. Jefferson, NC: McFarland, 1992.

Snyder, Robert. *The Voice of the City: Vaudeville and Popular Culture in New York*. New York: Oxford University Press, 1989.

Soule, George. *Prosperity Decade: From War to Depression: 1917–1929*. New York, Reinhart, 1947.

Staples, Shirley. *Male–Female Comedy Teams in American Vaudeville, 1865–1932*. Ann Arbor, MI: UMI Research Press, 1984.

Stott, Andrew. *Comedy*. New York and London: Routledge, 2005.

Sypher, Wylie, ed. *Comedy: "An Essay on Comedy" by George Meredith and "Laughter" by Henri Bergson*. Baltimore, MD: Johns Hopkins University Press, 1956.

Thorburn, David and Henry Jenkins, eds. *Rethinking Media Change: The Aesthetics of Transition*. Cambridge, MA: The MIT Press, 2003.

Toll, Robert C. *Blacking Up: The Minstrel Show in Nineteenth-Century America*. New York: Oxford University Press, 1974.

—— *On With the Show: The First Century of Show Business in America*. New York: Oxford University Press, 1976.

—— "Show Biz in Blackface: The Evolution of the Minstrel Show as a Theatrical Form." In *American Popular Entertainment: Papers and Proceedings of the Conference on the History of American Popular Entertainment*, ed. Myron Matlaw. Westport, CT: Greenwood Press, 1977, 23.

Walton, Lester A. "Bert Williams, Philosopher." *New York Age* (December 29, 1917): 6.

Watkins, Mel. *On the Real Side: Laughing, Lying, and Signifying – The Underground Tradition of African-American Humor That Transformed American Culture from Slavery to Richard Pryor*. New York: Simon and Schuster, 1995.

Watts, Jill. *Mae West: An Icon in Black and White*. New York: Oxford University Press, 2001.

Wertheim, Arthur Frank. *Radio Comedy*. New York: Oxford University Press, 1979.

White, Jr., Richard D. *Will Rogers: A Political Life*. Lubbock, TX: Texas Tech University Press, 2011.

Wilmeth, Don B., ed. *The Cambridge Guide to American Theatre*, 2nd edn. Cambridge, UK: Cambridge University Press, 2007.

Winfrey, Oprah. "Chappelle's Story: Dave's Moral Dilemma." *The Oprah Winfrey Show*, February 3, 2006, www.oprah.com/oprahshow/Chappelles-Story/.

Wright, Edward A. *A Primer for Playgoers*. Englewood Cliffs, NJ: Prentice-Hall, 1958.

Yagoda, Ben. *Will Rogers: A Biography*. Norman, OK: University of Oklahoma Press, 1993.

Zinoman, Jason. "A Comic Quits Quitting." *New York Times* (August 15, 2013), http://www.nytimes.com/2013/08/18/arts/dave-chappelle-returns-to-stand-up-with-stories-to-tell.html?pagewanted=all&_r=0.

Index